SHE LIVES!

SOPHIA WISDOM
WORKS IN THE WORLD

REV. JANN ALDREDGE-CLANTON, PhD

D1365343

Walking Together, Finding the Way

SKYLIGHT PATHS®
PUBLISHING
Woodstock, Vermont

She Lives!
Sophia Wisdom Works in the World

2014 Quality Paperback Edition, First Printing
© 2014 by Jann Aldredge-Clanton

Library of Congress Cataloging-in-Publication Data
Aldredge-Clanton, Jann, 1946–
She lives! : Sophia wisdom works in the world / Rev. Jann Aldredge-Clanton, PhD. — 2014 Quality Paperback Edition.
    pages cm
Includes bibliographical references.
ISBN 978-1-59473-573-8 (pbk.) — ISBN 978-1-59473-579-0 (ebook) 1. Femininity of God. 2. Feminist theology. 3. Women clergy. I. Title.
BT153.M6 A44 2014
230.082—dc23
                                    2014020625

10   9   8   7   6   5   4   3   2   1

Manufactured in the United States of America
Cover design: Jenny Buono
Interior design: Tim Holtz
Cover art: © Yuliya Koldovska/Shutterstock

SkyLight Paths Publishing is creating a place where people of different spiritual traditions come together for challenge and inspiration, a place where we can help each other understand the mystery that lies at the heart of our existence.

SkyLight Paths sees both believers and seekers as a community that increasingly transcends traditional boundaries of religion and denomination—people wanting to learn from each other, *walking together, finding the way.*

SkyLight Paths, "Walking Together, Finding the Way" and colophon are trademarks of LongHill Partners, Inc., registered in the U.S. Patent and Trademark Office.

Walking Together, Finding the Way
Published by SkyLight Paths Publishing
A Division of LongHill Partners, Inc.
Sunset Farm Offices, Route 4, P.O. Box 237
Woodstock, VT 05091
Tel: (802) 457-4000 Fax: (802) 457-4004
www.skylightpaths.com

Contents

Part 3: Wisdom's Works of Marriage Equality   65

Part 4: Wisdom's Works of Economic Justice   97

Part 8: Wisdom's Works of Interfaith Collaboration   203

Part 9: Wisdom's Works of Changing Hierarchies into Circles   229

Index of Inclusive-Language Hymns

Introduction

Growing up in the Baptist tradition, I learned from memory the hymn "He Lives." I loved singing this hymn to a lilting tune, increasing in volume along with everyone in the congregation as we came to the refrain after each stanza: "He lives, He lives, Christ Jesus lives today! He walks with me and talks with me along life's narrow way. He lives, He lives, salvation to impart! You ask me how I know He lives: He lives within my heart."

It would not be until many years later that I could even imagine singing or saying, "She lives." I had learned to worship a God who was named and imaged as male. But while studying in a conservative Baptist seminary, I was surprised to find Her. I discovered female names and images for the Divine in the Bible and in Christian history. Studying classic doctrines of the Trinity in my systematic theology seminary class, a voice within asked, "If God can include three persons, can't God include two genders?"[1]

After graduating from seminary and being ordained as a minister, I began researching, writing, preaching, and teaching to persuade people that we need to include female divine names and images in worship if we are to have social justice, peace, and equality.[2] Then She used another hymn, "O Come All Ye Faithful," to continue expanding my mind and heart. I started wondering what the world would have been like if we had sung "O come let us adore Her" in addition to "O come let us adore Him." So I began writing hymn lyrics and liturgies proclaiming that She also lives and that She is also worthy of our adoration.[3]

The title of this book comes from continual discoveries of Her, living and working in my heart and in all creation. The journey has led to experiences of the sacredness of all and of the dynamic nature of this Divinity—ever living, ever moving, ever growing. *She Lives!* moves Christian theology away from atonement to resurrection, focusing on abundant life and new creation. The subtitle of the book comes from one of my favorite female names for the Divine, "Wisdom," found in the Hebrew and Christian Scriptures and in many other spiritual traditions. Wisdom is *Hokmah* in the Hebrew Bible and *Sophia* in the Greek language of the Christian Scriptures. I continually see Wisdom working in our world and the great need for more of Her works. "Wisdom works" then plays on the word "works" as both noun and verb. Wisdom continually works within, around, and among all creation to bring justice, peace, liberation, love, compassion, hope, and joy. Works of Wisdom include gender equality, racial equality, marriage equality, economic justice, care of creation, nonviolence, interfaith collaboration, expansion of spiritual experience, and egalitarian faith communities.

Changing Church

Through writing my book *Changing Church: Stories of Liberating Ministers*, I continued to discover ways Wisdom is working in the world to bring social justice and peace.[4] In the years since that book came out, I have been writing a weekly blog, also titled "Changing Church."[5] In the blog I include stories of laypeople as well as clergy, believing that all are ministers and that everyone can take part in changing the church. In the book I included stories of ordained clergy, not from a belief that they are more important to changing the church than laypeople, but from a belief that they have the most to lose in advocating for change within the institutional church. Since writing the book, I have found many laypeople who also risk losses by advocating for change. And even though these laypeople may not risk losing their jobs or opportunities for promotion, they risk other losses by advocating for changes in church and in the wider culture.

For the book and blog on changing church, I have interviewed people who include female names and images of the Divine in their worship services and who believe this inclusive symbolism is connected to social justice. I have found that these ministers, both lay and clergy, who include multicultural female divine names and images in worship

are indeed active in social justice ministries. These ministers are changing the church through their inclusive and expansive theology, which
forms the foundation for an ethic of equality and justice in human
relationships.

Their stories demonstrate that social justice changes flow from the
foundational theological change of including multicultural female divine
names and imagery in worship. These ministers who use inclusive language and imagery take prophetic stands on race, class, gender, sexual
orientation, economic justice, ecology, interfaith cooperation, and
other social justice issues. They are working for freedom from interlocking oppressions, believing that it is vital to include biblical female
divine names and images in worship in order to have justice for women
and for all creation.

As I continued writing stories of these ministers on my blog, I
discovered more and more connections between theology, worship
symbolism, and social justice. I learned more about the ways in which
language and visual imagery reflect and shape our culture. I learned
more about the intersection and interrelationship of multiple forms of
oppression. But my hope increased as I continued to discover feminist
emancipatory groups who are working for freedom from various kinds
of discrimination and injustice.[6]

Language and Social Justice

As I interviewed these ministers who are changing church and society,
they taught me more about how language can limit as well as expand
understanding. For example, I learned that the term "Divine Feminine"
is limiting for some people, especially for women who do not feel that
they fit the culture's definition of "feminine." And I recognize how
this term too easily slips into traditional gender stereotypes and binary
views of gender. Mary E. Hunt, codirector of Women's Alliance for
Theology, Ethics and Ritual,[7] states: "I never use divine feminine language. I do not use 'feminine' anything as it seems to play into the sexist
trap of dividing people into masculine and feminine for which the latter
is almost always on the losing end of the equation."

Author Virginia Ramey Mollenkott comments on choosing language to include all genders: "When we use the male term 'God' along
with the female pronoun 'She,' we are including the people among

us who are transgender: who feel they are both female and male inwardly, or who were born intersexual, or who have crossed over from one gender to the other in order to match their inner understanding of their gender identity. Since Genesis proclaims both female and male to be made in the image of God, inevitably that image is inclusive of both female and male. Transgender people are often attacked, abused, and even murdered in our society, so including them as sacred beings along with women and men is important to our Christian witness."[8]

Others I interviewed prefer the term "Godde" (pronounced the same way as "God"), believing it to be more inclusive than "God." For example, Connie Tuttle and Mark Mattison have chosen the word "Godde" as a combination of "God" and "Goddess." They understand that the word "God," because of its long history of association with an exclusively masculine image of the Divine, implies to many people a masculine way of conceiving the Christian "God," and that "Goddess" is a word that Christians have not traditionally embraced. Others I interviewed, including Mary Ann Beavis and Stacy Boorn, embrace the term "Goddess" as a part of biblical and Christian tradition.

In *She Lives!* you will find a wide variety of designations that include the Female Divine. Prominent are biblical female names for Deity, such as the ones listed below.

- "Wisdom," *Hokmah*, the Hebrew word for "Wisdom" in the Hebrew Bible, and *Sophia*, the Greek word for "Wisdom," linked to Christ in the Christian Scriptures
- *Shekhinah*, a Hebrew word used to denote the dwelling presence of God and/or the glory of God
- *Ruah*, the Hebrew word for "Spirit" in the book of Genesis and elsewhere in the Hebrew Bible
- *El Shaddai*, a Hebrew name translated "God of the Breasts," "the Breasted God," or "God Almighty"
- "Mother"
- "Sister"
- "Mother Eagle"
- "Mother Hen"

General references include "God-She," "Divine-She," "Female Divine," "She Who Is," and "Divine Feminine."

Some of the people I have interviewed favor abstract over anthropomorphic names for Deity and suggest genderless designations like "Friend," "Spirit," and "Force." Others believe we need female names and multigender images to revalue females and all genders in the divine image. Rebecca Kiser, a Presbyterian pastor, advocates what she calls "gender-full" rather than genderless images of the Divine.

Angela Yarber, pastor and author, also believes that genderless divine names and images are not enough: "Neutral inclusive language continues to allow socialized patterns of domination to shape perceptions of God and humanity. If men and women were truly treated equally, and if an equal number of people perceived God to be female as well as male, then such neutral language could work. But women and men are not treated equally in society, and certainly not in the church, and most people still perceive God in male terms. Until this shifts, neutral language is not sufficient to gender the pulpit in the direction of justice."[9]

The title of this book and references to Deity throughout show my agreement that female language and images of the Divine are vital to justice and equality. "Wisdom" (*Hokmah* and *Sophia*), "Mother," *Ruah*, "Midwife," "Baker Woman," "She," and other biblical female designations give sacred value to women and girls who for centuries have been excluded, demeaned, discounted, even abused and murdered. Exclusive worship language and images oppress people by devaluing those excluded. This devaluation lays the foundation for worldwide violence against women and girls. Sadly, this violence is still all too prevalent. In the United States alone, every nine seconds a woman is battered or assaulted.[10] One in three women in the world experiences some kind of abuse in her lifetime.[11] Worldwide, an estimated four million women and girls each year are bought and sold into prostitution, slavery, or marriage.[12] Nicholas D. Kristof and Sheryl WuDunn write in *Half the Sky*: "More girls have been killed in the last fifty years, precisely because they were girls, than people were killed in all the battles of the twentieth century. More girls are killed in this routine 'gendercide' in any one decade than people were slaughtered in all the genocides of the twentieth century."[13] Two-thirds of the world's poor are women.[14] There are many more alarming statistics on worldwide violence and discrimination against women and girls. Theology and worship that include females as well as other genders can make a powerful contribution to a more just world.

The Diversity of Wisdom's Works

She Lives! collects stories from my blog and condenses stories from my book on changing church.[15] I have organized these stories by categories of Wisdom's works illustrated in them: gender equality, racial equality, marriage equality, care of creation, economic justice, nonviolence, expansion of spiritual experience, multifaith collaboration, and changing hierarchies to circles. These categories naturally overlap as they address interlocking oppressions. Thus a diversity of Wisdom's works can be found in each of the stories. This organizational structure, though somewhat artificial, serves to highlight specific works of Wisdom while acknowledging their interrelationship. In addition to stories, *She Lives!* provides worship resources that include female divine images and a list of feminist emancipatory faith communities in many locations.

One of Wisdom's works highlighted in this book is the movement from hierarchical to egalitarian faith communities, breaking down the separation between clergy and laity. However, because some of the clergywomen featured in *She Lives!* overcame many obstacles to their ordination, the title "Reverend" is important to their stories. Also, their clergy status and the educational achievement of clergy and laypeople in this book often increase their power for bringing change in church and society. Thus in *She Lives!* I have varied references to people to reflect this meantime period on the way to gender equality and to reflect the variety of ways they are addressed: by their first names and/or as "Rev.," "Pastor," "Bishop," "Dr.," "Rev. Dr."

This book comes from my location within the Christian tradition with the hope that people in other religious traditions will write stories of transformation through Divine Wisdom. More specifically, I am an ordained Anglo minister within the Baptist tradition, growing up in Louisiana and working in Texas. I have served mainly in ecumenical and interfaith settings as a chaplain, interfaith conference director, pastoral counselor, teacher, and speaker. While interfaith collaboration is an important part of my ministry and a common thread in the stories in this book, I have featured people from the Christian tradition because I can best work for change within my own tradition. When it comes to overcoming patriarchy and transforming society through Divine Wisdom, there is enough work for people in all religious traditions. I am a Christian feminist, trying to do my part from my tradition while collaborating with other traditions.

Some people think that the term "Christian feminism" is an oxymoron. Many feminists and others think that Christianity is misogynistic at its core and can't be reformed. And many Christians think that feminism is unbiblical or even ungodly. But as the Evangelical & Ecumenical Women's Caucus–Christian Feminism Today (EEWC-CFT) demonstrates, Christianity and the Bible clearly support the equality of the sexes. EEWC-CFT is one of many Christian organizations with a long history of working for gender equality and the equality of all. EEWC welcomes members of any gender, gender identity, race, ethnicity, color, creed, marital status, sexual orientation, religious affiliation, age, political party, parental status, economic class, or disability.[16]

Caryn Riswold, Lutheran theologian and author, also proclaims the compatibility of Christianity and feminism. In my interview with Caryn, she tells me that she wrote the book *Feminism and Christianity: Questions and Answers, in the Third Wave* for two main audiences: "the Christian who is either skeptical or uninformed about feminism's relevance for the religion today, and the feminist who doesn't see any need to talk about Christianity given its patriarchal history and tendencies." In the book she writes why she believes it's important to bring Christianity and feminism together:

> Feminism is the radical idea that women are equally human, and Christians everywhere should care that throughout human history, and still today, people have not in fact believed or acted as if this were the case.... Feminists should care about Christianity because it is simultaneously a religion with an egalitarian vision that has been and should continue to be liberating for women, and because it has been a major institution of patriarchy that remains a pervasive cultural force needing criticism.[17]

In *She Lives!* you will read the inspiring stories of Mary E. Hunt, Virginia Ramey Mollenkott, Connie Tuttle, Mark Mattison, Mary Ann Beavis, Stacy Boorn, Rebecca Kiser, Angela Yarber, Caryn Riswold, and many more. You will hear prophetic voices, witness transforming actions, and experience life-giving liturgies. You will find many resources for inclusive, expansive, creative worship. You will learn of feminist emancipatory faith communities in many different locations, and may find one of these communities near you or be inspired to create one.

She Lives! comes with the invitation to explore works of Wisdom in the world. It is my hope that these stories and resources will provide guidance to Wisdom's paths of peace, justice, and partnership. My vision is that emancipatory faith communities doing works of Wisdom will spring up all over the world.

Celebrate the Works of Wisdom
(Sung to the tune of "Joyful, Joyful, We Adore Thee")

Celebrate the works of Wisdom, shining forth in all that's fair;
Wisdom shows us peaceful pathways, calling us to dream and dare.
Like a vision bright and golden, Wisdom comes to light our way,
bringing us Her gifts most precious, leading to a better day.

Wisdom works in every nation, guiding us to live in peace,
teaching healing care and kindness, She will help all violence cease.
Wisdom works through daring people, prophets bold throughout
the years,
speaking up for truth and justice, crying out for all to hear.

Works of Wisdom bring abundance, lovely works beyond compare;
Wisdom opens doors of freedom, calling everyone to share.
Like a Tree of Life She blossoms, spreading beauty through the
earth;
we can join the work of Wisdom, new creation now to birth.[18]

Words © 2009 Jann Aldredge-Clanton   HYMN TO JOY

Part 1

Wisdom's Works of Gender Equality

"We don't need to do inclusive language anymore," some of the young women tell my professor friend in her seminary intern classes. "That was important when you were going through seminary because there were all men. Inclusive language isn't important anymore because now women can be leaders in church and are in the workplace big-time." My friend says that when they go out into churches, these students discover that gender discrimination, although often more subtle now than in the past, is still all too prevalent.

Although the connection between including female images of the Divine and gender equality may seem obvious, many people do not understand this connection. Language and imagery in the majority of churches, even those that espouse gender equality, still reveal worship of a male God. Even women pastors often do not see the importance of including biblical female divine names and images in worship.

But there are clergy and laypeople, both male and female, who know the importance of language and imagery in shaping reality. They recognize that our sacred symbols reflect and shape our deepest values. These people are bringing about change by breaking through the patriarchal foundation of a male God. By including female names and images of the Divine, they are creating a theological foundation for gender equality. Without this foundation, people will still view women in the image of the Divine in some secondary kind of way, and justice for women will still be lacking.[1]

In this book you will read stories of diverse people around the country who understand that the Female Divine is vital to gender equality. Their stories reveal their advocacy for female divine names and images as necessary for females to know we are created in the divine image and for all people to value females in the divine image so that gender justice and equality become reality. Wisdom and other female personifications of the Divine work for gender equality.

Celebrate a New Day Dawning

(Sung to the tune of "Love Divine, All Loves Excelling")

Celebrate a new day dawning, sunrise of a golden morn;
Christ-Sophia dwells among us, glorious visions now are born.
Equal partners 'round the table, we make dreams reality;
calling out our gifts, we nurture hope beyond all we can see.

Christ-Sophia lights the pathway to a world of harmony;
Sister-Brother Love surrounds us, nourishing our synergy.
Earth joins in our rich communion, grateful for our healing care;
leaping deer and soaring eagles, all Earth's fullness now can share.[2]

Words © 2009 Jann Aldredge-Clanton   BEECHER

Rev. Lori Eickmann

Intentional Interim Pastor, Sierra Pacific Synod,
Evangelical Lutheran Church in America

Teaching Female Divine Images in Scripture

"Church tradition has forgotten, ignored, or repressed the
feminine images of the Holy that are present *in the Bible*.
The truth of inclusive language for the Divine is *biblical*.
We risk impairing the witness of the good news of Jesus
Christ when we try to keep God in a box. Also, female
imagery for God is part of the Jewish and Christian
traditions (Woman Wisdom in the Hebrew Bible and Jesus
as Sophia's—Wisdom's—prophet or Sophia incarnate in
the Christian Scriptures). The exclusive use of masculine
names and imagery for God is the golden calf of this
century. We must teach people that the Divine Feminine is
truth, and justice will flow."

Rev. Lori Eickmann believes that her call as a minister includes
teaching this truth of biblical female divine images to as many
congregations as possible, and fulfills this call through serving Lutheran
churches as interim pastor. She expresses passion about teaching female
names and images of the Divine because of her strong belief that they
will lead to gender equality and deeper faith experience.

For thirteen years, Lori worked as a reporter for the *San Jose
Mercury News* in San Jose, California. The last year she was at the newspaper she wrote an article for the religion page about her search, as a

Christian woman, for her Heavenly Mother. The paper, she says, had "already run national stories about Jewish and Muslim women searching for Our Mother in their sacred texts." This article was published not only in the *San Jose Mercury News*, one of the top ten newspapers in the country, but also in other newspapers nationwide. In the article Lori tells about the pain she experienced from the exclusively masculine divine images in church: "I felt invisible, there in church. Maybe it was because I had children—one son and one daughter—and I was seeing the world through their eyes. I had to notice that the world offers a God, who, as someone wrote, 'is somehow more like my father, husband, and brother than like me.' I began to ache for all the daughters who couldn't see themselves reflected in the Divine. I ached for them and for myself, because I knew we were created in God's image, but mainstream Christian religion seemed unwilling to admit that."[3]

Lori grew up in a churchgoing family, but stopped attending when she went to college. "I left the church at age twenty not because of any spiritual crisis, but simply because I went away to college and got out of the habit," she recalls. "I returned to church a decade later because I yearned for a church home and wanted my young children to know God and grow up with a community of faith. But when I returned to church, I was shocked at how all the masculine names and descriptions of God made me feel: invisible. Although I'd grown up calling God 'Father' and 'Lord,' the lack of images of God as 'Mother' or 'She' now made me feel excluded, unseen, 'less than.' How could the One in whose image I was created be imagined as only male?"

At that time, Lori's pastors were a clergy couple. She asked the woman pastor, Jan, why everything about God and the Bible seemed focused on men and maleness. Jan replied, "There *are* feminine images of God in the Bible." Lori expressed surprise: "Nobody's ever told me that!" Jan gave Lori copies of *The Divine Feminine: The Biblical Imagery of God as Female* by Virginia Ramey Mollenkott, *Biblical Affirmations of Woman* by Leonard Swidler, and other books about female divine images in the Bible.[4]

Then Lori participated in a nine-month discipleship program created by her pastors. Through this program, Lori felt God calling her "to learn and to teach others that there are feminine images of God in our sacred scriptures." After the discipleship program ended, Lori went on a spiritual renewal retreat. There she met a woman who confirmed her call and labeled it a "call to ministry." Lori laughed and reminded the woman that the motto printed on their church bulletin each Sunday was "Every Member a Minister." The woman replied, "No, I mean *seminary*." Because Lori's children were in elementary school at the time, she decided that this call would probably come when they were in high school. She says, "If you want to make God laugh, tell Her your plans for the future."

A few years later Lori entered Pacific Lutheran Theological Seminary in Berkeley, "stunned but grateful that God wants the cosmos to know all Her names and faces." After graduating from seminary, Lori continued to look for ways to share her discovery of biblical female images of the Divine. While waiting for a call to a congregation of the Evangelical Lutheran Church in America (ELCA), she was asked to serve as interim pastor of Holy Cross Lutheran Church in Livermore, California. Through that experience Lori realized that her call to ministry was to serve congregations in transition as an intentional interim pastor. This ministry would not only allow her to use her gifts to guide congregations through a self-study process for twelve to eighteen months to help them prepare for a new pastor, but it would also fulfill her call to teach people about female images of God in the Bible. Lori comments on this unexpected opportunity: "God was surely laughing again! I now had an opportunity to educate many congregations about female imagery for God in the Bible. I developed a three-week class called 'Rediscovering Feminine Images of God in Scripture,' and I've been able to offer it to the congregations I've served so far." Shortly after beginning at her third interim congregation, Lori was ordained into intentional interim ministry.

Rev. Eickmann reflects on the benefits of teaching congregations about biblical female names and images of the Divine. "Educating people that there are feminine images of God in the Bible is part of helping people go deeper into their faith through Bible study. In the Lutheran church, the Book of Faith Initiative was begun to help Lutherans become more educated about the Bible, which many Lutherans (and other Christians) have never studied in much depth, if at all. People are more open to hearing feminine names for God if they have been taught that these are rooted in Holy Scripture and in the Jewish and Christian traditions. Ultimately, this will lead not only to gender equality but also to a deeper, richer, and more mature faith."

Multicultural images of humanity and divinity will also make a big difference, Rev. Eickmann explains. "Multicultural images of the Holy One *and* of women, children, and men are simply truthful and woefully absent in most of the white churches I've served. In my overwhelmingly Caucasian denomination, diverse images of God reveal a God who loves and is reflected in all people—male, female, many colors, young, old, and everything beyond and in between."

Although at one time Lori considered leaving the church because of the exclusivity she experienced, she now feels called to change the church. "I did consider leaving the church when I found, as a young mother, that not only did I feel invisible, confused, and angry each Sunday during worship, but I also began to realize that I could not raise my children to believe that God was a guy. I was not angry at *God*—it was *the church* that had it wrong. When my pastors asked me to be part of their discipleship program, part of me was afraid that by going deeper into Bible study I would find that God *was* a guy after all! So I prayed. I said, 'God, if I take this class and find out you really are all about men and maleness, you'd better help me see why that is—because otherwise I'm outta here.' But part of me knew from the start that Mom was about to take me on a big adventure. I've stayed with the church because I have experienced the love of my Mother, the grace of Her Son, and the inspiration of the Spirit of Wisdom (*Sophia* in Greek). I am called to be part of bringing the feminine faces and names of God into the church and into people's hearts."

Through her class and conversations and sermons, Rev. Eickmann brings female names and images of the Divine to the congregations she serves as interim pastor. In her class she discusses biblical texts such as Deuteronomy 32:18: "You were unmindful of the Rock that bore you; you forgot the God who gave you birth." Among the many other female divine images Rev. Eickmann teaches are Midwife and Wisdom. She points out that "God is praised as a caring midwife" in Psalm 22:9–10. And Lori elucidates the biblical parallels between Wisdom and Jesus: "In the gospel according to Matthew, Jesus speaks as Wisdom incarnate when he says, 'Wisdom is vindicated by her deeds.' He says this at the end of the passage that starts with the disciples of John the Baptizer asking Jesus, 'Are you the one who is to come, or shall we wait for another?' Jesus says they should tell John what they see—that the blind see and the lame walk; thus is Wisdom vindicated by her deeds. The Hebrew Wisdom tradition holds that Wisdom is a feminine personification of God, cocreating with God (Proverbs 8:22, to which John 1:1, 3–4 bears striking similarities)."

One time when Rev. Eickmann was teaching her class on female images of God in scripture at a small church of people mostly in their eighties and nineties, one of the older women remarked, "Imagine, learning all these new things at our age!" Lori recalls another time she offered the class at a larger church she was serving; this church was more diverse in age. "Some women, particularly, were very glad the class was offered, while others—both men and women—came even though they were very skeptical. At the end, one older man said, 'When I first heard about this, I thought it was going to be a bunch of hooey—but now you've shown that this *is* in the Bible!'"

Before Rev. Eickmann goes to a church as interim pastor, she usually has an opportunity to express her passion for helping people discover biblical female names and images of God. "Usually when I interview with a congregation to be their interim pastor, someone asks me why I left journalism to pursue ministry. I can't tell of my call to ministry without talking about feminine images of God. This is usually met with polite smiles and no follow-up questions. I come to a congregation as an intentional interim pastor with specific work to do with that congregation. I don't come in and demand that people start calling God 'She' or 'Mother,' but I do tend to neutralize the masculine language in the liturgy. Talking about female imagery for God and the need for inclusive language comes up in conversation, and I always offer my class. This is seed planting, and I pray that the seeds will sprout in individual hearts and maybe even in the congregation's life and ministry with the new pastor."

Rev. Eickmann appreciates the ELCA's statement on "Language and the Christian Assembly," calling for inclusive language and imagery for God in worship. "That's a big step into a just future," she acknowledges. "However, there still aren't any officially sanctioned worship resources and liturgies from the ELCA to support inclusive language, so many pastors and worship leaders struggling to promote female imagery for God have to constantly reinvent the wheel. Also, when I am serving as the interim in a congregation that is engulfed in conflict, introducing inclusive language isn't the first order of business. So in such circumstances I find myself letting the exclusive, male-centric language stand with few changes, and then I begin to feel I am part of the problem and not part of the solution."

Understanding, strength, and inspiration for all her challenges come from many sources, Lori affirms. "I get strength from prayer and meditation (spending time with my understanding and forgiving Mother), from friends and colleagues who share my struggles, and from books, articles, blogs, and worship services I may attend in which the Divine Feminine is named and celebrated."

Lori recounts an especially empowering experience. "I once participated in an intense, weeklong seminar on emotional intelligence for continuing education, and there discovered that because of the daily realities and pressures of interim parish ministry I was feeling too disconnected from my call to bring the feminine face of God to light. I felt guilty for not doing what God had called me to do. So the workshop leader had me kneel while the rest of the group laid their hands on me and commissioned me as a prophet of Holy Sophia. Remembering that always makes me smile, because it was so cool, but also because it reminds me that I had written into my ordination vows a vow to lift up the Divine Feminine. Truly, this is part of my calling as a Lutheran pastor."

Through her prophetic ministry in many congregations, Rev. Eickmann is fulfilling this calling. She offers a visionary prayer for the future of faith communities. "I pray that the Lutheran church and other Christian denominations and other faith traditions will all be inspired to write songs and liturgies that are inclusive—reflecting the truth that God is our Mother, Father, Inspiration, Love, Life, and Hope."

Rev. Sheila Sholes-Ross

Pastor, First Baptist Church, Pittsfield, Massachusetts;
Cochair, Equity for Women in the Church Community

Preaching Transformation
of Church and Society

"With traditional views, society appears hopeless; and in
the church, where there used to be hope, there appears to
be helplessness. I believe the use of female divine images
and the acceptance of women as pastors will lead society
and the church back to a venue of hope. Why? Because
hope incorporates a newness of doing things. And with
that newness there is justice, fairness, and equality. At
first, it may be uncomfortable for the masses; however,
once hope and newness are presented and the Holy Spirit
convicts, then the God in us can take over and lead us to
conduct the overall work of the Creator."

Rev. Sheila Sholes-Ross has a vision and a hope for multicultural
churches with women and men sharing equally in leadership and
with female divine images included. Sunday morning at 11:00 continues to be the "most segregated time of the week," many years after Dr.
Martin Luther King Jr.'s indictment of it. Rev. Sholes-Ross intends to
change that. And the majority of congregations continue to exclude
women from pastoral leadership and female divine images from worship. Rev. Sholes-Ross intends to change that, too.

Her big vision inspired her to initiate the Equity for Women in
the Church Community, begun in the Alliance of Baptists and reaching

across denominations and cultures. The purpose of this ecumenical, inclusive Community is to facilitate access and congregational receptivity so that clergywomen of all races find clergy positions in order to transform church and society. In partnership with Community members, Rev. Sholes-Ross organized a national conference that brought together clergy inclusive of ethnicities, genders, and denominations to create strategies for achieving equality. Conference participants and Community members are collaborating in the implementation of these strategies to accomplish the overall goal of equal representation of clergywomen as pastors of multicultural churches.

Rev. Sholes-Ross has an impressive history of "dreaming big" on justice issues and raising funds to make her dreams reality. When she served as executive director of Communities in Schools of Orange County, North Carolina, she wrote a grant for "The Green Awakening Math and Science Initiative" and received $180,000 to start the program. Sheila and her colleagues created this summer program to help middle-school students improve their skills in math and science while increasing their respect for the environment and their potential access to employment that supports eco-friendly projects.

Growing up in a Baptist church in New Orleans, Louisiana, Sheila never saw female clergy. At church and at home, she heard only male references to God. "As far back as I can remember, I had an interaction with an entity called 'God the Father,'" she says. "My mother had a strong faith in this God, and my father acquired a relationship with this 'God the Father' after marriage to my mother. Even today, I can clearly see them on their knees praying. I wanted that type of relationship."

However, this image of God as Father presented problems for Sheila. "My father was a very strict disciplinarian, so from an early age I had difficulty with this 'heavenly Father' image, who, I believed, was a strong disciplinarian and very hard on me. Being in a somewhat conservative African American Baptist faith, this could not be brought to light as a problem."

So Sheila found a more empowering divine image. "For as long as I can remember, I viewed God as Creator, a Creator of good things, such as springtime in New Orleans, and Creator of me, One who provided me with strength as an African American girl growing up in a racist society. I have always been involved with jobs that advocated on behalf of people facing injustices. I believe those jobs brought out the 'creator' in me, meaning having an ability to provide hope for others in situations that were not fair and just. I have been a counselor with a battered women's program, and since then, all of my executive administration positions have centered on advocacy on behalf of children and youth in areas of education and health care. Currently, I still view God as Creator, since for me that image creates in humanity the ability to address injustices and promote peace."

For many years Sheila says she felt God's call to ministry, but she believed 'He' was calling her husband, Nelson. "I told my husband that he needed to tell God that he could not accept the ministry call because I refused to be married to a minister. My husband kept reiterating that God was not calling him. It was not until I went to North Carolina and observed practicing female clergy that I recognized that God was truly calling *me*. When I told Nelson that God had called me into ministry, he said, 'I'm glad you have finally heard God's call.'"

When she was in seminary, Sheila preached a sermon that led her to include "Mother" and "She" in her references to the Divine. "I was invited to preach on Mother's Day at a multicultural church," she recalls. "I was burdened to preach 'God Our Perfect Mother.' I was terrified and begged God to give me another message, but She would not. It was storming that Sunday, and the only consolation I had was that I believed no one would show up due to the weather. Well, there was good attendance for such a horrible day. After the worship a parishioner stated that she had not come to church in many years on Mother's Day because of a poor relationship with her mother, but she was burdened to come that day. With tears in her eyes she said that after 'God's message' she would contact her mother, since the God I preached about was her perfect Mother and she did not have to try and find perfection in her biological mother." Sheila says that ever since she preached that Mother's Day sermon, she has believed the message was more for her than for the congregation. "I was having problems viewing God as 'He.' Prior to the sermon, I also had difficulty accepting the female images of God. After that sermon I began to view God differently."

Rev. Sholes-Ross believes in the importance of changing divine images because exclusively male imagery is a barrier for men as well as for women. "With the current church language and symbolism women are perceived as powerless, and men are perceived as having all the right answers relating to life. This is a burden because no one gender ever has all the answers. Whether a person is unable to view the image of God as male because of suffering emotional or physical abuse or because it hinders a person's true understanding of being created in God's image, changing to inclusive imagery is worth the effort, and most times an uncomfortable effort, in hopes of facilitating positive change."

With passion and persistence, Rev. Sholes-Ross preaches and teaches this hope of changing church and society. At an American Baptist Women in Ministry Conference in St. Louis, she led a seminar titled "Igniting the Flame: Taking Responsibility to Change the Status Quo!" She sounds this challenge: "As a preacher you must forget you are a woman, and as a preacher you must never forget you are a woman! Women do not need to become like men or submit to masculine definitions of their lives as women in the church. White and black women have joined in religious associations and secular clubs to bring about social reform. Black women have played a crucial role in making the church a powerful institution for social and political change. Women's voices are emerging and being heard on every continent of the world. Women will not allow our voices to be silenced."

This passion for women's voices being heard led Rev. Sholes-Ross to initiate the Equity for Women in the Church Community. Personal experiences of rejection of her pastoral calling have increased her determination to work for equality. With twenty-five years of administrative experience, many years of experience in speaking and preaching, three graduate degrees (master of administration and supervision; master of public health; master of divinity, magna cum laude) and two undergraduate degrees (bachelor of music and bachelor of music therapy), it seems obvious that everyone would see her as highly qualified to serve as a pastor. But this has not always been so.

"I have had rejection and more rejection, disrespect and more disrespect toward my calling and vocation," Sheila says. "Once when I attended a citywide revival with many well-known local preachers seated in the pulpit, other clergy arriving later were invited to join them. A seated clergyman denied me the seat next to him by placing his handkerchief on the seat. I moved to another vacant seat. With all of my preparation, gifts, talents, and abilities, I am still unacceptable in many venues. My conversations with God about this matter have been heated, but 'She whispers sweet peace to my soul'—a line I've adapted from an old gospel song. I was burdened to advocate on behalf of women in ministry because of the pain I have experienced and because of the hope I have that change is inevitable." Change finally came for Rev. Sholes-Ross when First Baptist Church of Pittsfield, Massachusetts, voted unanimously to call her as senior pastor.

Because of her personal experiences, Sheila remains resolved to advocate for clergywomen and to mentor them. "One struggle as an African American ordained clergywoman has included not acquiring an advocate on my behalf during or after seminary," she says. "It appeared that males were taken under the wings of senior male clergy, but there was no one to advocate on behalf of me. During my ordination interview process a clergy interviewer told me I must mentor young women entering ministry. I thought, 'What about me now?' She just thought the manner in which I presented myself during the ordination process, along with my educational background and administration experiences, would make me an asset to younger female clergy. Maybe that statement was the prophecy for the ministry with the Equity for Women in the Church Community."

Sheila says that she is finding advocates and mentors through the Community. "This one venue is providing such monumental emotional victories and interactions with strong women clergy. I am in awe of these women from varying ethnic, cultural, and denominational backgrounds—women whom I now call friends, colleagues, and also mentors. During Community meetings I am encouraged when strategies are discussed and efforts come to fruition."

Increasingly, Rev. Sholes-Ross feels confident to mentor other clergywomen. "Being affirmed as a writer and Bible scholar, I am becoming more self-confident as clergy, and I will pass encouragement on to other clergywomen. We all have a duty to be our 'sisters' keepers': the keeper who advocates on behalf of, the keeper who challenges with honesty and love, and the keeper who says, 'I understand the injustice associated with being a woman in ministry; just keep on standing and telling your story, for you are God's chosen vessel.' The injustices against qualified women in ministry will be eradicated, because 'The Creator' in me says so."

Having experienced the double discrimination of race and gender, Rev. Sholes-Ross also envisions racially inclusive faith communities to overcome injustices. "I cannot accept that Sunday is the most segregated time of the week. If because of differing worship styles, we are unable to feel a level of comfort with one another during our worship of God, then how can we truly work together to do God's work in the world? There must be an upsetting of our comfort zones. Yes, in many African American churches there is 'celebration'; however, in many Anglo churches there is celebration, too. We must come together to discuss our perceptions about worship and what celebration entails. This will not occur until we cross ethnic and racial lines to have the discussion about 'ism' against divine feminine images in relation to multicultural pastorates. Once this occurs, it will not be 'them' or 'those people,' but the conversation will focus on 'us' as the Body of Christ."

Inclusive leadership, language, and theology are closely connected to peace and social justice, Rev. Sholes-Ross believes. "This aspect of inclusiveness allows humanity to observe that we all have the same hopes, dreams, and even issues. If we become better connected during such an intimate time as worship, then maybe we will better understand one another and see the image of God within us all. We cannot have any aspect of social justice and peace if there is inequality toward any race or gender of humanity."

Rev. Sholes-Ross articulates her big vision: "My vision for the future of the church is that on Sunday mornings we will no longer say, 'Hey, we have a lot of diversity in this community because there's a black church on that corner, and there's a white church on the other corner, and there's the Latino community church on the opposite side and all of them now allow women to speak in the pulpit.' No, we will not have to make those statements because there will be multicultural churches including multicultural divine female imagery and women pastors. Is it too Pollyanna? I don't think so because it helps me to hold on to hope. I am like Abraham: even if I don't see the fulfillment of God's promise, I believe it will occur. I will be faithful in doing my part as pastor, clergy advocate, clergy mentor, clergy colleague, and woman-clergy friend." Through all aspects of her prophetic ministry, Rev. Sholes-Ross is indeed doing her part to fulfill the vision.

Dr. Kendra Weddle Irons

Professor of Religion and Philosophy, Texas Wesleyan University

Embracing Our Mother

"Living in this boundary where only a small number of
people have chosen to put down roots at the intersection
of feminism and Christianity can be lonesome. At least
for me, however, there is no going back and certainly no
desire to return to the narrow path of patriarchal claims.
But the question I continually struggle with is how to share
this perspective with others."[5]

D r. Kendra Weddle Irons's "feminist impulse" emerged when she
was growing up on a farm in Kansas and asked her father to teach
her how to drive a tractor. She had other childhood experiences that
gave her a strong sense of fairness. In her article "Fear, Fairness, and
Feminism: Does It Have to Be So Lonely?" she writes:

I expected to be treated like guys my age, and I did not want to be
treated as my mother was by my father and my grandfather, who
had both followed the traditional patriarchal belief that women
were subordinate to men and that wives were to submit to their
husbands. And, as I grew older and began studying the Bible as part
of my academic training, I began to see more clearly how Jesus
modeled a very different way of living: he respected women as
persons and he sought them out as companions on the Way. Over
time I became convinced! Jesus did not condone treating any group
of people as secondary and in fact demonstrated how going against
societal norms was often necessary to extend grace, love, and genuine hospitality, especially to the least and the last.[6]

When Kendra studied for her undergraduate degree at Friends University in Wichita, Kansas, in the late 1980s, all her professors in her field of religion and philosophy were men. "I never even for a moment thought about the implications of having no female role model," she writes in "Understanding Opposition to Feminism and What We Can Do about It." She continues:

> Nor did I consider how a woman might teach these subjects differently from a man. The feminist movement had rocked the world around me and I was completely insulated from its reverberations. None of my professors planted the idea that I might want to attend a graduate school where feminist thought was intersecting with Christian theology and history. And because my professors were silent about this movement, I did not know what possibilities existed. As I look back on my ignorance, I lament not knowing more. Not being aware of an entire movement underfoot resulted in my journey to feminism coming much later than I wished it had.[7]

With a master's degree in theological studies from Asbury Theological Seminary and a PhD in religion from Baylor University, Dr. Irons began teaching at George Fox University, a Christian school in Newberg, Oregon. While she was teaching there in the religious studies department, her study of feminist theology flourished, building on her interest in women in Christianity, reflected in her PhD dissertation, "Preaching on the Plains: Methodist Women Preachers in Kansas, 1920–1956," which later became a book.[8]

At George Fox University, Dr. Irons found little encouragement for her growing feminism. As the "only female religion professor among ten vocal males," she says that she felt "very much like a stranger in a strange land." When she told her male colleagues that she felt excluded in worship and in other venues, they questioned her feelings, indicating that there was "something wrong" with her, "not with traditional male theology." The preponderance of male images for God contributed to her feelings of exclusion, and she began to explore female images of the Divine. "When I read Sue Monk Kidd's *Dance of the Dissident Daughter*,[9] I knew I had to do something more, to not be complicit in what felt to be a silencing of the problem," she says. "Attending a church in Oregon with a female pastor was extraordinarily helpful. She served as a friend and mentor for moving beyond a masculine point of view."

Dr. Irons says she had a "terrible struggle" when she tried to bring feminist insights to students in her religion classes at George Fox University. "The resistance was so strong at Fox that I was labeled a feminazi, and the university paper ran a cartoon of me with the label." Her feminist theology almost cost Dr. Irons her job there. "I came close to losing my job," she says. "My theology was too liberal because I took a feminist stance. People from all parts of the campus were out to see me leave, including folks in the engineering department who had the ear of the president."

There were, however, some students who were receptive to Dr. Irons's feminist theology. She describes a highlight of her teaching at George Fox University: "I had a handful of students sign on to a project of praying to Sophia for a month and keeping a journal of their experiences. It was a powerful project."

Kendra expresses appreciation for theologian Elizabeth Johnson's book *She Who Is*[10] "as a helpful way of understanding how Sophia was eclipsed by the Word in the writings of John." Also, she appreciates Sister Joan Chittister's work that addresses the "church's sexism," including ways it refuses to take language seriously.

"Language shapes how we construct reality and not the other way around," Dr. Irons states. "I believe that until we change our language we will continue to live within the strictures of patriarchy."

In an article titled "Fearing the Feminine or Embracing Our Mother," Dr. Irons writes:

> It is easy to see how our culture reinforces male preference at the same time it methodically undermines any sense of well-being and confidence a woman works to cultivate. Our exclusive language continues to make women invisible and in some cases our derogatory language aimed at women reinforces an insidious sexism that is more difficult to expunge than the more easily located explicit variety. Adding to this difficulty is our deep resistance to embrace feminine language and images for the Divine. This rejection goes far beyond traditional theology and instead reveals a deeper-seated misogyny we are loath to address much less examine.... Churches,

theologians, and biblical scholars have probably contributed the most to this problem by their insistence upon a male deity and masculine language for God.... How often have I been told not to embrace Her; to see Her as a threat to what it means to be a true Christian? And, how often have I internalized the implicit message that because I am a woman I am naturally less valued than men?[11]

It is necessary to change male-dominated language and symbolism for Deity to change our patriarchal culture, Kendra believes. "While we may chip away at various corners of patriarchal expressions, we will not successfully create an alternative way of living and relating to one another until we change our thinking about both women and men alike as having been created in the image of God, and that this must surely mean that God is both female and male and that the male gender does not rank above the female gender. That means that we need to change both our language and imagery for Godde."[12]

Sexist traditions surrounding potluck dinners and other church activities are connected to exclusively male language for the Divine, Kendra writes:

Until we see and understand the relationship between the perception of God-as-male and subtle expressions of sexism (whether it shows up in potluck expectations or limitations on women's leadership in churches), we will not substantially change the way Christian communities are constructed. When we become as familiar with the image of God as Mother as the church has been with the image of God as Father exclusively, then and only then, will the long and painful history of patriarchy begin to fall. I think a failure to recognize this explains how churches who purport themselves to be progressive or egalitarian and yet fail to change their language for God will nevertheless continue to reflect patriarchy in Sunday school classes, nursery attendants, potluck dinners, vacation Bible school programs, and all the rest of it.[13]

One of the church's basic tasks, Kendra believes, is to create a worshiping community that does not follow sexist culture but embraces the call of Jesus to inclusiveness and wholeness. "Why does the church refuse to be countercultural here and why do women go along with their own exclusion? When women hear sermon after sermon based upon male experiences, why do they continue to listen? When churches sing songs and recite liturgy punctuated with male pronouns for God and people, why do women refuse to speak up about being left out?"[14]

Refusing to go along with exclusion of women, Kendra continues to speak up for change. But she has been dismayed to find resistance to changing exclusively male language for God even in churches with women pastors. The female pastor in Oregon, who was friend and mentor to Kendra, "continued to use the Lord's Prayer without alterations." When she moved to Texas, she visited what she thought was a progressive church with a woman pastor, a community garden, and a labyrinth. But she noticed a "consistent pattern of the father-only metaphor and masculine language" in the liturgy. Kendra discussed her concerns about inclusive language with the pastor, who promised to give more attention to language. But a few Sundays later, the pastor preached a sermon justifying her exclusive language by saying that Jesus used only the word "father" and by dismissing those concerned about inclusive language as having "some political correctness conviction." Kendra felt "bewildered" and "assailed."[15]

Now Dr. Irons seldom wants to attend church services because she has become "tired" and has "mostly given up" on finding a church with inclusive liturgy. But in Evangelical & Ecumenical Women's Caucus–Christian Feminism Today (EEWC-CFT), she has found what she has been looking for. "I met Anne Eggebroten at a conference in California several years ago," she recalls. "I made a presentation that had something to do with the sexism rampant at Christian colleges. She approached me afterward and suggested I look into EEWC." Now Kendra serves as a member of the EEWC-CFT Executive Council.[16]

Kendra describes her first experience of an EEWC-CFT Gathering:

What I encountered in worship with EEWC members from all over the United States is, as is all religious experience, impossible to convey through the limited construction of words. The closest I can come to describing this time is that of oneness; a deep and persuasive sense that even though I barely knew anyone, we were somehow fully connected to each other and to the divine mystery. As women read liturgy and sang and shared openly about their lives, as feminine imagery for God was employed and intention was given to exclude no one, the spirit of God surely was pleased. Throughout this holy weekend, I felt found. Found in this community of inclusivity. Found by a gospel of truly good news."[17]

Currently in her religion classes at Texas Wesleyan University, Dr. Irons has more freedom to introduce feminist theology and inclusive, expansive language than she had at George Fox University. In her course "Women and the Bible" she focuses not only on women biblical characters, but also on feminine imagery and gender issues in the Christian tradition, and in "American Women of Faith" she examines the intersection of American religious history and gender. But she wishes more students were interested in gender issues.

Undaunted by the resistance she has met in Christian colleges and in churches or by the apathy of students, Dr. Irons continues her work as a prophetic, passionate advocate for inclusive language and feminist theology.[18] "There is a direct connection between how we understand God and how we treat others," she states. "To the extent God continues to be understood in masculine terms, we will (unconsciously and consciously) see men as primary and women as secondary. There will be no gender equality and justice until our images of the Divine have shifted. Of course, this is why the resistance is so strong. Exclusively masculine images for God support sexism. Including female images will enable a different social structure."

Dr. Kendra Weddle Irons further articulates her vision of a transformed church and society: "I mostly think the church as it is currently constructed needs to die and in its place something entirely different will emerge. I imagine this to be not a church of buildings and programs but more organic groups who migrate from places of need to new places of need. Maybe the church will become more like how I imagine Jesus and his followers were—people who moved around seeking to spread compassion and justice." Through her writing, teaching, and advocacy, Kendra joins Divine Wisdom's work of bringing this transformation.

Mark Mattison

*Author; Lay Theologian; Coeditor, Divine Feminine
Version of the New Testament*

Reclaiming Biblical Female Divine Images

"Be careful not to publicize your pursuit of justice to be
noticed, or you will have no reward from your Mother who
is in heaven. So don't blow your own horn when you make
donations, like the hypocrites do in the synagogues and in
the streets, so that people might praise them. Believe me
when I say that they have already received their reward. But
when you make donations, don't let your left hand know
what your right hand is doing, so that your donations may
be made secretly; then your Mother who sees in secret will
reward you.

This is how you should pray:
'Our Mother in heaven,
we honor your holy name.
Let your Reign come.
Let your will be done on earth as it is in heaven.
Give us our daily bread today.
Forgive us our debts as we forgive our debtors.
Do not put us in harm's way,
but rescue us from evil.'"

MATTHEW 6:1–4,9–13, DIVINE FEMININE VERSION[19]

A new translation of the Christian Scriptures—the Divine Feminine Version of the New Testament (DFV)—is one of the ambitious initiatives of the Christian Godde Project, an organization cofounded by Mark Mattison, who is also coeditor of the DFV. The Christian Godde Project is "the work of women and men who are called by the Holy Spirit to help restore gender equity in churches by exploring the Divine Feminine within the Christian Godde."[20]

The word "Godde" combines the words "God" and "Goddess," Mark explains. "The word 'God,' because of its long history of association with an exclusively masculine image of the Divine, implies to many people a masculine way of conceiving the Christian God, and 'Goddess' is a word that Christians have not traditionally embraced. The term 'Godde' seeks the middle ground between 'God' and 'Goddess,' combining a feminine-type ending with the traditionally masculine-type word. It's intended as a more gender-inclusive term, something broader than both 'God' and 'Goddess' and yet transcending both as a term that points beyond itself to a divine reality that we can grasp only by metaphor. This term serves as a constant reminder that the Godde of whom we speak is not the ancient man with the white beard so quickly recognizable as a traditional Christian stereotype."

The Christian Godde Project states a solid biblical and theological foundation this way:

> We believe that since women as well as men are created in Godde's image (cf. Gen. 1:27), Godde is revealed in scripture using feminine as well as masculine imagery (cf. Isa. 66:13). In addition, we believe that Divine Wisdom reveals the Divine Feminine in all three 'persons' of the Trinity: as a feminine personification of Godde in the Jewish Wisdom literature, Divine Wisdom reveals Godde as Mother (cf. Prov. 8:1–9:6); as the incarnation of Godde in the New Testament, Jesus is identified with Divine Wisdom (cf. Matt. 11:19; 1 Cor. 1:24, 30); and as the Holy Spirit, Divine Wisdom is revealed as Godde in action (cf. Wis. 7:22ff).[21]

The Christian Godde Project includes a collection of online essays exploring female divine images along with the Divine Feminine Version of the New Testament, which is gender-inclusive in reference to humanity and feminine in reference to Godde. Mark explains: "Recognition of the Divine Feminine in Godde not only signals a willingness to consider seriously the criticism that churches have historically suppressed women, but goes a long way to help restore the rightful place of women as equal partners with men in the task of building up the Church."[22]

Mark believes that a biblical translation that gives precedence to the Divine Feminine is needed as a balance to all the translations with mostly masculine language for the Divine. He tells about meeting a Christian Scriptures professor for breakfast: "When I told him about the Divine Feminine Version of the New Testament he seemed, well, unenthused. He asked me what I thought of the idea of a Divine Masculine New Testament. I think he expected me to respond on a gut level and balk at the idea. What I told him at the time was that I didn't have a problem with masculine language for Godde; I just wanted to see feminine language used as well. Looking back on that conversation, I wish I had pointed out that nearly every other Bible version is *already* a divine masculine version!"

There are, Mark acknowledges, two gender-neutral translations of the Bible on the market: *The Inclusive Bible*, a translation by the Priests for Equality, and *An Inclusive Version*, a modification of the New Revised Standard Version. "Both are very good," Mark says. "However, in relying so heavily on gender-neutral language for Godde, they offer only a partial concession to those of us who long for a recovery of the Divine Feminine within the Christian tradition. They don't distract us by using masculine terms, but they don't nourish us by using feminine terms either, nor do they challenge those who repudiate the Divine Feminine entirely. There are as yet no Divine Feminine Bibles on offer. With so many translations of the Bible, it seems inconceivable to me that there is no Divine Feminine Bible." For this reason Mark is working with others to develop a Divine Feminine translation of the Christian Scriptures. So far, DFV translations of many books of the Christian Scriptures are available free of charge online.[23]

Mark Mattison grew up as a "pastor's kid" in the Church of God General Conference, a conservative branch of the Adventist movement, but not part of Seventh-Day Adventism. Because his father moved around to pastor various churches, Mark lived in Illinois, Michigan, Texas, and Louisiana as he was growing up. He was a fifth-generation member of this denomination, distinguished by its rejection of Trinitarianism. Mark says that feminist theology not only gave him a way to speak of Godde in feminine terms, but it also provided an ecumenical bridge for him into historic Trinitarianism by giving him the "biblical theological tools to describe the preexistence of Christ as Lady Wisdom."

Mark first heard about biblical female divine images not from feminist theologians but from a chapel preacher when he was at the conservative Oregon Bible College (now Atlanta Bible College). "A guest preacher spoke in our chapel once, and I talked with her about theology afterward," Mark recalls. "She was very concerned about women's ordination, which I didn't have an opinion about at the time. She also told me about the Holy Spirit as the Divine Feminine. That was something I had never heard of before. I filed it away in the back of my mind, where the idea lay dormant for many years. The first seed had been planted, but the conditions weren't yet ripe for it to take root. Though I had a strong sense of morality at that time, I had not yet developed a meaningful consciousness of social justice."

More than ten years later, Mark encountered the Female Divine again while he was driving with two other members of the Michigan Peace Team to Terre Haute, Indiana, to work with capital punishment abolitionists. "One of the people I was driving with was a womanist named Melody," Mark recounts. "She described the need for a new ecumenical council to establish the Divine Feminine in the form of the Holy Spirit. This time the idea took root; I was intrigued."

Mark began reading dozens of feminist articles and books; Elizabeth Johnson's *She Who Is* had the greatest influence on him. "That book is just about the most profound work of Christian theology I've ever encountered," he says. "I was completely and overwhelmingly convinced, and have been deeply indebted to the spiritual wisdom of Christian feminist scholars ever since."

Around the time Mark embraced feminist theology, he and his wife, Rebecca, and son, Gabe, joined a Disciples of Christ congregation. They appreciated being part of a denomination that didn't subscribe to any creeds and that had copastors, husband and wife, who avoided using masculine pronouns for Godde. After the copastors left, the congregation hired an evangelical Reformed Church pastor. "I didn't really agree with his theology or his approach to the Bible," Mark says. "And he used divine masculine pronouns all the time. I remember counting how many times I heard words like 'he,' 'him,' and 'his' in reference to Godde. I never heard 'she,' 'her,' or 'hers.' That's about the time I became interested in a divine feminine version of the New Testament. When our son found that his spiritual needs weren't being met either, we left." They have remained in the mainline Protestant tradition, currently attending Trinity Lutheran Church in Grand Rapids, Michigan, where they reside.

Mark would like to see more churches include female divine names and images in worship. When, "occasionally," he has seen the Divine Feminine in worship, he says the experience has been profound. "At a local ELCA church the associate pastor, who's a woman, enacted a sermon illustration by inviting a mother to bring her infant in front of the congregation, and she talked about how this mother's love for her child illustrates Godde's love for us. What a powerful image!"

In trying to change the church through theology inclusive of female divine images, Mark finds that being a layperson has disadvantages and advantages. Although he tries to talk to pastors about inclusive Godde-language, he feels his influence is limited because he's a layperson and not a worship leader. On the other hand, the risks of advocating for inclusive language are minimal for him because his livelihood isn't tied to a religious organization. "So I don't have to walk that tightrope that a lot of others do," he says. "No one is going to threaten to cut off my funding or deprive me of a job based on my religious convictions."

An independent scholar and author, Mark currently makes a living as an administrator with Farmers Insurance. Working in the insurance business and with Ministry School Publications, Mark has had extensive experience in designing, writing, editing, proofreading, and publishing books, newsletters, journals, websites, announcements, and other documents. Recently he has published two illuminating Christian feminist books: *"Because of the Angels"* and *The Gospel of Mary*.[24]

Because of his deep belief in the power of inclusive language and leadership in the church, Mark works many hours as a volunteer on the Christian Godde Project. "The leadership of the body of Christ has to be as diverse as the body of which it's a part," he says. "Otherwise the body just isn't healthy. Strictly male images of Godde, conveyed through a strictly male leadership, distort the reality of Godde and undervalue the sense of identity of those who don't fit the supposedly ideal model that is set before them. I believe that's why so many churches are anemic! I'm honestly disheartened by how many churches seem to devalue peace and social justice, and I don't think it's a coincidence that often these are churches that don't celebrate diversity."

Resistance to inclusion of female divine names and images, Mark believes, stems from "overly literal approaches to the Bible," especially in interpreting the Christian Scriptures' use of the word "Father" to describe Godde. Mark suggests asking what the scriptures are trying to communicate with this "familial description." He wonders, however, whether or not critics are ultimately motivated by fidelity to the biblical text. "The fact that their reaction is so strong suggests to me that there's more to their resistance than that, something on a gut level. The divine masculine image of Godde is just so ingrained; it seems like it's not easy to dislodge."

In his efforts to overcome this resistance, Mark points out biblical female images of Godde that need to be reclaimed. "The Divine Feminine has a long and venerable history within the Christian tradition, all the way back to the beginning. Biblical images of Godde as a nurturing Mother, or as Wisdom calling people to follow Her, or as a Spirit groaning in the pains of childbirth, are all over the place. These images and others need to be reclaimed in order to bring spiritual healing to the church."

To bring healing change to the church through reclaiming these female divine images, Mark works diligently with the Christian Godde Project team on the Divine Feminine Version of the New Testament, generously made available free of charge online. He has a big vision for the DFV: "I'd love to see quotations from this Bible version popping up across the Web and in publications, and to see commentaries and devotionals using this version as their text. I'd love to see congregations using this text in their liturgies. My hope and prayer is that this translation will provide a much-needed tool to integrate the Divine Feminine within the church."

Rev. Dr. Angela M. Yarber

Scholar; Dancer; Artist; Minister

Embodying the Divine Feminine

"God of many names, who is not constrained by gender or
the binaries humans construct, thank You for the diversity
that You imbue in each of us, Your beloved children.
We are grateful that You love unabashedly and without
discrimination, celebrating the wondrous diversity of
humankind: women, men, trans, gay, straight, bi, lesbian,
queer, and those not limited to the finitude of our
language. In a world where many of us feel constrained by
socially constructed categories, we implore You to set us
free. In a world where some are valued more than others,
we beg You to liberate, overturn, subvert the status quo.
And we ask You to embolden us to liberate, overturn, and
subvert. Empower us to be Your people, people called to
set the captives free, basking in Your never-ending, life-
changing, always-accepting love that unites us all. Mother,
Father, Friend, Lover, and Guide, incarnate Yourself in us
we pray."[25]

Rev. Dr. Angela M. Yarber's prophetic book *The Gendered Pulpit*
demonstrates that "gendered and sexualized bodies" are "a vital
part of proclaiming the Word, so that the body and the experiences
of women and the LGBTQ[26] community are affirmed in preaching
and worship." In addition to providing liturgical resources, like this
section's opening prayer, Dr. Yarber engages readers with personal

narrative and scholarly examination of scripture, church history, theology, and theories of preaching and worship.

In the introduction to *The Gendered Pulpit*, Rev. Dr. Yarber states that through her experience "as an ordained lesbian Baptist preacher," she has discovered the importance of highlighting marginalized voices.

> Since I firmly believe in the notion, "if you can't see it, you can't be
> it," I have devoted all my adulthood to shifting the status quo when
> it comes to preaching and worship, doing my best to gender the
> pulpit in a manner that creates pathways for women and LGBTQ
> persons to see that they, too, can be called to proclaim the Word.
> When I step into the pulpit, I do so on behalf of countless people
> who never dreamed that they were affirmed and beloved of God,
> let alone that they, too, have a Word to share.[27]

In addition to being a minister, Rev. Dr. Yarber is an artist, a dancer, and a scholar. I met Angela at an Alliance of Baptists Gathering in Greenville, South Carolina. I was amazed to see her powerful female divine paintings all around the large church where we met. Even though the Alliance is progressive and the language in worship usually avoids masculine pronouns for God, there are rarely any female divine names and images included in worship at the annual meetings. So I was surprised and delighted to see Angela's female divine paintings displayed throughout the church and to watch her paint on the platform during worship services, illustrating the sermons and readings.

Dr. Yarber's first book, *Embodying the Feminine in the Dances of the World's Religions*, addresses the importance of embodying the Female Divine as a part of interfaith dialogue by looking at four dances from four different faith traditions.[28] In *Dance in Scripture: How Biblical Dancers Can Revolutionize Worship Today,* she also celebrates dance as a creative and empowering way to affirm the body in worship.[29]

Angela didn't grow up in the church, but she became very active in a conservative church when she was a teenager. "My family isn't religious, but I come from a long line of feminists," she says. "Though church was not a part of my upbringing, my mother always taught me the importance of harmony, compassion, love, and openness. When I did become involved in a very conservative church in my late teens, I accepted the brand of Christianity they taught for a brief period because

I thought that their version of Christianity was the only version. I gave up some important parts of myself—including feminism—for a couple of years until I was exposed to feminist theology and Baptist history in college. It was then that I realized my original feminist-artist-vegan self could also be Christian. The two weren't mutually exclusive like I was taught. I've been proclaiming the Feminine Divine ever since!"

After earning a bachelor of arts in religion from Brewton-Parker College, Angela went on to earn a master of divinity degree from McAfee School of Theology at Mercer University and then a doctorate in art and religions from the Graduate Theological Union at UC Berkeley. She has taught undergraduate and graduate courses at colleges and seminaries in Georgia, North Carolina, and California, and pastored local churches.

Rev. Dr. Yarber comments on ways she brings theology inclusive of the Female Divine to theological education and to the church. "The most obvious example is the inclusive language policy I have on all my syllabi and in worship. I do all my own translations for worship services, so that language about God and humanity is inclusive. Feminists and womanists are well represented in readings assigned to my classes. As a queer woman, I also think that my very presence in a classroom or pulpit illustrates elements of the Feminine Divine. My bodily being speaks to this inclusion before I even open my mouth and proclaim a word."

Female divine names and images are imbedded in Christian history, scripture, and tradition, Rev. Yarber believes. "It's simply that patriarchy and heteronormativity have ignored or neglected them and it's our responsibility to uncover these seemingly hidden truths. When I do change the church's tradition regarding language or symbols, it's in the spirit of openness, inclusion, and justice. I believe that justice and equality are at the heart of our tradition, so our language and symbols should reflect and honor that."

In *The Gendered Pulpit*, Rev. Dr. Yarber states that "gender-neutral" language is not enough to promote justice.

> Neutral inclusive language continues to allow socialized patterns of domination to shape perceptions of God and humanity. If men and women were truly treated equally, and if an equal number of people perceived God to be female as well as male, then such neutral

language could work. But women and men are not treated equally in society, and certainly not in the church, and most people still perceive God in male terms. Until this shifts, neutral language is not sufficient enough to gender the pulpit in the direction of justice.[30]

Instead, Angela advocates the use of biblical female divine names and images like *Ruah*, *Hokmah*, *Sophia*, *El Shaddai*, and *Shekhinah* in worship. These names and images have the "potential to gender the pulpit in a manner that promotes equality, justice, and empowerment."[31]

Angela says she also paints multicultural female divine images to promote justice, inclusion, and empowerment. "It's important for women, LGBTQ persons, and racial and ethnic minorities to be able to see images that reflect who they are in worship. Worship that only includes images from traditional iconography, for example, ignores the experiences of women and LGBTQ persons, while also 'white-washing' many persons of color out of our history. If the church truly values all of humanity, then one should be able to look at the images the church displays and see all of humanity." She continues, "If a woman, LGBTQ person, or person of color can step into the church and see an image of the Divine that looks like them, they can be empowered to know that they can become the God they adore. This empowerment extends beyond the walls of the church and into the world so that oppressed minorities can be emboldened, validated, and liberated. The liberation that occurs at church is not limited to the church, but can expand beyond it; as it should, the church can lead the world toward justice."

Although Rev. Dr. Yarber has at times considered leaving the church, she feels a responsibility to stay. "When I receive regular hate mail that tells me I'm damned to hell simply for who I am, and when I experience sexist, classist, and heterosexist microaggressions within my own congregations, communities, and denomination, I often consider leaving! But I return to the notion: 'If you can't see it, you can't be it,'" she remarks. "I think of the women and LGBTQ persons who have never looked into the pulpit and seen anyone like them preaching behind it. I think of the way the church has maligned and oppressed their bodies. And I think of the privilege I've had to be a queer woman proclaiming the Word. I feel a responsibility to stay and create pathways for other women and LGBTQ persons to find affirmation, liberation, and justice."

By working to create new pathways in church and society, Angela acknowledges that she takes risks. "When a feminist theologian received an award for her work on pneumatology and referred to the Spirit by saying 'bless Her,' the room filled with nervous laughter. When I gender the pulpit in the direction of justice, many respond with nervous laughter, as though what I'm saying isn't valid, true, scholarly, meaningful, or important," Angela relates. "Worse, people sometimes respond with anger and disdain. This is a small risk: people thinking I'm foolish, people regarding my work as nonacademic or unchristian, or people disregarding it all because they think feminism isn't needed. The bigger risks come with some of the hate mail I've received. These deal less with issues of gender and more with sexuality. I can take the standard quotation of six Bible verses ripped out of context and condemning me to hell. I can even take the writer of one of my pieces of hate mail describing the way my flesh will smell when I burn in hell. But when people name my partner, or our adopted baby, they have gone too far. This is a risk I am not willing to take."

Apart from the extreme responses she receives in hate mail, Rev. Dr. Yarber also experiences criticism of her inclusive, progressive theology. "Less extreme, but often annoying, is when someone says, 'I'm just not comfortable changing scripture' or 'You just don't take the Bible seriously.' These comments are annoying merely because I've chosen to dedicate my entire life to taking scripture seriously. I translate it weekly and read it nearly every day; I spend a great deal of time researching its historical contexts and do my best to live by the virtues of love, compassion, peace, and justice that come from much of scripture," Angela explains. "If people aren't comfortable 'changing' scripture, then they should translate it themselves and acknowledge that every translation is an interpretation. If people choose to translate *anthropos* as 'man' rather than 'human,' for example, they are ignoring the broader and truer meaning of the scriptural text. And given that the dictionary deemed it 'academically archaic' to refer to humanity as 'man' more than forty years ago, I'd hope the church could stop resisting and update their antiquated language."

Inspiration and strength to meet the resistance, struggles, and challenges come to Angela from many people. "I often think of the many women and LGBTQ persons who have gone before me, living authentically into their callings, so that I, too, can live into mine," she says. "Many of these women are found in my Holy Women Icons,[32] and I think of them as the 'great cloud of witnesses' who strengthen, embolden, inspire, liberate, and empower. I think of the eighth grader who participated in the 'Day of Silence' and has grown into a fabulous straight ally. I think of more than thirty women at Baptist Women in Ministry who initiated a letter-writing campaign to write me 'love letters' to combat the hate mail I receive. I think of the peacemakers who gather each year at the Baptist Peace Fellowship's annual conference who make protest signs that read 'Jesus Loves All Cocoa Farmers' and inaugurate the Baptist Equal Exchange partnership for fair trade chocolate." She continues, "Anytime someone has told me that my teaching or preaching has helped her or him live more compassionately, more justly, more peacefully, it is a rewarding experience. I'm also inspired and strengthened daily by people in my own life, namely my mother and my partner. My partner is an ethicist, and she inspires me to be more compassionate to all creatures, to wonder at the earth, and to stand in solidarity with the poor."

Rev. Dr. Angela Yarber articulates a hopeful, expansive vision for the future of the church: "I hope and dream of the day when women, LGBTQ persons, and the Feminine Divine are an integral part of the church and church leadership. I hope that one day our visions of the Divine and of what it looks like to be a church leader are equal and inclusive. I hope that one day people will not giggle or become angry when God is referred to as 'She.' I hope that one day when churches post signs that say 'all are welcome,' they'll truly mean all: gay and straight, black and white, rich and poor, university educated and life educated, English speaking and non–English speaking, young and old, abled and differently abled, male and female. Unfortunately, I think this day is in the far-too-distant future. Until then, I continue to rage, work, paint, write, and dance toward justice."

Part 2

Wisdom's Works of Racial Equality

Worship language and symbolism all too often contribute to racism as well as sexism. A friend told me that he was appalled to hear the children in his church singing these words: "Who's that dressed in white? It must be the children of the Israelites. Who's that dressed in black? It must be the hypocrites turning back."

Religious worship services and the wider culture symbolize black as evil or ominous and white as purity and holiness. In many hymns, prayers, scripture readings, and sermons, images of darkness carry negative connotations while images of light carry positive connotations. Visual images of a white God fill many churches. This symbolism gives greatest value to Anglos while demeaning and devaluing people of color.

On the other hand, multicultural images of the Divine contribute to racial equality by affirming the equal value of people of all races and ethnicities. Liturgies that symbolize darkness as creative bounty and beauty affirm the sacred value of people of color. Language and art that symbolize darkness as sacred power contribute to equal power and opportunity for all races.

Multicultural images of the Divine combine with female images of the Divine to form a foundation for equality and justice. Gender and racial equality go hand in hand. As the stories in this book reveal, female names and images of the Divine open doors to multicultural images and vice versa. When people begin to expand imagery for divinity, they discover a multiplicity of names and images in scripture, church history, and tradition.

There is a strong connection between female images of Deity and multicultural images. For example, depictions of Sophia ("Wisdom") have traditionally been dark or a combination of dark and light, drawing from both Egyptian and Greek sacred images.[1] *Ruah* ("Spirit") and other female divine images are also often represented as dark. Wisdom and other female personifications of the Divine work for racial as well as gender equality.

O Holy Darkness, Loving Womb
(Sung to the tune of "O Little Town of Bethlehem")

O Holy Darkness, loving womb, who nurtures and creates,
sustain us through the longest night with dreams of open gates.
We move inside to mystery that in our center dwells,
where streams of richest beauty flow from sacred living wells.

Creative Darkness, closest friend, you whisper in the night;
You calm our fears as unknown paths surprise us with new sight.
We marvel at your bounty, your gifts so full and free,
unfolding as you waken us to new reality.

O Holy Christ-Sophia, your image black and fair,
stirs us to end injustice and the wounds of Earth repair.
The treasures of your darkness and riches of your grace
inspire us to fulfill our call, our sacredness embrace.[2]

Words © 1996 Jann Aldredge-Clanton   ST. LOUIS

Rev. Dr. Grace Ji-Sun Kim

Associate Professor of Doctrinal Theology, Moravian Theological Seminary

Healing Racism, Sexism, and Classism Through Sophia Christology

"Every woman in North America has experienced the life of powerlessness to some degree, but visible minority women experience it in greater intensity. Sophia can help transform this life. Korean North American women need to hold on to this promise and hope as they respond to the grace of divine Sophia, who will unconditionally accept and love them."[3]

R ev. Dr. Grace Ji-Sun Kim's powerful book *The Grace of Sophia: A Korean North American Women's Christology* addresses Korean North American women specifically, but also offers hope to all who suffer from sexism, racism, and/or classism. Dr. Kim analyzes racism and sexism in North American culture and patriarchy in Korean society, drawing from multifaith understandings of Wisdom (Sophia) to provide a liberating Christology.

Korean North American women have been silenced and subordinated for too long. They have endured hardships through their Confucian heritage and also from their immigrant lifestyles. Torn between two different cultures, they do not seem to fit in comfortably anywhere. To make matters worse, the church has rarely helped these women to become liberated. Instead, the church has reinforced their subordinate status by perpetuating notions of a masculine divinity. The imagery for God needs to expand to include more liberative metaphors from the Christian faith tradition. Female images of God are essential for maintaining the fullness of the image of God and for the promotion of equality between women and men. For a liberative understanding of God, Korean North American women need to break away from the present patriarchal framework and move to a more inclusive understanding of God and of Jesus Christ. Sophia Christology is already a major feature of white feminist theology.... Sophia Christology may also serve as a meaningful and liberative way forward for Korean North American women's Christology, particularly because of the wisdom tradition of Korean women's own religious and cultural roots.[4]

Born in South Korea, Grace Ji-Sun Kim immigrated with her family to Canada at the age of five. Religion has always played an important part in her life. In Korea, her parents followed the Buddhist tradition. Soon after immigrating to Canada, her family converted to Christianity and became members of a Korean Presbyterian church. She writes:

Our membership in a Korean church kept our Korean heritage alive. The church plays an important role in the lives of immigrants, as it becomes a haven away from the problems and difficulties of living in a foreign world.... At church I learned Korean language, history, and music. The church is an essential gathering place where Korean immigrants experience likeness, similarity, and bonding. On the other hand, the church is an institution that also perpetuates patriarchal and oppressive teachings. My Christian upbringing made me question why I was experiencing racism from the wider society and oppression from the patriarchal Korean society.[5]

In part, Grace's personal experiences of injustice led her to write *The Grace of Sophia*. Growing up in Canada, she experienced classism as well as racism and sexism. Her family lived in a small apartment while her school friends lived in large homes. In addition to enduring poor living conditions, Grace had her first experience with racism when she was in kindergarten. Classmates teased her about the way she looked, talked, and dressed, and they called her hurtful names, such as "chink," that "penetrated deeply, becoming unhealable wounds."[6] She acknowledges that she has experienced racism and sexism throughout her life.

Grace draws from these experiences in her prophetic work for others who suffer oppression. Her teaching and research focus on giving a voice to the marginalized and those on the underside of history. She earned her master of divinity degree from Knox College and her doctor of philosophy degree from the University of Toronto. She has served on the faculty of Knox College and is currently an associate professor of doctrinal theology and the director of the Master of Arts in Theological Studies program at Moravian Theological Seminary in Bethlehem, Pennsylvania. Dr. Kim is the author of five books and more than fifty journal articles, book chapters, and book reviews.

An ordained minister of word and sacrament within the Presbyterian Church (USA) denomination, Rev. Kim sees the church as a community of believers who "need to work together to get a better understanding of the Divine whom we worship and are in relationship with." She believes in changing the church not only for her generation but also for the ones to follow. Rev. Kim and her husband, Dr. Perry Y. C. Lee, a mathematics professor at Kutztown University, have three children: Theo, Elisabeth, and Joshua. Rev. Kim states: "As we think about our children, it is imperative not only to write about the problems of racism, but also talk about them so we can work toward eliminating racism. In addition, as we also work towards a more equal society for both men and women, we also need to talk about male privilege, supremacy, and structural 'isms.'"[7]

Her personal experiences of racism and sexism inform Dr. Kim's work. She writes:

> Much of my personal life intersects with race, religion, and gender issues. In some ways the word *intersects* is too gentle. Perhaps *collide* better captures what occurs in my life as an Asian North American woman theologian, writer, minister, and mother. As I try to engage in theological dialogue, living in community with the dominant, unfamiliar culture, and raise my kids with concerns on how to be just in this world, I realize that the lives of all people, especially people of color, collide and clash with others on the critical issues of race, religion, and gender.[8]

Rev. Dr. Kim believes that we need inclusive images of the Divine in order to create a more equal, just, and peaceful society. "If we are to work for social justice and peace, we need to work towards the inclusion of all people," she states. "This includes people of different ethnicities, genders, sexuality, and so on. If our spirituality includes only a masculine understanding of the Divine, this is problematic. Therefore, to be inclusive of all people, it is important to include and embrace the feminine divine images. These feminine divine images are already present in our biblical and Christian tradition. Therefore, we are not presenting anything new; we are retrieving and incorporating them into our present theology."

Inclusive language for the Divine is vital to bringing justice and equality into church and society, Rev. Kim says. "Language forms our thoughts. If language restricts or limits our understanding of the Divine and each other, then it needs to be changed or reexamined. Using feminine language for the Divine isn't something new but rather has existed and is already part of our tradition. Therefore, it is more of a retrieval and an embrace of our tradition that was already in place two thousand years ago."

Because of her belief in the importance of language, Dr. Kim requires all her seminary students to use inclusive language for humanity. She also pushes them to use inclusive language for divinity. But she meets resistance from her students and from her church to changing language to include biblical female names for the Divine.

One of the biblical female divine images Rev. Kim finds especially empowering is Wisdom (*Hokmah* in Hebrew, *Sophia* in Greek). "Sophia Christology provides hope and empowerment for those who have suffered sexism, racism, and classism because it provides a more inclusive understanding of the Divine, which embraces all people," she says. "We are limited in our understanding of the Divine. Furthermore, there is a mystery when it comes to the Divine. Therefore, understanding our own limitedness and the mystery that surrounds the Divine, we should move forward and not neglect the powerful images that exist and are part of our Christian tradition. We need to welcome these images because they are powerful and life-giving. God is both male and female, and we need to try to grasp this understanding. As I struggle with my own experiences of sexism within society and the church, it is important to understand that God is both feminine and masculine."

Another biblical female divine image that Rev. Dr. Kim finds empowering is the Spirit. In her book *The Holy Spirit, Chi, and the Other* she explores the female dimension of the Spirit.[9] Connecting the Spirit in the Hebrew Bible with the Eastern concept of Chi, she writes: "Because God as the Spirit manifests herself as wind, or *ruach*, she is also Chi."[10] The purpose of this book is to widen the scope of theological discourse to include those whom Western religion and culture have considered "others" and embrace them on common ground.

In her book *Colonialism, Han, and the Transformative Spirit*, Dr. Kim also focuses on the image of the Spirit and expands her prophetic work to include caring for the earth.[11] She demonstrates how colonialism, globalization, and consumerism have devastated large parts of our world and how inspiration for work toward a safer, sustainable planet can come from the transformative Spirit who gives, sustains, and empowers all life.

Rev. Kim believes that multicultural as well as female divine names and images are changing the church. "These multicultural names and images are opening up the church and making us realize that it is the universal church and not just a European church."

Multicultural female names and images for Deity will help change not only the church but also the wider culture, Dr. Kim asserts. "Our society is heavily entrenched in patriarchy. Patriarchy has been devastating as it continues to subordinate and subjugate women in all aspects of society. One way to overcome this patriarchal culture is to move toward understanding the Divine as feminine. This movement will help society realize that women and men are equal and need to be treated equally in all aspects of life."

Grace experiences many struggles and challenges in her creative, prophetic work to change church and society.[12] She says that her inspiration comes from "other women who are in solidarity" with her "in the struggle to fight against patriarchy and patriarchal understandings of the Divine." Rev. Dr. Grace Ji-Sun Kim articulates a powerful, hopeful vision for the future of the church. "My vision is that the church will understand and embrace the Feminine Divine in all aspects of the life of the church." Embracing biblical female imagery and language for the Divine will contribute to the "reign of God, which receives all people as equal regardless of class, age, ethnicity, or gender."

Rev. Christine A. Smith

Senior Pastor, Covenant Baptist Church, Wickliffe, Ohio

Creating Multicultural Churches

"The concept of the glass ceiling is not new. In the secular
realm, the glass ceiling represents the barrier that
prevents qualified individuals from excelling beyond a
certain level due to their race, gender, or orientation.
For those of us who serve in the sacred or religious
realm, we know it as the stained glass ceiling, referring
to the barriers imposed by churches.... Contrary to
some reports, female clergy have not yet arrived. While
a few denominations such as United Methodists, the
Presbyterian Church (USA), United Church of Christ,
Disciples of Christ, and American Baptist Churches
USA have accepted and called women to serve as senior
pastors, many qualified and well-equipped sisters still
struggle to have their gifts of preaching and pastoring
recognized. Among those who have become senior
pastors, remnants of the stained glass ceiling persist."[13]

R ev. Christine A. Smith wrote her prophetic and practical book
*Beyond the Stained Glass Ceiling: Equipping and Encouraging Female
Pastors* in order to "address the barriers and injustices that female pastors still encounter as they prayerfully pursue the senior or solo pastor-
ate." Rev. Smith cites studies showing that females represent only about
9 to 10 percent of senior or solo pastors in America and that females
who serve as pastors receive much lower compensation than male pastors, although clergywomen are more likely to have seminary degrees.

In addition to statistics, the book includes insights from interviews and surveys she conducted with 150 female pastors.[14]

Because of the inequities clergywomen experience, Rev. Smith enthusiastically accepted the invitation to participate in the Access and Equity for Women Clergy Conference, held at Wake Forest University School of Divinity. Participants at this historic gathering developed strategies to make reality the big vision of equal representation of clergywomen as pastors of multicultural churches. "This conference was an answer to prayer," Christine says. "My desire is to have opportunities to positively influence the church, the academy, and communities regarding increasing opportunities for women to pastor, preach, teach, and lead."

Rev. Smith's book, *Beyond the Stained Glass Ceiling*, provides much-needed wisdom for the conference's purpose of addressing the interlocking injustices of sexism and racism that women encounter in pursuing their call to pastor. She writes:

> Sexism and racism have some tragic similarities. Racial minorities have been given "compliments" such as "You are so intelligent! You are not like *them*. You are different!" The implication is obvious: "*You people* are usually ignorant and incapable, but somehow you're not like the rest." What an insult! Many persons of color have heard these words not as insults but rather as a reprieve from oppression—a welcomed affirmation, a hint of praise. Women have dealt with the same dynamics as they have reached higher levels. Out of extreme thirst for acceptance, they drink in patronizing words such as, "You aren't like those other women; you can preach," or, "I like how feminine you are; you aren't trying to act like a man." When one is psychologically and emotionally hungry, it is tempting to be drawn into the illusion of acceptance and relish the thought of being a part of the upper crust.[15]

In response to my interview questions, Rev. Smith draws additional similarities between sexism and racism. "Both have set up formidable systems that perpetuate oppression, self-loathing, economic injustices, and pain that we have yet to overcome. Sexism and racism blind power brokers to the true value of minorities and women. Their gifts and talents are frequently boxed in all or most of their lives."

When she was sixteen, Christine was called to the ministry. She expresses gratitude that her home pastor was very supportive of women in ministry. Not until she was in her twenties and in seminary did she begin to understand the discrimination against women in ministry. "It was there that I heard the horror stories of other women and faced the stark reality, particularly as a Baptist woman, that women were not welcomed in the pulpit by many of our churches."

While she was in seminary, Christine won a scholarship for an internship in a program called "Black Women in Church and Society." Among Christine's responsibilities as an intern were visiting homeless shelters, counseling students identified with behavioral disorders, and assisting in food distribution in a church pantry. In this program Christine also read books such as *Ain't I a Woman*, *In Search of Our Mothers' Gardens*, *God of the Oppressed*, and *The Courage to Be*.[16] These books spoke to Christine about God's call to women and men to serve the present age and about gender not thwarting God's work.

Christine's story makes clear that she has worked hard not to let gender or race thwart her call or her gifts. After graduating from seminary, she served as a staff minister for several years and then was ordained. Rev. Smith served three years as a minister of education at Olivet Institutional Baptist Church in Cleveland. She continued her training through a clinical pastoral education residency and then through psychology courses at Cleveland State University. For a year she served as a pastoral counselor to homeless women and then for five years as a hospital chaplain. For many years she has served as a trustee for Cleveland Baptist Association. In addition, she served as executive leader for the Association and now serves as acting administrator in a transitional time. Currently, Rev. Smith also serves as senior pastor of Covenant Baptist Church in Wickliffe, Ohio. She is the first female pastor of Covenant Baptist, the first African American pastor of this church, and the second female pastor in the greater Cleveland area of American Baptist Churches USA. Rev. Smith states that her challenges at this church "have been both racial and gender based."

In *Beyond the Stained Glass Ceiling*, Rev. Smith writes about the challenges that she and other minority female pastors face:

> With few exceptions, African American clergywomen will find most opportunities to pastor in Euro American congregations. In a perfect world, race and culture may not matter, but we do not live in a perfect world. At the onset, both pastor and people

may be willing to work together; both, however, may wrestle with the fact that they would like to have it another way.... Some might retort, "We should not be concerned about race—we are all God's children, and heaven is diverse!" Nevertheless, diversity should be an intentional goal that is sought out of a vision and passion for racial and cultural reconciliation, not the result of two parties that have few other choices. For minority female clergy who have been brought up, nurtured, loved, and supported by churches of their own culture, the pain of rejection after announcing the call to pastor, coupled with the fresh struggles of pastoring and compounded by the realities of cultural differences, can be daunting. Often, major differences exist in perceptions of leadership ... administration ... and worship styles.... It can be very discouraging. Yet, in a deep desire to fulfill her calling, many a clergywoman will press through the challenges, make the most of what she has, and cultivate something beautiful. If individuals are honest, however, the ugliness of deep-seated prejudices can make crossing the hurdles of cultural diversity tricky. A pastor may experience that the church has a burst of growth, numerically, financially, and culturally, only to have that growth cancelled by an exodus from those made uncomfortable by what is perceived as a potential power shift.[17]

Given these challenges, leaders from eight Christian denominations gathered at a conference at Wake Forest School of Divinity to plan strategies for creating culturally diverse churches where clergywomen have increased opportunities to serve as pastors. Rev. Smith brought wisdom for this process: "If we are serious about creating true multicultural churches representative of various cultures in styles of worship, teaching, preaching, mission work, and so on, and not just cosmetic diversity (people of different cultures attending the same church, but using the dominant culture's worship style), then we have to be intentional about incorporating a variety of worship styles into the process." Rev. Smith also brought her experience as pastor of a multicultural church. She received the "Living the Legacy" award at a conference, sponsored by American Baptists, for her work as a pastor of a multicultural church, an author, a community leader, and an advocate for social justice.

With deep faith and passion, Rev. Smith expresses the biblical and theological foundation for her inclusive ministry. "Genesis 1:27 declares, 'In the image of God, God created humankind, male and female, God created them.' It is critical that leadership reflects both male and female imagery because the church is both male and female," she says. "Additionally, male and female leadership is important to the balance of perspectives in ministry. Women tend to be multitaskers, can be positive role models for other women and men, can provide pastoral care more easily in certain settings and highlight the feminine attributes of God's love such as mercy, sensitivity, and compassion. Throughout history, women have been among the oppressed, abused, and disenfranchised members of society. God-endorsed feminine leadership highlights the message of the gospel that God hears the cries of the oppressed, answers them, and exalts them—giving them a seat of honor at the banquet table. As the church and the broader community become more willing to make room at tables, conversations surrounding 'doing justly, loving mercy and walking humbly with God,' as Micah 6:8 suggests, will increase."

Including all the female images of God in the Bible, Rev. Smith believes, is important to this theology of justice and inclusiveness. "Imagery is both powerful and important. I preach and teach using all of the imagery given in the scriptures." She specifically mentions the image of God as a mother eagle "stirring her nest." Also, she emphasizes an image used particularly in the African American tradition: "God is a mother for the motherless and a father for the fatherless."

Just as God comes in varied ways to minister to people with varied needs, female and male ministers are necessary to minister to diverse people, Rev. Smith asserts. "God uses both male and female to address the multiplicity of needs coming from God's people."

Christine has risked disapproval and exclusion because of her advocacy for clergywomen. "Both men and women become uncomfortable and sometimes angry if you dare suggest that there is still much work to be done," she says. "Contrary to common belief, we have not yet arrived! My risks have involved daring to write a book that addresses this issue, continuing to raise questions and suggest new approaches even when people get sick of me, and continuing to be an advocate even when it means being dismissed from certain circles."

Rev. Smith indicts our churches and culture for patriarchy and racism that exclude women from pastoral positions:

> In many ways, churches have remained captive to the patriarchal character of the larger culture. Although women have made great strides in recent decades, society in the United States remains patriarchal, and women still lag behind men in top-level positions and salaries. The complex dynamics of racism also play a role in the oppression of women of color. For communities of color in the United States—especially the African American community—the church is one of the few places where men hold positions of power and influence. These men may be considered of nominal influence on the job or in the marketplace, but when they come to church, they are deacons, elders, bishops, or pastors. Men may be reluctant to share these leadership roles with women.[18]

In the midst of all these challenges, Rev. Smith remains hopeful and confident in her call to change the church. She affirms that God has called her, anointed her, and appointed her for this prophetic ministry. She also gains encouragement, inspiration, and strength from other women and men who have worked "in the heat of the day, stood for what is right, and remained faithful in the midst of opposition and struggle."

Rev. Smith articulates a powerful prayer for the future of the church: "My prayer is that the people of God will put aside the foolishness of discrimination, oppression, and cowardice and get busy being the hands and feet of Jesus in a lost, broken, and dying world." In her book she connects her vision for the church to the "beloved community" envisioned by Dr. Martin Luther King Jr. "While Dr. King was referring to racial integration, the concept is also appropriate for bringing about equality and integration of women into the pastoral ministry," she writes. "In order to press on, the need is for more than rules and regulations that may begin the process but will not be transformative in the long run. What is needed is a change of heart and attitude through love."[19] Through her prophetic preaching, writing, and pastoral ministry, Rev. Smith contributes to this transformation.[20]

Rev. Virginia Marie Rincon

Episcopal Priest; Founder and Executive Director, TengoVoz

The *Virgen de Guadalupe* at the Forefront of Justice

I am a Chicana
I dance and chant my prayer.
My roots call me to a simple
but deep and compassionate
faith.

I love the prayer that comes via my culture,
bright colors, images of *Nuestra Virgen de Guadalupe*
and the smell of tamales and tortillas on the stove.

I am a Chicana
and
I believe I have much to offer.
I love to dance and chant my prayers.
These visions are not just mine they are
also yours—
come, dance and chant my prayer.

In her strong, lyrical voice, Rev. Virginia Marie Rincon reads "I Am a Chicana," a poem she wrote when trying to discern whether to enter the ordination process. In TengoVoz gatherings, she begins the liturgy with a poem, often one that she has written. The women in this group then continue the liturgy by reflecting on the poem. Rev. Virginia

Marie Rincon founded TengoVoz ("I have voice") to advocate for Latina women and children and to facilitate women's groups.[21]

Around her neck Rev. Rincon wears a gold medal with female divine images on each side. "It's the *Virgen de Guadalupe* and the *Virgen de San Juan*," she says. "The *Virgen de San Juan* has a shrine in Texas; she is very strong for me because my grandmother used to go there every year and pray for me that I would fulfill my call. And the *Virgen de Guadalupe* is so important to me because I've always seen her first as a feminist, but then later when I was able to articulate that I was a *mujerista*,[22] I realized that she's a *mujerista* I can really relate to with all her different complexities, her fusion of Aztec culture and Catholicism."

Rev. Rincon tells how this image of Guadalupe has also been empowering for the women in TengoVoz groups. "They're looking at the *Virgen de Guadalupe* in a different way, not as the submissive *Virgen*. Most Roman Catholics will put her up there in this little nice space, but the women of TengoVoz are seeing her as very different, a strong woman of action. They use her story for their own image of themselves, and they're like, 'Wow! Women in the church could create change.'"

When she was about seven years old, Virginia Marie first knew she had a call to ministry. In a Catholic school in Houston, Texas, she was praying at the communion rail. "I remember thinking, 'I want to go see what the priests do back there.' So I jumped the communion rail, opened the closet, and put the vestments on. Then I came out and said something like, 'The peace of Christ be with you.' Of course, all the kids started laughing. The nun came in and was very upset. She had a conversation with my grandmother, and I was sent back to public school," she recalls. "I've always been drawn to the altar and the sacrament. Until I was seven, I was mostly raised by my grandmother, who was a shaman, a *curandera*.[23] Now I look back and realize that there are similarities in how she gathered and approached people and how I do. It wasn't unusual for me to wake up in the morning and my grandmother would have all these women sitting at her table drinking coffee, talking, praying, doing healing ritual, chanting, singing. When I was a little girl, my grandmother would always say that I was special, that I had the gift of healing. And she would teach me things, like to listen. As a kid of five or six years old, I didn't know what I was listening for, but now I know."

In high school Virginia Marie decided that she wanted to be a nurse and went to the counselor, who told her, "You could never be a registered nurse (RN), but you could probably be a licensed vocational nurse (LVN)." As a member of the National Honor Society with straight A's, Virginia Marie could have gotten scholarships and easily completed the RN requirements. Although Virginia Marie can now see the racism in the counselor's advice, at the time she accepted it. "Back then, that's the way it was. So I went ahead and did the LVN course at Houston Community College."

As a public health nurse in Houston, Virginia Marie's call to ministry continued to unfold. "That's when things started moving for me in terms of looking at healing and spirituality, especially in the maternity and well child clinics. The women would come and ask me for prayer," she relates.

Continuing to explore her call, Virginia Marie went to a discovery weekend at the Seminary of the Southwest in Austin, Texas. "I was feeling God calling me to something, and I wasn't sure what it was," she says. "I'd been a nurse. I'd felt a call, and I was trying to decide if this call was about ordination or a call to a different career." At the seminary discovery weekend she learned that Rev. Judith Liro was one of the priests at St. George's Episcopal Church. When Virginia Marie visited the church, she saw a woman at the altar for the first time. "I was so moved," she recalls. "I was so emotional, and shed some tears."

When she enrolled in Episcopal Divinity School, in Cambridge, Massachusetts, Virginia Marie at first felt alone and overwhelmed. "It was a whole different world," she recalls. "I remember not seeing myself at all in the seminary; I was the only Latina on campus. I walked into a class on feminist perspectives of the Bible with Rev. Alison Cheek. It was my first day of class, and I realized that I was sitting with all these white women who had studied the Bible maybe back and forth. It was my first real critical analysis of the Bible class. I left the class and went to my apartment, and I cried my eyes out because I thought, 'I can't keep up with them. There is no way that I could ever do this.'"

The next morning Virginia Marie went to see Rev. Cheek to tell her she was going to drop the class. "I'm dropping because I was not able to hear my voice in it. I felt like I didn't understand what these women were talking about. They never talked about the poor. They never talked about the oppressed. They never talked about suffering. And I just don't think I fit in that class."

Rev. Cheek replied, "Virginia Marie, yours is the voice that we need in that class. And if you can hang in there for two or three more classes, I think you're going to find your voice."

Virginia Marie tells one of the most painful experiences she had while she was in seminary. A campus maintenance worker who was "very white" called her a "wetback." Devastated, she didn't return to campus for two weeks. But with the encouragement of an African American student, Virginia Marie invited people of color at the seminary to her apartment, and they organized a protest. In addition to the African American student, "there were people from Africa, India, and Korea," she recalls. "We sat in my apartment, and they asked me, 'How many times a day do you face racism on this campus?' We stayed up till one o'clock in the morning talking about our experiences. Then we decided to organize a protest. We each wrote a sign such as, 'I come from poverty,' 'I come from the oppressed,' 'I am this or this,' or whatever. We decided that giving voice to the voiceless would be our contribution to the Thursday liturgy. At the point where we were to receive communion, we all pulled out our signs and walked out. And we put our signs in front of the chapel. It was a very powerful statement. A couple of months later I was called to be on a task force. Out of that task force, the position of pastoral counselor to people of color was created, and I was one of the first to get that position."

While she was in seminary, Virginia Marie began the ordination process. "I started noticing that some of how I viewed myself in the world was difficult for church officials to understand. How could I bring my understanding of *curandismo*, of healing, to the Episcopal Church? Where do I fit in there? I would get upset when I heard people preach that we need to help the poor and oppressed, or those who are marginalized, to come forward to become priests, and yet they would be looking right at me and couldn't comprehend me," she says. "What they wanted was for me to become like them. I was already to some degree angry with myself because I had assimilated so much. Bishop Tom Shaw asked me, 'If you become a priest, what are you going to do for a broken world?' I said, 'Tell the truth—why people are dealing with racism, why people are suffering in Mexico, how NAFTA affected the people in Mexico, why they come to the United States, why they sacrifice themselves in the desert to come here. Look at what we're doing to them—tell the truth. I think we forget that there is an enormous amount of suffering in this world, and we just go around with blinders on. That has to be preached from the pulpit, too.'"

During her struggle with the ordination process Virginia Marie found support from women at Greenfire Retreat Center. "The women there helped me so much," she recalls. "They would do women's church. We had a ritual where they ordained me. And even though my later official ordinations as deacon and as priest were very important, that ordination to me was so symbolic of women ordaining each other to use our voices. It helped me to be able to start doing the work without waiting for a bishop to say, 'Okay, now you can do it.'"

On September 18, 2005, Virginia Marie became the first woman of color to be ordained to the priesthood in the diocese of Maine. "The bishop asked me what I wanted to happen on that ordination day, and I said, 'I want the community where I minister to feel that they're part of this. I don't think they've ever seen a Latina being ordained.' The bishop said, 'Then we're going to have a bilingual service, and I will lay my hands on you and call you forth into priesthood in Spanish.' That was a beautiful moment," she says. "A lot of Latinos came. My family came—my daughter and my brother and my sisters and my nephews." Shortly after her ordination, a newspaper article titled "Rev. Virginia Marie Rincon Looks to Foster Latino Connection" celebrated her groundbreaking accomplishments: "She is the first woman of color to be ordained in Maine. Since 2000, Rincon has worked to empower Latina women and their families through her ministry in Portland. She uses spirituality, education, and the arts to connect with Latinos and meets with them on the street or at their workplaces."[24]

One of the ways Rev. Rincon has empowered Latina women is through her creation of TengoVoz. "It came to me that the women needed a place," she says. "So I organized the first gathering of women in a basement of a Unitarian Universalist church. I read some poems, and the women began to talk about their struggle. I encouraged them to create the sacred space." She says that she named this organization TengoVoz because Latina women "need a voice."

In her vision for the future of the church, Rev. Rincon includes a gathering of Latina clergywomen. "I want to get the Latina clergywomen together and just talk. I believe it's important for the healing to begin before we do big-picture work: the whole immigration thing, what's going on politically," she explains. "But we can't share it if we're exhausted from pushing up against the system, all the resistance that we get. I feel that if we can make this gathering of women happen, then we'll be in positions of power in different places where we can impact change. It's unfortunate that the Latina women priests don't have the resources that other women clergy have because most of us are in Hispanic ministry, where there isn't a lot of funding. I think it's going to take coming together and asking what we have to offer out of our experiences as Latina clergy. The church is not going to work any longer the way it's being done. We've got to think about who's coming if we just stand in the pulpit in a nice comfortable church. We've got to go wherever the people are and listen to what the people are experiencing in their lives. We've got to change."

To Rev. Rincon, female images of the Divine are vital to this change. "These images need to constantly be put in front of people's faces. Not just women clergy, but divine images, like the *Virgen de Guadalupe*," she claims. "As clergywomen, we walk into a meeting, and here we sit with mostly men who are running the meeting. So I believe it's important to put those divine feminine images in front of them in our liturgies and in our meetings. Men dominate the Hispanic ministry. And they're not talking about the different shapes the *Virgen de Guadalupe* can take, like the Guadalupe with big breasts and big hips. I am a *Virgen de Guadalupe* admirer in every way. She is always at the forefront of immigration marches and other justice actions."

Joining with the *Virgen de Guadalupe*, Rev. Virginia Marie Rincon is at the forefront of justice ministry. Her prophetic preaching, writing, and advocacy for racial, gender, and economic justice continue to transform church and society.

Dr. Melanie Springer Mock

Professor of English, George Fox University

Gathering Everyone
under Her Wings

"If we see only white male images for the Divine, this will shape our understanding of God and our ability to relate to the Divine. This is personally important to me because my children are Asian Americans, and I want them to know that they too are created in the image of the Divine. They haven't really encountered many images of God that look like them, and this makes me very sad. I want them to have these encounters, and I want the church to be ready and willing to do this for them and other children who are not white."

Dr. Melanie Springer Mock believes that including multicultural female divine language, images, and symbolism in church will contribute to peace and social justice in the wider culture. "I think truly understanding and believing that we are all created in God's image means that we will be more likely to work for justice for all people," she explains. "Using gender-inclusive leadership, language, and theology affirms in real, concrete ways that we are all created in the image of the Divine, rather than suggesting that we are all created in God's image, but some are more than others. If we believe that all of us reflect the Divine, we are less likely to marginalize those who are different because of gender identity, sexual orientation, race, class, and so on."

In her moving article "God's Gift of Motherhood Comes in Different Ways," Dr. Mock writes about the joys and challenges of adopting two sons: Benjamin Quan from Vietnam and Samuel Saurabh from India. She concludes with this biblical metaphor of God as Mother Hen:

> When I was a child, my mom played a game with us called hen and chicks. Covered by an old blanket, she would spread her arms wide and call out, "Where are my chicks?" My brother and sister and I would run under her wings, and she would wrap her arms, and the blanket, around us; we giggled in the darkness of her flannelled embrace. Because of this game, the metaphor of God as a hen gathering her chicks has been especially powerful for me, a reminder of my mother's care for me, and of God's care for all God's children: for me, yes, and also for Benjamin Quan and Samuel Saurabh, and for the mothers who once bore them and entrusted them to me. And so I imagine a day when God will gather us all under her wings—including all the people who have been a part of Ben's and Sam's lives, from their very beginning—and we will feel God's warm embrace together, laughing, rejoicing in our imperfect love for each other, and in God's perfect love for us.[25]

When she first heard about language that included female metaphors for God, Melanie resisted it. "I had gone to an evangelical Quaker college, and so the Divine Feminine wasn't really part of the discussion there," she explains. "At first I was really resistant when several progressive Christians introduced the idea to me, in great part because I found them pushy and aggressive. Because the idea was so new to me, and because I didn't really trust the people who were telling me I *had* to use inclusive language, I became more entrenched in the idea of using Father God language."

While working on her master's degree in English literature, Melanie became more open to the Divine Feminine. "I read some feminist theology in a feminist literature class, taught by an agnostic who was my mentor, and who helped shape my belief system in a Divine Feminine, despite her lack of spirituality," she recalls. "But what really opened my heart and mind to new ideas of the Divine Feminine was reading Alice Walker's *The Color Purple*, and seeing in the character Shug Avery the characteristics of a feminine divinity I found really appealing. So it was through an agnostic mentor and an author's novel that I was transformed, rather than through the relationship with some folks a few years earlier. I'm not sure what that means, except that I have tried to refrain from aggressively forcing people to use feminine language for the Divine, figuring that doing so might make them more entrenched in their ways of seeing, as I was."

In "God's Gift of Motherhood Comes in Different Ways," Dr. Mock writes about her continued discovery of the power of female language for the Divine:

> After long, prayer-filled waits, I have been given the gift of motherhood, and this, in turn, has allowed me to comprehend God's nature in profound ways. I experience biblical metaphors describing God's love for her children more powerfully now. My children do not bear my genetic code, but this matters not at all: I love Ben and Sam as God loves me, fiercely, overwhelmingly, unconditionally. As God is to me, so I am to my boys; I am as the she-bear in Hosea, the mother hen about whom Jesus speaks, the comforter in Isaiah, and so know God more fully in those terms as well.[26]

Melanie grew up in the Midwest with a father who was a Mennonite pastor and a mother "who was always fighting against traditional expectations for women," Melanie says. "My mom taught me from a young age that I needed to be my own self, even when that meant going against what was expected. I don't think I appreciated what she gave me at the time, but I have more and more: the gift of letting me become all I was meant to be."

After graduating from George Fox University, Melanie went on to earn a master's degree in English literature from the University of Missouri–St. Louis and then a PhD from Oklahoma State University. Currently, Dr. Mock teaches a wide variety of courses in the English department of George Fox University. Among her publications are *Writing Peace: The Unheard Voices of Great War Mennonite Objectors*; *Just Moms: Conveying Justice in an Unjust World*, a book about teaching children the values of peace, equality, truth, simplicity, and love; and essays in both popular and academic presses. In addition, she blogs with Kendra Weddle Irons on "Ain't I a Woman? De/Constructing Christian Images."[27]

Language and symbolism have great power to shape our beliefs about humanity and divinity, Dr. Mock asserts. "I believe strongly that language reflects reality, and that language shapes reality. I talk about this in really simple terms with my students—and in terms that I think will be met with less resistance. When students write about the 'men' and 'girls' in their classes, I challenge them to consider the reality that even that simple language creates. We can then progress to talking about how masculine images for God can create our sense that men are created in God's image more than are women and that men are closer to God because God is male like them."

In addition to teaching inclusive language to her students, Dr. Mock expresses hope that she contributes also to change in her church. "I attend an evangelical Friends church that is just opening to some new ways of thinking, in part because of some young people who are being more vocal about their understanding of God. We used inclusive language in an alternative worship service in the fall at our church, and I wept because I never thought such would happen at my church. This one service gave me hope that things are changing."

It's easier to take risks in advocating for inclusive language and theology through her writing than through other ways, Melanie acknowledges. "I take risks in my writing, but I'm fairly conflict-averse. I was on a panel about work, religion, and women at George Fox, and expressed my beliefs about inclusive language, but I'm more comfortable writing about what I feel. At my pastor's invitation I wrote something about how I felt the church was excluding women; he wanted me to preach, but agreed instead to read what I'd written. This was also a risk for me, and made some people angry. I thought the message was important, and worth the anger, though in the moment I also regretted hurting some people's feelings."

Resistance to her inclusive theology has come not only at church but also at home, Melanie says. "I've tried to talk with my husband and family about why this is important to me. I think he's learning, too, but is resistant. I've certainly experienced resistance in my church. I need to get to the point of letting go of my own desire to people-please and to embrace this resistance. I'm getting there!"

Melanie expresses appreciation for the inspiration and strength she has received from feminist colleagues and friends, especially Letha

Dawson Scanzoni and Kendra Weddle Irons and others in Evangelical &
Ecumenical Women's Caucus–Christian Feminism Today (EEWC-CFT).
"Letha is an amazing encourager, and has always been so supportive of my
writing," Melanie says. "Kendra has been huge in helping me learn more
about the importance of inclusive language and has always been encouraging. When I went to my first EEWC-CFT board meeting, and met other
women on the board, I was amazed, transformed. I came home from the
following year's Gathering also feeling entirely new, kind of like how I
felt at church camp as a kid. Amazing women and men who have amazing stories, and who have done extraordinary things. I've been trying to
introduce my students and colleagues to this extraordinary organization."

Especially rewarding to Dr. Mock are positive responses to her
writing and teaching. "Any time I get a good response to something on
my blog, I find that really rewarding—knowing that my writing has
transformed folks' lives. Also, I get the opportunity every year to work
with students and to see their own thoughts about faith, gender, and the
Divine be changed. That is always, always rewarding: especially when
someone comes to George Fox University fairly conservative in her
beliefs about 'God's Design for Women' and leaves feeling empowered
to be a strong, independent woman."

The purpose of the "Ain't I a Woman?" blog that Melanie writes
with Kendra is "to examine the many ways Christian culture lets women
know exactly who they should be, deconstructing those messages that
we find troubling—and, in the process, constructing a different message: one that allows Christian women to be all that God intended."
Melanie writes this story to further illustrate the purpose of this blog:

> Several days ago, I had a conversation with a George Fox University
> senior, one of our college superstars. She received an impressive
> scholarship to attend George Fox four years ago, and when I met
> her the summer before her first year, I knew she'd be successful.
> The student is smart, articulate, thoughtful, an on-campus leader.
> She will certainly make something of her life post-graduation, and
> I can easily imagine her some day assuming an important role in
> government, a field that interests her. It might seem hyperbolic to
> say she might be president of the United States, but yeah—she's
> that kind of person.

So I was (somewhat) surprised to hear that, seven weeks short of graduation, this student feels like she's failed. She'll be graduating from George Fox with a B.A. degree, but no M.R.S. degree...

She's heard the pervasive messages from Christian culture telling her a woman's worth is found solely in her ability to land, marry, and care for a spouse and children. Although she recognizes the problematic messages Christian culture sends women about what and who they should be, she also wonders if, maybe, Christian culture is right: that because she values independence at this point in her life, she is going against God's wishes; that because she wants to be a leader in some capacity, she is going against biblical mandate; and that because she hasn't found The One, God hasn't blessed her.

It is for people like this amazing woman that Kendra and I continue to write. We meet folks every day who have been damaged by Christian culture's insistence that men and women have particular, distinct, and—at least for women—limited roles. We also believe strongly that God wants us to freely explore the gifts God has given us; and that too often, Christian culture has demanded that women not have that freedom, all in the name of biblical (mis-)interpretation.[28]

Dr. Mock expresses her feelings about the future of the church: "I feel hope for the future, and the ways the church might become more inclusive. I want these changes to come quickly, so that my boys will grow up believing that women and men of all races are created in the image of the Divine, and that they will grow up to become feminists interested in fighting for justice and equity. Inclusive language and feminist theology will help them on this journey, but when I look at the Sunday school curriculum, for example, I feel despair that these changes may not come quickly enough for them."

Still, in her conclusion to a recent article, she sounds this passionate note of hope: "There are people everywhere pushing back against the cultural mythologies that have, for too long, told women who and what they could and could not be.... I still have hope that someday soon, young women and men will truly be free to be all God intended them to be."[29] Through her prophetic writing and teaching, Melanie Springer Mock contributes to Divine Wisdom's work of freeing people of all races and genders to become all they are created to be.

Patrick Michaels

Composer; Minister of Music, St. James's Episcopal Church, Cambridge, Massachusetts

Celebrating Her Dark Gracefulness

Antiphon: Lifetime Partner, Loving Friend,
      Fount of Wisdom, Source and End,
      She is God, Holy One: Glory!

Look! Behold her dark gracefulness,
moving between worlds with ease—
anywhere she is, her home is!
In her wake the waters roll and part
and slaves are made a people.

Look! Behold her great openness,
seeing and embracing all,
welcoming each new encounter!
In her presence, strangers speak and hear
and learn from one another.

Look! Behold her full radiance,
shining out from depths of love,
blessing the weak and the timid!
In her spirit, wine and bread are shared
and life is given freely.

Look! Behold her hard suffering,
knowing what she cannot say—
eloquence bruised and then broken!

In her silence, sorrow fills the ears;
the world awaits her story.

Look! Behold her quick liveliness,
taking pleasure in all things,
singing and dancing and playing!
In her laughter, joy and peace abound
and health becomes contagious.

Antiphon: Lifetime Partner, Loving Friend
  Fount of Wisdom, Source and End,
  She is God, Holy One: Glory!

In his hymns, Patrick Michaels celebrates the biblical truth that all human beings are created in the divine image. Imaging God as a dark female contributes to overcoming the racism and sexism that have led to the denial of the sacred image in women and in people of color. "When we include images of God that are black-positive and dark-positive and when we include images of God that affirm nighttime as a time of God's own creation and mystery, we affirm our understanding that all humans are created in the image of God," he says. In writing "Lifetime Partner, Loving Friend," Patrick focused on one of his friends: "As a person of color, she impressed me in the way that she could live in different 'worlds' and be at home in different settings. This seemed to me to be a spiritual gift, and one which I had never as a white person been required to recognize or name before. I named others of her spiritual gifts in succeeding stanzas. I gained spiritual insight by staying fixed on the female images for God that I had right in front of me. New language, like 'her dark gracefulness,' then became both obvious and necessary to remain true to my task."

Language and images for the Divine are foundational to our social justice work, Patrick believes. "The imagery that we use for God must affirm our highest dreams and aspirations. God is the source of our freedom and liberation from oppressive structures. God wants us to be free of the prejudice of racial or gender inequalities and the effects of institutionalized racism and sexism and homophobia. These are our common sins, and we name them in community by singing and preaching and praying and by working to eliminate them in our common life. Language for God can set the stage for this work, and remind us that we are all in it together."

Patrick Michaels grew up in a Roman Catholic family and attended Catholic parochial schools through the eighth grade. "Critical thinking was part of that inheritance," he says. "I continued a time of questioning and discerning that has brought me this far." He trained as a classical pianist, earning a music degree from the University of Minnesota. When he was serving as music director for the Episcopal Center at the University of Minnesota, he met his future spouse, Laurie Rofinot. When she decided to pursue ordination in the Episcopal Church, they moved to Cambridge, Massachusetts, so she could attend Episcopal Divinity School. Patrick began serving as minister of music at St. James's Episcopal Church in Cambridge and has continued in that position for thirty years. For eight years he also served as director of chapel music at Episcopal Divinity School.

When he was working at the Episcopal Center at the University of Minnesota, Patrick first encountered inclusive language. "I was not entirely receptive to it, as the process of changing language in hymns was messy and entailed more work," he recalls. "However, I was never against the idea, and I learned that change could be done at a grassroots level. When I started reading feminist theology, my eyes were opened to the painful reality that women and men were not treated equally in most arenas in the United States. Mary Daly made a particularly great impression on my thinking. I formed and joined men's groups to discuss and wrestle with what it means to be a man in this time. I was introduced to new attitudes about church, gender, and sexuality." When Patrick and Laurie moved to Cambridge, he continued expanding his thinking. "This was a formative period for me, as I had time to read and reflect on my place in society and the privileges accorded men in this world."

In the 1970s, Patrick began writing hymn tunes and texts and now sees this creating of new hymns as one of his main ministries. "I love introducing new hymns and songs, often with female imagery for God, to congregations and have had the opportunity to do that in workshops, consultations, and conferences," he says.

At the Hymn Society Conference in Winston-Salem, North Carolina, I attended Patrick's workshop titled "Hymns with Female Imagery for

God." I delighted in the female divine names and images in his hymns that are missing in the majority of traditional and new hymns. At another Hymn Society Conference, eleven years later, in Richmond, Virginia, I reconnected with Patrick and was glad to learn that he was still writing hymns with female divine imagery.

Patrick relates his personal journey to inclusive divine language and imagery. "I discovered that the image of God as Father was empty to me and didn't carry with it any of the expected associations of fatherhood. This was not because of deficiencies in my own father, but because connections between human and Divine had never been made explicit. When I encountered the image of God as Mother, it immediately brought my own mother to my mind, and very slowly, I began to understand the power of language to form our thoughts and feelings. Only then did the image of God as Father begin to take on new meanings for me. I believe that by naming God as Father or Mother or Friend, we allow those actual people in our lives the freedom not to be gods to us—we can expect to have finite, flawed, loving, and forgiving human relationships with them, and not require them to be our saviors—or perfect in any unhealthy way."

For his hymn "The Holy Spirit Came to Me," Patrick says he drew from relationships. "I decided to write each stanza that describes the Holy Spirit by focusing on a particular woman in my life—mother, teacher, friend, spouse—and seeing what I could say about God based on who that person was to me. This allowed me to think 'outside the box' in a very natural and simple way." Here are the lyrics of this hymn:

> The Holy Spirit came to me—
> she fed and clothed me, worked and played;
> she showed me how to look and see
> the world, and not to be afraid.
>
> The Holy Spirit came to me—
> she taught me music of the soul,
> and showed how time and sound and touch
> combine to make a radiant whole.
>
> The Holy Spirit came to me—
> and soon became a trusted friend;

though springs and winters come and go,
her constant love will never end.

The Holy Spirit came to me—
she loved me as I was, but said
she loved me more, and sought to bring
to life the me I'd left for dead.

The Holy Spirit came to me—
she knew my worth and saw my need;
she lifted lids, she opened doors,
we swept the house and planted seeds.

The Holy Spirit comes to me
in every time, on every side;
wherever I may turn, she is
already there: my friend, my guide.

Our imagery for Deity influences our relationships with one another, Patrick believes. "Language is a tool that we use to step closer to people or away from them. Using female imagery for the Divine is one way to step closer to others because it affirms our communal ability to discern and judge for ourselves what is life-giving and what we have in common. This is as equally valuable for men as for women and children."

Patrick also comments on the value of multifaith and multicultural language and imagery in hymnody. "When we sing from many diverse traditions, we affirm our belief that God created all of us and loves us with all the things that give us life. Language inclusive of these images allows us to remember that God is greater than any one tradition, and that God delights in the diversity of all creation." Indeed, his church posts this description of the worship music on its website: "Alongside traditional church hymnody, we incorporate music from several different traditions into our worship service. In the last year, we surveyed several Christian hymn traditions: Asian, Hispanic, Celtic, and African. We draw upon the diverse cultural history and original material of our parishioners."[30]

Expansive language and imagery for Deity are important for people of all ages, Patrick asserts: "Children are comfortable with expansive language for God, as their world is expanding every day as they grow and mature. It makes sense to them that God is beyond any language, but that language can help us learn about God. If adults want to continue to grow and mature, then expansive language for God will help them grow and stretch. Adults need to remind themselves that their childhood understandings of God will not be sufficient for continued growth and spiritual maturity and that the new experiences they have as adults will require new understandings of who God is. We refer to this when we say 'the living God.'"

When people are not open to expansive language for Deity, Patrick responds with biblical education and personal stories. "Some people are resistant to female images of divinity. Showing them biblical passages that use female images for God is the simplest way to educate them. They can absorb the parts of tradition that they have neglected and have a new relationship with scripture—which can open them to see other things in new ways, too. I have found that telling my story, sharing my insights, and leaving room for others to speak is the most rewarding experience of my church membership," he says. "We have had hymn sings of pieces with female images for God. I assembled ten or fifteen songs, and we sang through each piece together and then broke into small groups and shared our reactions to the piece. This was very successful. Most interesting to me was that many people had never been given an opportunity to share their feelings and thoughts about hymn texts and tunes! The female images for God became only one aspect of people's reactions. They commented on a wide range of other material as well. This exercise brought people closer; everyone's voice was heard and respected."

The creative ministry of Patrick demonstrates his belief in the power of music to transform individuals and the church. "Music is one of the best ways to revive people, bring them together, and educate them," he says. "Singing engages the senses and the mind. New theology is most easily taught and absorbed through musical and poetical forms. I consider the musical repertoire of the congregation to be an essential and ongoing project in the work of liberation. And the choice of that repertoire is the church musician's biggest challenge and greatest reward. Wonderful music is accessible to most of us who are looking for ways to nurture and challenge our congregations. Resources abound at both local and global levels. Musical connections to others are waiting to be made, and insights about how to work together are abundant."

Patrick Michaels contributes to liberating music resources through his prolific work as a hymn writer. Some of his hymns are published in hymnals with worldwide audiences. One of these hymns is "Who Comes from God? (Sophia)" to a familiar tune often used with the traditional Catholic hymn "Hail, Holy Queen Enthroned Above." Here are Patrick's new lyrics:

Who comes from God, as Word and Breath?
Holy Wisdom.
Who holds the keys to life and death?
Mighty Wisdom.
Crafter and Creator too,
Eldest, she makes all things new;
she ordains what God will do,
Wisest One, Radiant One,
Welcome, Great Sophia!

Who lifts her voice for all to hear?
Joyful Wisdom.
Who shapes a thought and makes it clear?
Truthful Wisdom.
Teacher, drawing out our best,
magnifies what we invest,
names our truth, directs our quest,
Wisest One, Radiant One,
Welcome, Great Sophia!

Whom should we seek with all our heart?
Loving Wisdom.
Who, once revealed, will not depart?
Faithful Wisdom.
Partner, Counselor, Comforter,
love has found none lovelier,
life is gladness lived with her,
Wisest One, Radiant One,
Welcome, Great Sophia![31]

Part 3

Wisdom's Works of Marriage Equality

Male-dominated worship language and imagery contribute to hetero-sexism as well as to racism and sexism by exalting the traditional "masculine" and devaluing any traits that have been traditionally labeled "feminine." This exclusively male symbolism forms a foundation for the exclusion, devaluing, demeaning, and abuse of LGBTQ persons. But when Deity is named and imaged as female, as well as male and much more, then all will be seen in the divine image and thus given greater value and respect.

Wisdom's works expand to include everyone. People of all genders, races, and sexual orientations are created in the divine image and thus have equal value. Divine Wisdom affirms sexual and gender diversity as sacred gifts, and marriage equality as a basic right. Wisdom works for the full equality of LGBTQ persons in all areas of religious and public life.

Biblical revelation includes a wide variety of names and images of the Divine to suggest the immensity of the Creative Spirit and the wide diversity of creation. Holy Wisdom, other female divine images, and divine images of many genders work for equality for people of all genders. The search continues for sacred symbolism to celebrate this wondrous diversity.

Praise the Source of All Creation
(Sung to the tune of "Come, Thou Long-Expected Jesus")

Praise the Source of all creation, giving life throughout the earth,
blessing every love relation, filling all with sacred worth.
Celebrate all forms and colors, varied beauty everywhere,
streams of goodness overflowing, wondrous gifts for all to share.

Many genders, many races, all reflect Divinity;
many gifts and many graces help us be all we can be.
Partners on this path of freedom, taking down each stifling wall,
we will open doors of welcome, bringing hope and joy to all.

Long have many been excluded, judged and scorned by custom's
    norms;
everyone will be included as we work to bring reforms.
Let us end abuse and violence, bringing justice everywhere,
joining Holy Wisdom's mission, helping all be free and fair.

Equal marriage, healing, freeing, nurtures body, mind, and soul,
reaffirming every being, all created good and whole.
Come, rejoice and sing together, celebrating life and love;
praise the great Creative Spirit, living in us and above.[1]

Words © 2012 Jann Aldredge-Clanton   HYFRYDOL

Rev. Dr. Nancy Petty

Pastor, Pullen Memorial Baptist Church, Raleigh, North Carolina

Challenging Unjust Marriage Laws

"Every time I sign a marriage license for a heterosexual couple and act as an agent of the state, I am reminded of those couples I marry who are denied the basic human right to legally marry the person of their choice. Do we, Pullen Memorial Baptist Church, want to continue to participate in offering religious ceremonies that carry with them civil and human rights that are not afforded to all people? Or will it be our practice and the practice of our ministers to honor all marriages equally by only offering religious ceremonies, thus not acting as agents of the state and perpetuating the unjust marriage laws of our state?"[2]

R ev. Dr. Nancy Petty, pastor of Pullen Memorial Baptist Church, took a stand that few other pastors have taken. She refused to sign marriage licenses for heterosexual couples until same-sex couples can legally marry in her state of North Carolina. With her leadership, the congregation voted unanimously to affirm this prophetic statement:

Pullen Memorial Baptist Church has a longstanding tradition of supporting the rights of all citizens to equal protection under the law. We find that current North Carolina law and the proposed amendment to the North Carolina constitution that "Marriage between a man and a woman is the only domestic legal union that shall be valid or recognized in this state" discriminates against same-sex couples by denying them the rights and privileges enjoyed by heterosexual married couples. As people of faith, affirming the Christian teaching that before God all people are equal, we will no longer participate in this discrimination.

Consequently, the members of Pullen Memorial Baptist Church affirm the following:

1. Marriages between same-sex and opposite-sex couples will be treated equally, and marriage ceremonies conducted at our church will reflect the spiritual nature of the solemn commitments between two people in a loving relationship.

2. To obtain legal sanction for their union, heterosexual couples may obtain their legal marital contract from another source such as a local magistrate until such time as the State of North Carolina recognizes the legal union of both heterosexual and same-sex couples.[3]

This stand for marriage equality is only one of many prophetic stands for diversity that Rev. Dr. Petty has taken. She partnered with Rev. Dr. William Barber, president of the North Carolina chapter of the NAACP and pastor of Greenleaf Christian Church, to oppose the Wake County school board's plan to dismantle the district's policy designed to promote school diversity. For participating in sit-in protests at school board meetings, Rev. Petty and Rev. Barber have been arrested several times.

In an article in Raleigh's *News & Observer*, Rev. Petty states her reasons for involvement in these protests: "We must not fool ourselves by thinking that the issues at hand are not issues of race, economic status, privilege, and power. If we allow our elected leaders to return us to a place of segregation and intolerance within our schools—a place where the gap between the haves and have-nots is widened rather than closed—it is ultimately our children who will suffer."[4]

From the positive experience of her own children attending diverse schools, Nancy says she knew this was an important issue for her to speak out on. "The majority of school board members are now very conservative and doing away with our socioeconomic diversity policy, which was a nationally recognized school system model. I see the value in my children going to school with people not like them, and what they've learned and who they've become because of that."

In taking stands for justice, Nancy sees the importance of women and men in partnership. "Women need to be willing to partner with men because they do have power," she says. "And if we want to share that power, then it's important to nurture those relationships and be in partnership with them. On the school board issue, Barber reached out to me, and I reached back out to him. Together we've been able to tap into a power that's much greater than either one of us alone."

Rev. Petty has also found that she makes a prophetic statement by just being who she is. Before a wedding where she was officiating, a little girl spotted her in her robe, and they had this exchange:

"So you're the priest!" the little girl hollered out.

"Yes, I'm the minister here, and I'm going to marry Jessica and Ronnie today," Nancy said.

"I've been watching you since you got here. When I saw that robe, I knew you were the priest."

A little while later, while they were still waiting for the ceremony to begin, the girl began running around Nancy in a circle, saying, "You're the priest! You're the priest! You're the priest!" Nancy says she doesn't know the girl's background: "If she goes to a Catholic church, she probably has never seen a woman priest, and she was paying close attention to who's in this role."

Nancy Petty grew up hearing her father tell her, "You can do anything you want to do." Nancy lived with an older sister and her parents in the small town of Shelby, North Carolina, and went to a small Southern Baptist church. "This little church bought a bus, and Dad and I did a bus ministry together, and always planned Vacation Bible School together from the time I was really young," Nancy recalls. "My world in that small community centered on my church."

When Nancy was in high school, she felt called to be a missionary. "I knew that my love for church was deep, but I'd never seen anyone other than a man in the role of pastor or in any other leadership role in the church," she says. "Growing up I never saw a woman in a ministerial role. When I got to high school and was so invested in church and leadership in my youth program, I had this sense of connection to church. I did what many other young girls who feel that nudge and that calling probably did; I said I wanted to be a missionary. My calling continued as a process, more of just living into it, and being open to it."

After graduating from Gardner-Webb College with a religion major, Nancy began to explore other ways of fulfilling her call. She served as a youth minister while earning a master of divinity degree from Southeastern Baptist Theological Seminary. At Southeastern, Nancy for the first time experienced a woman teaching theology and biblical materials. "I was amazed," Nancy recalls. "I tried to take every class Dr. Barnes taught, because it was different hearing theology from her. I don't know how to explain it, except that she spoke with an authenticity and from an experience that I connected to."

Although the Baptist tradition does not connect the gender of the Divine and of ministers as closely as the Catholic tradition does, Rev. Petty often speaks of women ministers and women in general as synonymous with the Female Divine. Beginning in seminary, Nancy saw Dr. Elizabeth Barnes as the face of the Divine Feminine. "I go back to how significant it was in my own experience to have that encounter with Dr. Barnes, to see a woman and hear a woman's voice and hear how women's stories intersect with the biblical stories," Nancy says. "Representing the Divine Feminine is really important to me because I know how much Dr. Barnes meant to me and how she changed the way I see myself as a theologian and as a pastor. And a number of women have said to me, 'You don't know what your presence means; I can look up there and see myself there.' Over the years I've continually listened to women tell me what a difference it makes to have a woman in the pulpit, that it in some way symbolizes their story, their experience."

As pastor of Pullen Memorial Baptist Church, Rev. Petty started a women's group with the female divine name *Ruah*.[5] "The purpose of the group at the beginning was to look at the stories of women in the Bible," Nancy says. "It's important to connect with the biblical stories. To do that, women have got to be able to see ourselves in these stories. That's where I think the church has failed our daughters and our mothers. We are in those stories, but the church hasn't told those stories and taught those stories. As we look to the present and future about how to bring in the Divine Feminine, we really need to rethink how we're teaching the biblical texts. The *Ruah* group spent about a month rewriting the creation story from a feminist perspective. That was such a liberating experience because we found ourselves in a different way in that story. We read other creation stories and tried to understand how different faiths have interpreted the creation. The group then moved from looking at biblical stories to telling our own stories."

The *Ruah* group also initiated a committee to expand the visual imagery in the sanctuary to include the Divine Feminine and to include the diversity of creation. "It's important for our images to be in alignment with who we say we are as a church and what our theology is," Rev. Petty explains. "We say that here all people are equal, that women are just as important in the church as men, that women's stories are important. And yet none of our imagery in this church tells that story. And it's not just women that we need to represent in the imagery, but children and creation. Our church has a Care of Creation mission group. Nothing in our imagery speaks to that value as part of our theology. There's nothing in our church that persons with disabilities would visually see that makes them feel welcome. I don't know that the person who is privileged in our world understands how significant that is for other people to see themselves represented in worship so that they feel they belong."

Nancy explains the church's plans for including diverse imagery: "The committee set out to include the Divine Feminine as the top priority, and then to move to make the imagery inclusive of children and creation. Also, two women together and two men together would represent a large part of our story as a church. It's important for us to model in a visual way and with our words what we say we believe, as opposed to saying one thing and then walking into a sanctuary where everything is about men."

At Pullen there's been more resistance to inclusive visual imagery than to inclusive language, Nancy says. "We have people who don't want anything in the sanctuary to change. Some people ask, 'Why do we have to bring feminine imagery in? We have a woman pastor, and we know what we believe. Why is it important to put stuff on the walls?' I keep saying, 'Because it's theologically the right thing to do.'"

Balancing her prophetic and pastoral work proves challenging, Rev. Petty says. "Change takes time, but my preference is to move forward when I see something that needs to be done. I go back to Martin Luther King's 'Letter from Birmingham Jail.' King writes about being 'disturbers of the peace and outside agitators.'[6] That's what the church is called to do, and that's what we as ministers are called to do. So when I come to this issue of divine feminine imagery and language, I know I need to agitate people about this, that it's not about trying to comfort people," she explains. "At the same time it's important to meet people where they are and to try to understand what it is within them that's resistant. That delicate balance of being pastor and prophet is a constant challenge."

Inclusive language, visual imagery, leadership, and theology can liberate men as well as women, Rev. Petty believes. "I don't think it's just women who've been oppressed by our patriarchal culture and church. Men have been oppressed too, because they've had to carry this load and power all by themselves and have been cut out of being able to nurture and care and connect on a different level. When we talk about changing church, I wonder what it would mean for the church not to think of roles and gender together, but to think of who's best suited in various places. Being a welcoming and affirming church, like Pullen, helps to change traditional gender roles."

Rev. Nancy Petty articulates an expansive vision for the future of the church. "As I think about my vision for the future of the Divine Feminine and how we talk about our faith, it's my hope that the church can represent all people as equal. I want our children to know that when we say we are made in the divine image, that means all of us. It doesn't matter what gender you are, what your sexual orientation is, what color you are, how well you're educated or not educated," she says. "Everyone has gifts to offer. If there's one vision that points me in my ministry, it's that we are all equal. My vision is for the church to live into that and believe it in a way that's counter to our culture. I don't think our culture really understands that, because there are systems in our culture that require that hierarchy of leadership. Instead of the church reflecting the culture, it's my hope and vision that we can represent something different and be a different voice in the world." Through her prophetic ministry, Rev. Petty continues to be a voice for equality and justice in church and society.

Rev. Dr. Susan Newman

Associate Minister of Congregational Life and Social Justice,
All Souls Church, Washington, D.C.

Claiming Our Divinity

"The Bible teaches that we are made in the image and likeness of God; therefore, I must believe that there is a male and female expression of God. Behave like the goddess you are.... God's Spirit has often felt like a nurturing mother, and I want to honor God by living like a goddess. Claim your divinity and walk in it every day, because you are fearfully and wonderfully made."[7]

Claiming her power and her divinity, Rev. Dr. Susan Newman worked to pass the Marriage Equality Law in Washington, D.C. She expresses her delight in working with other ministers and community leaders to achieve this social justice victory. "We passed the Marriage Equality Law so that gay and lesbian people could get married legally. I was one of the ministers who worked on it, and we had that victory."

Growing up, Susan didn't feel so powerful. Her father was an alcoholic who often abused her and her mother. "It was to the point that Monday through Friday at 3:00 p.m., when the school bell would ring, my heart would freeze inside of me because I didn't know what to expect when I went home, whether my father would be there, how he would be," Susan recalls.

In Goodwill Baptist Church in their home city of Washington, D.C., Susan found a safe place, especially with her Sunday school teacher. "I sat there in Sunday school class and looked in the face of this woman and saw the love of God," Susan says. At the age of twelve, Susan became the

Sunday school superintendent, because she knew more about the Bible than most of the adults at the church.

When she was a teenager, Susan joined Mt. Sinai Baptist Church in D.C., where the pastor didn't support women ministers. "He belonged to the D.C. Baptist Ministers Conference, an African American group that wouldn't even allow women to come to the meetings," she says. "If any man ordained a woman to the ministry, he was excommunicated from the fellowship and stripped of his standing."

When Susan first felt a call to preach, she thought she was mistaken because of all the negative messages she had heard about women preachers. Her mother was happy to hear about her call. But Susan was surprised by her pastor's response when she told him that God called her to preach. "The whole church knew that when you walked in here quoting the Bible like you wrote it," he said.

"But I'm a woman! Don't you think I shouldn't preach?"

"Susan, if God has called you, we're going to do a trial sermon, and we'll see the gifts and graces of God on your life."

At the age of nineteen, Susan preached her trial sermon. "When I finished preaching, the whole church was up on their feet," Susan recalls. "They didn't wait to have a church meeting the next week to vote to license me to the ministry. It was a unanimous vote. The pastor had already gotten my ministry license at the Baptist bookstore. He had crossed out with a magic marker every 'he' and put 'she,' every 'him' and put 'her,' because all the pronouns were male."

Although Rev. Newman had gotten a standing ovation on her sermon and a unanimous vote by the church to be licensed to ministry, she had few opportunities to preach. "I only preached at the 3:00 a.m. Halloween service," she laughs. "There was no way I was going to preach at the 11:00 a.m. service. Women were not allowed in the pulpit unless it was Women's Day." Later she wrote: "There is a sickness in the Black church, and it is the sometimes subsiding, but never dying, sexism. Women have been told we should be grateful that we are granted a Women's Day, that women are allowed in the pulpit, that the woman preacher can preach from the pulpit rather than from the floor. We should not complain or even speak of any dissatisfaction. This reminds me of white America during segregation, telling us that we should be thankful for what they have afforded us, and that coloreds need to remember their place."[8]

After graduating from George Washington University with a double major in journalism and speech communication and a minor in religion, Susan began Wesley Theological Seminary, the only black female at the school. Because her pastor and the male officers of the church discouraged her from completing seminary and being ordained, and because she didn't know of a Baptist church in D.C. that would allow her in the pulpit on Sundays to do the required seminary internship, Susan dropped out after one semester. A little later, with the encouragement of several other ministers and professors, she entered Howard University School of Divinity. She had found a church, Zion Baptist Church in D.C., to hire her as seminary intern and allow her to participate in worship leadership every Sunday, not just on Women's Day. When she preached at the church for the first time, she received a standing ovation.

After Susan graduated from seminary, Peoples Congregational United Church of Christ in D.C. ordained her and hired her as assistant pastor. Her ordination was especially meaningful to her because professors and ministers who knew her family participated. In seminary she had discovered a book on outstanding African American preachers that included her grandfather and six uncles, who were all United Methodist ministers. She hadn't known before that she came from a line of preachers because her father, the only child who was not a preacher, didn't talk about them as ministers. Susan became the first black woman ordained by a mainline denomination in D.C.

Several years later Rev. Newman became associate pastor of Shiloh Baptist Church, one of the largest churches in D.C. "I was the first woman on staff at Shiloh Baptist," she recalls. "The Sunday I came to preach before the church voted on me, you could hear a rat piss on cotton, it was so quiet! I wondered, 'What do you think I'm going to do in the pulpit, take my bra off and swing it in the air over the Bible?' All the deaconesses and missionaries were sitting on the front row with their white uniforms on. They told me later that they were just sitting there praying that I would be so good the church would vote for me." Again, she got a standing ovation on her preaching.

After completing a doctor of ministry degree at United Theological Seminary in Dayton, Ohio, Rev. Dr. Newman accepted the position of religious coordinator for the Children's Defense Fund, working with

Marian Wright Edelman. Susan helped plan the opening worship service, called "A Moral Witness for Our Children," for a Democratic National Convention in New York and a Republican National Convention in Texas.

A few years later, Rev. Dr. Newman accepted the call to serve as pastor of First Congregational Church in Atlanta, Georgia. All the "movers and shakers" of the African American community belonged to either Ebenezer Baptist, Dr. King's church, or First Congregational. Susan relates a story about teaching a Sunday school class for the officers of the church. She was excited, focused on teaching the lesson from the book of Romans on not conforming to the world but being transformed. She called on a trustee who looked like she wanted to speak.

"Sister, do you have something you want to say?"

"I don't like your lipstick. From where I'm sitting in church on Sunday, it looks like you don't have any lipstick on."

After the worship service one Sunday, a member of the church commented on Dr. Newman's shoes. "I had on a beige suit and beige pumps to go with my suit," she recalls. "During the service I had on my black robe. After the service, I was standing shaking hands with people. One woman said to me, 'Dr. Newman, we only wear black shoes with our robe in the pulpit.' I said, 'Well, did you hear the sermon?' It was that kind of thing constantly. They felt free to comment on my dress, my style, how I looked. They would never do that with a man."

Although Rev. Newman became well known and loved in Atlanta, the church did not follow her leadership. She was especially disappointed that the church voted against an adopt-a-school program, delineated in her book *With Heart and Hand: The Black Church Working to Save Black Children*.[9] The church had been willing to call a woman, but it had become obvious that parishioners would not follow a woman's leadership.

She left First Congregational Church to serve as executive director of Georgians for Children, a statewide child advocacy organization. When she moved back to D.C., she worked with the Campaign to Prevent Teen Pregnancy, Planned Parenthood, and the Virginia Department of Health, and served as senior advisor for religious affairs to the D.C. mayor and on the mayor's HIV/AIDS Task Force.

During this time when she was serving in faith-based communities, Rev. Newman also interviewed with churches. Although her preaching drew standing ovations and *Ebony* magazine named her one of the Top Black Women Preachers in America, many churches rejected her as pastor. "The churches were not ready for a woman as a senior minister," she says. "It's very difficult as a black woman to get called to a church. There are churches that don't mind your being the assistant, but they're still not ready for you to be senior pastor."

Rev. Dr. Newman is now associate minister of congregational life and social justice at All Souls Church in D.C. She expresses appreciation for this opportunity because of the church's inclusive leadership. "We don't want the pulpit to be all vanilla on any one Sunday. We make sure our worship leaders are male and female of various races and ages. It's important what people see in the pulpit of our congregations. When they see people who are their race and their gender, that's very empowering. The images you see—that's what your dreams are made of."

To keep her standing as a minister in the United Church of Christ denomination, Rev. Newman also preaches and participates in the ministry team at Covenant Baptist United Church of Christ. "All Souls and Covenant are social justice churches, intentionally inclusive in worship leadership and language," she says. "The leaders of these churches use inclusive language as a model for laypeople. They hear us say, 'God who is Mother and Father to us all.' So I can be with these two churches that I feel are great models of the 'beloved community' that Dr. King spoke of."

Consistent with her theology of the Divine within us all, Dr. Newman often connects the human and the Divine when she speaks about inclusive language and leadership. "It's important for women to be in the pulpit. I think it's important for people to see themselves, that we're all created in the image of God and that God is male and female, and that God is black, brown, yellow. I address God as 'He' and 'She,' 'Father' and 'Mother.'" Susan also balances female and male references to God in her writing: "If God did not want us to enjoy sex, She would not have made Barry White. If God did not want us to enjoy sex, He would not have made the Isley Brothers, Stevie Wonder, Smokey, Will Downing, the Dells, Harold Melvin and the Blue Notes with Teddy Pendergrass, Jeffrey Osborne with LTD, Luther, Marvin, D'Angelo, Maxwell, Lenny Kravitz, Prince, and R. Kelly. If God did not want us to enjoy sex, She would not have let us ever hear and slow drag to 'Stay in My Corner,' 'Stairway to Heaven,' 'The Love We Had Stays on My Mind,' 'If Only for One Night.'"[10]

Many people tell Rev. Newman that they had never thought of God as female until they heard her say it. "I think including female imagery of God is so powerful that Jesus did it in the parable of the lost coin; God is the woman sweeping the house.[11] I think that was very powerful that Jesus used female divine imagery while teaching even in that time," she says. "Words are powerful because our world is shaped by our language. The way we communicate with people through our language and through our images—that is powerful; that is what creates our mind-set."

Inclusive leadership and language empower marginalized people, Rev. Newman believes. "People of color and women have been marginalized by our dominant white male culture. I would love to get to the time when we would no more see in the news the 'first black this,' or 'the first female that.' There is room at the table for everyone. Every voice should be heard; no particular voice is greater or more valued because of gender or sexual orientation or race. I often joke that a whole lot of folks are going to be very upset when they find out that God really is a heavy-set black woman in her mid-fifties!"

Rev. Dr. Susan Newman articulates an expansive vision for the future of the church. "I hope for a truly ecumenical, interfaith church. When we are able to do justice and work to uplift suffering humanity, put aside our differences and find common ground, I feel we're working toward that 'beloved community.'" Through her prophetic preaching, writing, and advocacy, Rev. Newman works to make this dream reality.

Rev. Paul Smith

Author; Teacher; Minister

Releasing the Divine from the Male Prison

"We have to let the Divine out of the male prison. Locking the Divine in a male prison as the big guy upstairs blocks transformation. Including feminine divine images is connected to other justice issues. Valuing the feminine will value all people, wherever they are on the scale from homosexual to heterosexual."

For many years, Rev. Paul Smith has been connecting female images of the Divine and justice for all people. At Broadway Church in Kansas City, Missouri, where he pastored for forty-six years, he took many prophetic stands. He initiated controversial changes such as movement from hierarchical to team leadership, ordination of women as pastors, inclusion of female divine images in worship, and complete affirmation of LGBTQ persons. When Broadway Church (formerly Broadway Baptist Church) began doing holy unions for people of all sexual orientations, the church was ousted from the Missouri Baptist Convention and the Southern Baptist Convention (SBC).

Local, state, and national Baptist groups had been threatening to oust the church for about twenty years. "Finally when we became gay affirming and started doing holy unions, and that made the newspapers, then the Missouri Baptist Convention voted to remove us from the SBC," Paul recalls. "That made the news. We were on TV—heresy, local Baptist church removed from the SBC! I just loved it! We were hoping that we could wait long enough to be thrown out and make the news. Then the word would get out that they're some Baptists who think it's okay to be gay." Paul says he felt a new freedom when the SBC ousted the church for becoming welcoming and affirming.

The inclusive ministry of Rev. Smith is also reflected in the church's "Faces of Jesus" art collection, impressive in its scope and diversity. For forty years Paul has been collecting these images, now totaling 240, installed in hallway galleries in the spacious church building. The collection includes multicultural images of Jesus as female and androgynous, as well as male.

Among the female images is *Ruach* by Lucy Synk, displayed with these comments by the artist: "This was inspired by my discovery that the Hebrew word 'Ruach' ('spirit,' 'breath') is feminine in gender, and is used in the Hebrew Bible to speak of the Spirit of God." Another female image in the collection is Robert Lentz's *Christ Sophia*, with this inscription: "In this portrayal Christ Sophia is placed in an egg-shaped mandala to connote her fertility. She holds the ancient Cro-Magnon statue, Venus of Willendorf, a prehistoric figure of the Divine as female. The Greek letters in her halo stand for 'I am who I am,' the divine name given Moses at the burning bush. She points to herself as if to say, 'I am She; know me now more fully.'" Another Lentz painting, *Dance of Creation*, portrays the connection between "Hagia Sophia, Holy Wisdom, and Logos, Pattern of all Creation, incarnate in the Cosmic Christ." In *Compassion Mandala* by Robert Lentz, we see "the androgynous Cosmic Christ holding the world in loving arms."

The "Faces of Jesus" collection includes passion images that challenge cultural prejudices. In Becky Harrelson's *The Crucifixion of Christ*, the plaque on the cross above Christ's head reads "faggot" in capital letters. The artist explains in the caption: "Today gays are socially acceptable and religiously justifiable targets for hate. And just like gays, Jesus was made a hate target in his time because he dared to be different, to tell the truth even though his words and his position subverted the religious establishment." Paul comments on this picture: "The artist is not saying that Jesus was gay. One could substitute other words that condemn and express violence toward others. Homophobia is the last acceptable prejudice, widespread in our culture and bolstered by a heretical distortion of Christianity. We must see rejection of gays for what it is—violence toward that which God has created and called 'good.'"

Also in the collection are two female passion images: a photograph of Edwina Sandys's bronze statue *Christa*, depicting a woman on the cross, and *After El Greco* by an unknown artist who has replaced the male Christ figure on the cross in El Greco's familiar painting with a female Christ figure. "Christ on the cross identifies with all the persecuted of the world," Paul says. "Women are the largest group on earth who have been and today are consistently persecuted and denied opportunity to be all that they are meant to be. Ironically, it is often religion itself that supports this oppression."

In *Is It Okay to Call God "Mother"? Considering the Feminine Face of God*, Paul makes clear the importance of including female divine names and images in public worship. "Churches have been making God exclusively masculine in public for a long time, and changing in private will not reverse the damage," he writes. "This is a decidedly public issue. Nothing will change business as usual in our churches unless those of us who are convicted by the Holy Spirit first change our own behavior and then work towards change in the church."[12] Paul goes on to give a sequence of steps for changing worship language: stop using gender-exclusive words for people, stop using masculine pronouns for God, start calling God "Mother" in personal prayer life, experiment with using female pronouns and metaphors for God with others, ask others to study this issue, encourage worship leaders to use gender-inclusive language for persons, promote the adoption of a church service policy of gender-neutral language for God, and encourage incorporation of female divine metaphors and pronouns into worship services.

At the conclusion of this book, Paul quotes Teilhard de Chardin: "Faith has need of the whole truth." Then Paul makes his final call to action:

> Now is the moment in history for the church to see more of this truth in the awesome light of God's revelation of herself as recorded in Scripture. Is it okay to call God "Mother"? It is not only okay but it is just and holy, righteous and necessary. Now is the time to break the conspiracy of silence about the feminine face of God. God's Word is rousing itself again, wrestling itself free from the grip of patriarchy and sexism.[13]

In a more recent essay titled "The Cover-up of the Divine Feminine: Is it Okay to Call God 'Goddess'?" Rev. Smith sounds an even stronger call for inclusion of female names and images of the Divine. He refers to Dan Brown's popular book *The Da Vinci Code*, saying that its premise is true: there has been a cover-up of the Divine Feminine.

> The feminine has been demonized and called unclean for thousands of years. As long as the worst thing you can call a boy or man is "sissy" or "gay," the war on the feminine is still going on. The most sexist hour of the American week is on Sunday morning. An observer going into most church services would notice that they have only men as priests, pastors, and deacons. As long as God is male, then male is God. Using exclusively masculine words to the exclusion of feminine words such as "Goddess" says something that Jesus never intended, that God is more like a man than a woman. As long as we refuse to challenge the male-only divine images deeply imbedded in our psyche, women will not be seen or treated as equals with men. "God" has become a male word. If you don't think "God" is a male word, just use the word "Goddess" and see the reaction. If the word "God" included both male and female, there would not be that reaction. So the answer to my beginning question today—Is it okay to call God "Goddess"?—is yes, of course. This is an exciting time for all of us as the Spirit of Goddess is calling us to continue the revolution that began in the early church and was stopped and covered up. It's a great time for women, for gays, for all of us to grow in our understanding of our Creator and Her creation.[14]

Rev. Smith elaborates on including female divine names and images not only to support gender justice and equality but also to expand spirituality: "It's the first opening to include feminine as well as masculine divine images. Exclusively masculine symbols have been so degrading for women. Now I see the Divine Feminine connected to expanding the whole image of the Divine to include the infinite, intimate, and inner dimensions." Paul believes that experience is a key to people's including female images of the Divine. "One good experience would take care of it all. The medieval Christian mystics can refer to Jesus as feminine because of their experience. You can go only so far with the cognitive, and the other has to be experienced and practiced. I think Jesus really did experience God as a Daddy and a Mama. And we all experience and feel our divinity more when we hear 'She' and 'He' in church."

Changing both language and visual symbols will help people expand their experiences of the Divine, Paul says. "It's very important to have the words 'She,' 'Mother,' and other feminine references. Many Catholics relate to God as Mary. They found a way when the church said 'no' to the Divine Feminine. They found a way—good for them. Others find the way through 'Sophia' or 'Mary Magdalene.' Like words, visual images are powerful. It seems to me that today we are more in a period similar to that of the medieval church where the only Bible people had was in the form of statues and images at church because few people could read. Today everybody can read, but they don't. So it's more about images. The reason for the 'Faces of Jesus' exhibit is that people are going to remember these images."

Paul mentions one picture in the "Faces of Jesus" collection that people either love or hate: *Virtuous Giving,* by Michael Floyd, a former member of Broadway Church and graduate of Midwestern Baptist Seminary. Paul comments on this picture: "Jesus is seen as a pregnant woman on a birthing table ready to give birth. Meister Eckhart said, 'What does God do all day long? God gives birth.'" Eckhart also serves as inspiration for Rev. Smith's book *Integral Christianity: The Spirit's Call to Evolve,* in which he elaborates a mystical spirituality, applying integral philosophy to Christian faith and practice.[15] In addition to his books, Paul is reaching a worldwide audience through his writing on the "Integral Life" website blog.[16]

"I think prayer is becoming conscious of Divine presence," Rev. Smith says. "The deepest form of prayer is what I call 'being prayer' or 'abiding prayer.' Mystics in the Eastern traditions and Christian mystics teach us about contemplative states. In the deepest state we experience God as pure consciousness, that divine consciousness that was in Jesus and is also in us. Jesus said that we are all gods.[17] The goal is to live in that consciousness and then manifest it, like Jesus did, to change the world."

Dr. Caryn D. Riswold

Professor of Religion; Chair, Gender and Women's Studies Department, Illinois College

Connecting Feminism and Christianity

"A big part of why I started writing and speaking more about issues like marriage equality and reproductive justice in recent years was in fact to untangle the hold that right-wing and conservative evangelical Christianity has when it comes to public god-talk and the politicization of sexuality. So in some way, every time I write about being pro-faith and pro-choice, I'm saying that Christians are not all like that. Every time I point out that what Jesus had to say about homosexuality can be summed up in zero words, I'm saying that Christianity doesn't have to be like that."[18]

In her writing and teaching, Caryn Riswold, a feminist theologian in the Lutheran tradition, illuminates the shared values of Christianity and feminism, demonstrating ways Christians and feminists can collaborate in advocating for social justice. In *Feminism and Christianity: Questions and Answers, in the Third Wave,* Dr. Riswold makes a compelling case for the connection between Christianity and feminism:

Feminists should care about Christianity because it is simultaneously a religion with an egalitarian vision that has been and should continue to be liberating for women, and because it has been a major institution of patriarchy that remains a pervasive cultural force needing criticism. The first two waves of feminism demonstrated

how various institutions of patriarchy promoted injustice and inequality especially for women, and they helped bring about positive change in many of them. The work of criticizing the negative
elements of Christianity while uncovering its positive legacy must
continue today with third-wave feminist insights and strategies....
Myths and stereotypes fuel the resistance that Christians have toward feminism. Stripping them away is a first step toward seeing
why feminism matters, and why in fact it is good for Christianity.
Feminists are not the man-hating, family-destroying feminazis that
conservative ideologues like Rush Limbaugh believe them to be.
Feminism is the radical idea that women are equally human, and
Christians everywhere should care that throughout human history,
and still today, people have not in fact believed or acted as if this
were the case.[19]

In this book Dr. Riswold presents thorough scholarship in a clear and
engaging style accessible to lay and clergy, as well as academic audiences. She describes her purpose for this book: "I wrote *Feminism and
Christianity* for two main audiences: the Christian who is either skeptical
or uninformed about feminism's relevance for the religion today, and
the feminist who doesn't see any need to talk about Christianity given
its patriarchal history and tendencies. I divided the book into 'feminist
questions of Christianity' and 'Christian questions of feminism' as a way
to start addressing the questions that I know to be out there. I don't
claim to have answered or even asked every question perfectly, but I
do hope to have sparked conversation and discussion in classrooms,
churches, and living rooms that will live on beyond the covers of the
book."

For more than a decade Dr. Riswold has taught religion and
chaired the Gender and Women's Studies program at Illinois College
in Jacksonville, Illinois. While Dr. Riswold realizes the value of her
academic writing, she feels called also to write for a wider audience. "I
intentionally wrote the book to be accessible to a wide range of readers.
My previously published writing had been much more tailored to an
academic reader and an audience more familiar with terminology and
'insider' issues in the field of Christian theology. I've come to realize in
recent years, though, that while that work remains vitally important,
I am called also to speak and write to people who are not experts. In

fact, this is what I do in the classroom with undergraduate students every day. So, I realized, why not take the skills and passions I bring to my classroom every day into the public realm of writing, speaking, and publishing?"

Caryn grew up in Lutheran congregations in South Dakota. She was in the first generation of her family who earned a college degree, completing her bachelor of arts at Augustana College, a liberal arts college of the Evangelical Lutheran Church in America (ELCA), in her childhood hometown of Sioux Falls, South Dakota. When Caryn was about to leave for graduate school, the pastor of her home church remarked about her interest in feminist theology: "You're not one of those feminazis, right?"[20]

In the introduction to *Feminism and Christianity*, Caryn also relates this more recent incident: "I travel through the rural Midwest proudly wearing a black T-shirt proclaiming in hot-pink letters: 'This Is What a Feminist Looks Like.' The manager of the Cracker Barrel in Missouri said to my husband: 'She doesn't look any different than my wife.'"[21] This remark, like that of Caryn's pastor, indicates that many people still have distorted images of feminists.

In her graduate studies Caryn connected feminism and Christian theology. She earned a master's degree in theological studies from Claremont School of Theology and master of theology and doctor of philosophy degrees from Lutheran School of Theology at Chicago. At Lutheran School of Theology, where her advisors were all male professors, she took the risk of declaring that for her qualifying exam she wanted to write on radical feminist philosopher and theologian Mary Daly. "To put this in context, know that most of my classmates wrote on more typical male giants in the field like Wolfhart Pannenberg or Karl Barth or Albrecht Ritschl," she says. "My faculty advisors agreed, and I was off and running. It's just one moment in my journey where supportive communities made a significant difference. It has been important throughout my journey that I've been a part of educational and ecclesial communities that recognize and support feminist work."

I met Caryn at an annual Faith and Feminism, Womanist, Mujerista Conference at Ebenezer/herchurch Lutheran in San Francisco. She was engaging, knowledgeable, and witty in her presentation and in personal conversations. In her presentation she was so persuasive about the importance of social media in spreading the egalitarian, liberating messages of Christianity and feminism that I increased my activity on Facebook and signed up for Twitter when I got back home.

Practicing what she preaches, Dr. Riswold continues to find wider audiences for her messages. "Bringing more thoughtful people into conversations about justice and God and church and religion and social change is crucial to any movement," she explains. "So I started trying to do that in *Feminism and Christianity*, and I've taken it to another level now with my blog, 'feminismxianity,' on the Progressive Christian *Patheos*.[22] Since that launched, I've been amazed by both the gratitude and the resistance for feminist perspectives on Christianity, politics, and pop culture."

That resistance is especially evident in some of the reactions to the posts on her blog. "Resistance to feminist theology is still quite real," she says. "Even on something as seemingly innocuous as the Women's Ordination Conference's parody of 'Call Me Maybe' video titled 'Ordain a Lady,' the number and level of negative comments is pretty stunning. I've made a decision as a blog administrator to allow comments when they are negative, when I vehemently disagree with what they say, and even when they are personally insulting to me. I do that in part to allow others to see the real resistance to justice and women's empowerment that exists today. It may be just a few comments here and there, but it represents a broader opposition to our work for justice that we need to name, read, and resist collectively."

In addition to her writing and teaching, Caryn's justice ministry includes serving as one of twenty participants in the Faith and Reproductive Justice Leadership Institute at the Center for American Progress in Washington, D.C. Caryn identifies herself with "third-wave feminists," whom she describes as "the generation of feminists active in the twenty-first century who were raised during and with the benefits of second-wave feminism," who work "to include awareness of race, class, sexuality, age, ability, and many other factors that shape human identity," and who focus on "social problems like safeguarding marriage equality, ending race- and gender-based violence, and ameliorating the effects of global capitalism on the poorest of poor women."[23]

Many women in Caryn's generation don't want to be called feminists because of negative stereotypes they associate with feminism and because they believe that women have already achieved equal rights. But Caryn points out that women still don't receive equal pay for equal work and that sexism is often more subversive than ever before. She lists other inequities: "Women make up about 17 percent of the United States Congress. Every U.S. president has been male. One in four women is raped or assaulted by an intimate partner at some point in her lifetime. Women earn approximately 77 cents for every dollar that men earn. Women cannot be ordained into leadership in the Roman Catholic Church, the Lutheran Church–Missouri Synod, the Christian Reformed Church, and many other sizable Christian denominations."[24]

In her prophetic writing and teaching, Dr. Riswold challenges Christians of all ages to see the continuing importance of feminism and to join with feminists in justice work:

> Recognizing the important and culturally beneficial work that feminism has done for both women and men takes little more than a cursory glance at history. Realizing that feminism is one reason why multitudes of women have had access and choices that they have had is important. Understanding how multitudes of women around the world and in our own neighborhoods still do not have all of the privileges afforded to men is also important. Feminism and the advocacy for women's equality remain culturally and politically relevant and necessary.[25]

In the conclusion to *Feminism and Christianity*, Dr. Riswold expresses some ways she hopes that Christians and feminists will apply what they learn from her book:

> Church reading groups and their pastors might be inspired to examine the language that they use to talk about God on a daily and weekly basis in worship, prayer, and public communication. If language does not reflect the fullness and diversity of the human community, they may take steps to change it. Young third-wave feminist activists might be willing now to see how some Christians can be partners in advocating for federal marriage equality, debunking the popular misuse of God's word to discriminate against gay and lesbian Americans. They no longer need to accept the way the Bible is invoked by heterosexist political foes.[26]

Caryn cites Ebenezer/herchurch Lutheran as an example of a church creatively connecting Christian tradition and feminist theology in worship that includes biblical female names for the Divine, such as "Mother," *Shaddai*, "Sophia," "Womb," "Midwife," *Shekhinah*, and "She Who Is." Caryn explains that "feminism challenges Christianity to understand its history of suppressing concepts of a female deity as well as to open itself up to a rich storehouse of images and names for God that more fully represents human experience."[27]

As she connects Christianity and feminism in her justice work, Caryn says she draws inspiration and strength from grateful responses to her teaching, writing, and speaking. "Years ago, I heard writer and Holocaust survivor Elie Wiesel speak at the University of Chicago. A question posed to him at that event was 'Where do you find joy?' His slow and thoughtful response was something like this: 'When I am teaching ... when I am in the classroom ... and there is a student ... maybe even back there in the corner ... who *gets it* ... that is my joy.' This resonates with me so much. It sometimes happens with the young people I teach and advise and talk to in my daily work. It sometimes happens with a reader who writes back to me that they are so happy to have 'found' my work. It sometimes happens on Twitter when someone thanks me for saying the things that not enough other people are saying. It sometimes happens off to the side at a conference when a female colleague says, 'Thank you for saying something real in a room full of suits.' When someone gets it. As long as I have a voice and a platform, I will continue to tell stories and speak to the justice that needs to more fully pervade our world."

Rev. Stacy Boorn

Pastor, Ebenezer / herchurch Lutheran, San Francisco, California

Changing the World by Changing the Church

"It would be wonderful if even half of all Christian churches included the Divine Feminine in worship, if this were not an alternative to the norm but the norm. The whole structure of the church will change. Persons who have been kept in their place by the patriarchal structure won't be kept there anymore. Equal partnership at the table will reap good rewards, resulting in just structures. Women and others who have been marginalized within religions will reclaim their identity and connection to the Holy Other, giving a different reality to the church."

R ev. Stacy Boorn's voice rises as she expresses her excitement that the vision of equality and justice in the church is "happening in many places." Several years ago she envisioned a purple church as another symbol of equality and justice. This vision became reality when Ebenezer/herchurch Lutheran chose to paint the outside of the church building purple "to honor the Divine Feminine, to be in solidarity with empowering women and all persons who are oppressed and denied equal rights, to advocate for marriage rights for all people."[28]

When she was only nine years old, Stacy announced, "I want to be a pastor. God wants me to do this." Even though she was growing up in a church that was part of the Missouri Synod Lutheran denomination, which still doesn't ordain women, she didn't realize then that women were prohibited from being pastors. As she grew older, she observed that there were only male pastors in the congregations in her town and only male Sunday school teachers and male elders in her church, but she still believed that women could share leadership with men.

At a Missouri Synod college, Stacy was one of just three women studying to be ministers. The three women did not get the scholarships that the male pre-seminarians were given. But her Lutheran congregation and pastor became supportive. After her first year in college, she declared that she wanted to preach the sermon in a Sunday morning service at Trinity Lutheran, her home church in Schenectady, New York. She describes Trinity Lutheran as a beautiful little German church with slate floors, wooden pews, and stone walls with buttresses—like a miniature cathedral. Stacy, only nineteen years old, climbed up the steps into the elevated pulpit to preach her first sermon to a congregation of about eighty people. When she reached the pulpit, three women raised their bulletins, looked at one another, stood up, stamped their feet, and walked out. Their high heels went *clunkity, clunkity, clunk* on that hard floor. Stacy stood there bewildered, but the pastor said to her, "You just go on; never mind."

After graduating from Pacific Lutheran Theological Seminary, Stacy was ordained by the Association of Evangelical Lutheran Churches, a breakaway group from the Missouri Synod denomination that became part of the Evangelical Lutheran Church in America (ELCA). Stacy's first opportunity to serve as solo pastor came at Grace Lutheran Church in Richmond, California. When she was teaching in the children's program, a Laotian girl looked at a picture in the Sunday school curriculum and said, "None of these children look like me." Rev. Boorn at first thought the little girl meant that the children surrounding Jesus in the picture were all Caucasian, but then realized that they were also all boys. "Not only was Jesus a male, but all the children around Jesus were all boy children," Stacy exclaims. "In the curriculum there were no children of color, very few images of girls, few role models of women of faith, and certainly no feminine images of God. I tried to introduce pictures of God other than masculine, but these kids, ages three and four, told me, 'That's wrong! Jesus was a boy, and God's a boy; that's all there is to it!' The whole society still teaches this masculine God."

Ten years later, Rev. Boorn began serving as full-time interim mission-assessor pastor of Ebenezer Lutheran in San Francisco, and a few years later as called pastor. About the time she began serving this church she discovered feminist theology. One of the first books she read was Rosemary Radford Ruether's *Sexism and God-Talk*.[29] She remembers thinking, "Oh, my goodness, what have I missed? Why didn't anybody in my seminary experience point this out?" Stacy began wondering how she could integrate feminist theology into the liturgy but found the church "very entrenched in traditional liturgy."

When she had been at Ebenezer Lutheran less than a year, Pastor Boorn, with the parents' permission, baptized a child "in the name of God who is our Mother and our Father and in the name of Jesus, who is the child of God." This baptism stirred controversy in the congregation. "One woman really became upset and said that I was 'not naming the God of the ELCA,'" Stacy recalls. "I wondered, 'Does she mean that God is the God of the ELCA and every other church has their own God?'"

Four years into Stacy's tenure at Ebenezer Lutheran, the church put a large banner across the front of the building with these words: "Everybody welcome at the table. Sunday morning worship at 10:30 a.m. God loves all Her children!" Then church members thought it was time to have a website, and Stacy suggested naming it "herchurch.org" to connect with the banner statement. Soon thereafter the church became Ebenezer/herchurch Lutheran. After the banner was up, people started calling the church to say, "God is not a She!" Pastor Boorn says she has also received emails filled with condemning words: "You're going to hell. How dare you change the nature of God! You're not doing God's will; you're leading your congregation astray."

In teaching children at the church, Pastor Stacy referred to God as "She," and had this interchange with a seven-year-old girl:

"You can't call God 'She.' God's a 'He,'" the little girl declared.
"How do you know that?" Stacy asked.
"Everybody knows that."
"How do you feel about that?"
"Well, I don't like it because I'm a girl!"

Stacy says it's sad that this little girl "had already figured out this was the way it was supposed to be, and there was something less about her." But Stacy believes that continuing to hear the Divine referred to as female at Ebenezer/herchurch will make a difference in the self-worth of this little girl and others because it's clear that the pervasive male language for divinity in the culture has had the opposite effect.

"Language helps create who we are," Rev. Boorn says. "Words have so much meaning, especially in the Protestant tradition because we don't have icons. But words can be even stronger than pictures. We can pretend that we don't have a domination structure because we don't have male icons, but our words have become icons. Words for Protestants have become icons. Some people say that all the masculine words in worship don't matter because they don't believe that God is male. How can they believe that God is gender-neutral if they call God only 'He' and refuse to call God 'She'? I'm convinced that you cannot possibly believe that God is neither he nor she if you cannot call God 'She.'"

Because the two worship books in the Lutheran tradition do not offer inclusive language for Deity, Ebenezer/herchurch prints liturgies, collecting them from a variety of sources. "Mother-Father," "God/dess," and "Christ-Sophia" are among the wide variety of divine images the church uses. "Christ-Sophia is one way to refer to the Risen One," Pastor Boorn says. "There are many different ways of looking at the Divine Feminine. Darkness is another image for the Divine Feminine, reclaiming Darkness as being as holy as Light."

Ebenezer/herchurch includes many other divine feminine images, such as "Midwife," *Shekhinah*, and *Shaddai* from the Jewish tradition. "We especially love the name *Shaddai*, meaning 'mountain,' 'most high,' and 'the breasted one,' because the church is in the shadow of what are called the 'twin peaks' of San Francisco, two peaks on the northeast side of the church that from a distance look like breasts," Stacy explains. "So we look out and say, 'There She is, *Shaddai*, right over there!' Another image that has been powerful for us is the 'Baker Woman' in one of Jesus's parables.[30] We have people who have been well educated in the biblical tradition but who have never realized that the Baker Woman in the parable is an image of God. They've learned that the male images in the parables, like the Shepherd, are God, but not the female images. When we start using the female images, like Baker Woman, as a God-name, people say, 'Why wasn't I told that was in the Bible? No one ever told me that was God. Who told me I could only read the Bible certain ways?'"

Pastor Boorn expresses her strong belief that the role of the pastor is to be prophet and priest at the same time. "The prophetic word is as important as the healing word or the comforting or pastoral word," she says. "The mission of Ebenezer/herchurch Lutheran is to be a prophetic voice within the patriarchal church. Inclusion of the Divine Feminine will change the whole structure of the church. Eventually the clergy structure will be dismantled. The inclusion of the Sacred Feminine empowers women and men to look at alternative structures, to change power structures that leave people out or belittle them or give a person power over others. Exclusively masculine language for Deity supports those structures. Egalitarian language for the Holy Other supports egalitarian communities. There will never be full equality or justice for woman and girls globally as long as the religions of the world continue to personify the Holy Other exclusively or unevenly as male either metaphorically or literally."

For that reason, Ebenezer/herchurch worship services include female names and images of the Divine. Pastor Boorn explains:

> It is not the intent or goal of the Sunday liturgy in this place to seek the eradication of masculine metaphors for God from Christendom but rather to speak and seek the holy liberation that is the core of the church and the One to whom the church gives witness. Claiming and celebrating female images of God in the scripture and the continued revelation of the presence of the Divine is an attempt to balance the predominantly androcentric and hierarchical images of God that abound in our biblical tradition. The use of feminine images and language for the Divine underscores the issue of justice. There is a direct correspondence between the church's attitudes and actions towards women and the abuse of women.

The liberating ministry of Pastor Boorn reaches out beyond Ebenezer/herchurch Lutheran. She has organized seven Faith and Feminism, Womanist, Mujerista Conferences, bringing people from around the world to experience the healing love, peace, and justice of the Female Divine. One of these conferences celebrated the sacred value of the earth and inspired spirituality, politics, and praxis for a sustainable world. "Religious feminism includes direct focus on ecofeminism," Stacy says. "At herchurch we make the connection between feminism and care of the earth. We see the earth as Sacred Mother or the way the Holy

Other is embodied, so that any abuse of the earth would be an abuse of She Who Is." Stacy celebrates the sacredness of the earth through her photography as well.[31] She is especially drawn to trees that symbolize for her "the Tree of Life and its connections to the Divine Feminine."

Multicultural female divine names and images provide a foundation for social justice and equality, Rev. Boorn believes. Even though she recognizes the intersection of justice issues, people have tried to discount her by calling her a "one-issue person." She responds: "I think that one issue is the groundwork for everything else; along with others in the Christian tradition, I've come to understand that feminism and the gospel are actually the same. Feminism means an egalitarian world, so there would be no racism, sexism, classism, and economic disparities. Feminism means economic justice and good stewardship of the earth." Although the Evangelical Lutheran Church in America did not name a connection between feminism and the vote that lifted the denomination's ban on openly lesbian, gay, bisexual, transgender, and questioning (LGBTQ) clergy in committed relationships, Stacy sees that connection. "The total acceptance of LGBTQ persons in the clergy and in all aspects of church and society connects with the feminist vision of an egalitarian world." She continues, "But I know of a few primarily LGBTQ pastors and congregations that are pretty traditional in their language, pretty male chauvinist. They don't make the connection between what we do to women and what we do to LGBTQ persons. I believe that the oppression that happens, especially with gay men, comes from their being seen as women-like. Gay men are demeaned because they act like women, and women are not seen in as high a realm as men."

Pastor Stacy Boorn believes that in order to bring justice in the world for females and for all people, we must change the church to include multicultural female images of the Divine. "I don't see how the world is going to change until the religious institutions change because they are so much a part of who the world is," she says. "The more we can provide church in a different way, the more we can hope things change." Pastor Boorn continues to provide church in a different way, a prophetic and creative way. Through her boldness in reimaging divinity to include female language and imagery, she makes major contributions to justice for people of all genders and races and for the earth.

Part 4

Wisdom's Works of Economic Justice

M any women suffer the triple discrimination of sexism, racism, and classism. Womanist and *mujerista* theologians have illuminated this triple discrimination and focused on ways to overcome it. Some women suffer the quadruple discrimination of sexism, heterosexism, racism, and classism. Women suffer from economic injustice disproportionately: 70 percent of the world's poor are women.

Wisdom calls us to work with Her for economic justice for all. She calls us to change our sacred symbolism. Many traditional male divine names and images, such as "Lord," "Master," and "King," sanction classism as well as sexism. These images support kyriarchy (rule of lords or masters), a hierarchical class system with rich, white, straight men dominating from the top.[1]

Wisdom guides us to sacred symbolism that supports equal partnership instead of domination. Multicultural female divine names and images, such as "Holy Wisdom," and other nonhierarchical divine images, such as "Friend" and "Partner," contribute to overcoming sexism, heterosexism, racism, and classism so that there will be economic justice for all.

Where Are Liberty and Justice?

(Sung to the tune of "We Are Travelers on a Journey")

Where are liberty and justice when so many live in need?
Let us rise to caring action, showing faith and love through deeds.
Holy Wisdom, give us courage; help us be Your prophets bold,
joining You to end oppression, truth and fairness to uphold.

Now the rich are growing richer, while the poor cry in distress;
heads of corporations flourish, while the poor have less and less.
Millions suffer unemployment; many more are underpaid;
give us power, Holy Wisdom, so that changes can be made.

How unjust that some make millions, crushing others with their
  greed,
basic rights of workers flaunting, never hearing those in need.
Holy Wisdom, come to help us; give us power to unite,
moving hearts and changing systems, joining hands to work for
  right.

Holy Wisdom, send us forward, working for equality,
economic fairness bringing, making dreams reality.
As we join with those who suffer, fill us with Your loving care;
may we take Your peaceful pathways, bringing justice everywhere.[2]

BEACH SPRING

Rev. Dr. Isabel Docampo

Professor of Supervised Ministry, Perkins School of Theology

Sophia Wisdom Making All Things New

One: Listen!

Many: The shout for liberation breaks forth,
   and the bell of God's freedom is ringing.

One: *Eschucha!*

Many: The joy of celebration erupts,
   and the salsa of God's love is dancing.

One: Listen!

Many: The promise of anticipation beckons,
   and the kinship of God is birthing.

One: Listen!

Many: Sophia-Wisdom-God has set the table; it is round,
   bountiful and set for all!

One: Come, let us feast on the bounty of Her Holy Wisdom,

Many: That we, like Mary, may sing of joy,
   and labor with hope for a new world—

One: A world where Christian worship sets people free so that

Many: The poor and immigrant have dignity, work and food;
   women do not worry about politics in their health care
     nor rape as a weapon of war;
   gay, lesbian and transgender people live with dignity and
       respect;
   religion is not used as a weapon of subjugation,

**and Christianity stands with the least of these in every
corner of the world.**
One: Come, let us feast on the bounty of Her Holy Wisdom,
Many: And be filled with God's peace, justice, and compassion.
All: Behold! Sophia-Wisdom-God; She makes all things new!

Rev. Dr. Isabel Docampo has been sounding the call for gender and economic justice for many years. She created and led this call to worship for an Alliance of Baptists Annual Convocation.

From the time she was in seminary, Rev. Docampo has been advocating for social justice. "It's probably the same sermon I've been preaching all my life," she says about her first sermon, delivered in her seminary preaching class. It was a "justice sermon," inviting "people to look at the scripture from a different perspective, not the dominant one, but the perspective of people who are hurting."

Later at Grace United Methodist Church in Dallas, Texas, Rev. Docampo preached a prophetic "justice" sermon titled "The Essence of the Divine is Shalom/Peace." In it, she urges us "to overcome the subtle ways that the ugly manifestations of homophobia, ageism, sexism, racism, and classism arise" and to express "outrage and stop politely tiptoeing around the elephant of injustice in a world where little girls are killed by their father in a Dallas loft apartment or where the immigrants we serve in our clinics are denied civil rights because they lack legal immigration status, where gay and lesbian sisters and brothers are victims of hate crimes and are denied access to the church as full members." In this sermon, Rev. Docampo emphasizes the difference including the Female Divine in worship makes to justice and equal relationships:

> The names we use to address the Divine in prayer and song, Sunday after Sunday, affect not only our relationship with the Divine, but also our relationship with all of humanity, and how we see and understand ourselves. Women who never hear God as female unconsciously integrate that they are not totally created in God's image, limiting their sense of worth and power. Men who never hear God as female unconsciously integrate that they have greater knowledge and worth because they always hear their male gender equated with ultimate power and wisdom.

Words make a lot of difference. The first time I heard God described as female Creating, Loving, Powerful, Forgiving, tears streamed down my face. It was like my soul had been touched in a new and powerful way. I felt in that sacred place that I was being affirmed for the first time as truly created in the image of the great Divine. I had already felt very certain of God's calling me to give my life to serve the Christian church. But for the very first time, I felt truly created in the image of God with the full blessing of the Divine.

Three years later when I was being told that my gender made me inherently sinful because of my connection as a woman to Eve's role in the Garden of Eden, and therefore, could not serve as an ordained clergy teaching men, but only in other prescribed roles, I found strength and courage as I remembered that Sophia-God created the earth, sent Jesus to redeem us, and had placed Her hand upon me. I didn't give away my God as Father, but now I had Sophia-God as my Friend and Soul Guide as well. You see, God as Father was unapproachable for me at that time because I was facing so many Christian men who used "God the Father" to try to silence me. It was easier for me to address the feminine God, and She gave me strength. I could approach Her in prayer. It was profoundly important. And I can tell you many stories from my ministry with very devout Christian women, victims of domestic violence, whose only reference to God was a male, giving males more power and dominance in their eyes and keeping them at risk for their lives. How we address the Divine makes a big difference.

Isabel's story reveals that she has indeed been preaching a justice sermon all her life through her actions as well as her words. Her parents were first-generation immigrants from Cuba. When they came to the United States, her mother was four months pregnant with Isabel. Born in New Orleans, Louisiana, Isabel was baptized Roman Catholic. Later, her family joined Primera Iglesia Bautista Hispano-Americana. Growing up in this church, Isabel listened to *testimonios* of Latina and Latino immigrants from Panama, Honduras, Nicaragua, Ecuador, Puerto Rico, and Guatemala, as well as from Cuba. These stories wove together deep gratitude to God for the United States and heartbreak over family left behind and injustices still endured.

Most of the families in her church were lower income day laborers and domestic laborers. Even though poor, "they were trying to send money back or to get their family members to the United States," she says. Her parents, like most others in the church, struggled to make a living. They had left Cuba because they couldn't make a living there, even though they worked hard. They saw America as a place where they could give their children a future. Isabel says that the "struggles of the underclass" became part of who she is, along with a sense of gratitude for being in America.

As Isabel grew up, she began "to lose that naïveté of how wonderful this place is and started to understand the institutional racism, classism, and other injustices." But she says that the shattering of her childhood view didn't make her cynical. "What it did was make me believe that my patriotic and Christian duty was to help America be the best it can be," she explains. "My work to change injustice comes from my understanding of what God is calling me to do, of what God is calling all of us to do. When I'm working for justice issues, I feel that I'm working for my country to preserve freedom. We have to hold on to that freedom to live fully, freedom from being a racist society, freedom from sexism, gender inequality."

Isabel's ordination at Broadmoor Baptist Church in Baton Rouge, Louisiana, created a firestorm. "All hell broke loose," she says. During this time fundamentalists, who opposed the ordination of women, were gaining control of the Southern Baptist Convention. Isabel had been serving as director of Christian Social Ministries for Judson Baptist Association in the Baton Rouge area. Her ministry included working with women and children who experienced domestic violence, starting the Greater Baton Rouge Food Bank and serving as the first board president of the Food Bank, teaching English literacy classes to Muslim women, and giving pastoral care to her elderly volunteers. Even though her ministry was exemplary, protestors against women's ordination stirred a yearlong controversy, culminating in a meeting of the Association where delegates voted on two questions: whether to fire Rev. Docampo and whether women should be ordained to ministry. "The meeting was packed," she recalls. "This had been the talk of the town. It had been in the state and associational Baptist newspapers." The vote went against the ordination of women, but the delegates voted by an overwhelming majority for Isabel to keep her job. Nevertheless, several months later the Association had to eliminate her position when the Southern Baptist Home Mission Board withdrew its portion of the funding because she had been ordained.

A little while later, Rev. Docampo moved to Washington, D.C., where she served in the outreach program of Baptist Senior Adult Ministries. "We did caregivers' support groups and advocacy groups with the National Coalition on Aging to get laws changed and to help seniors with all kinds of health care issues and ageist issues in the workplace," she recalls. While in D.C., she also had her ordination transferred from Southern Baptist to American Baptist.

Nearly two decades ago, Rev. Docampo joined the faculty of Perkins School of Theology in Dallas, Texas, where she now serves as professor of supervised ministry and associate director of the intern program. Her doctor of ministry degree program included a project on the integration of the Hartford Institute of Religion's congregational studies method into the internship curriculum. Rev. Dr. Docampo's ministry has included serving on the task force that led to the Center for the Study of Latino/a Christianity and Religions at Perkins, chairing the Perkins Committee on Gender, Racial, and Ethnicity Concerns, and her publications.[3] Her justice ministry has also extended into the Dallas community through her cochairing of the Workers' Rights Board, through her service with the Workers Defense Project, and through her activity on the board of the Dallas Peace Center and on the advisory council of the Dallas Women's Foundation's Faith, Feminism, and Philanthropy project.

Over the years Rev. Dr. Docampo has been at Perkins, many of her students have discounted the importance of gender-inclusive language by calling it "just political correctness." She invites students to go deeper to discover that language forms our identity, affecting our self-worth and our relationships with the Divine and with others. Isabel gives an illustration of her belief in the power of language to shape identity. Recently she and her mother watched Don Francisco interview children on the Univision program *Sábado Gigante*.

> "Who's the boss at your house, your mom or your dad?" he asked the children. "Who should be the boss, your mom or your dad?"
> "It has to be the dad," a little girl answered.

"Why?" he questioned. "We've all been talking about how mothers have the babies and how mothers are smart and run the house."

"Because men are better," she said.

Disheartened, Isabel said to her mother: "Now where did she get that idea that men are better? It's everywhere. But it's definitely in the Divine. We go to church and hear, 'God the Father knows best,' and never hear 'God the Mother.'"

In her mentoring of students one-on-one and in small groups, Dr. Docampo challenges them to see the connection between gender issues and other social justice issues. She encourages them to grapple with the hard questions about the underlying structures that create injustices and guides them to see the difference between social charity and social action. She is honest with them about the risks of social justice ministry. "We talk about the institution of the church, that if we really want to help people engage with these tough issues, the risks we take sometimes involve even the denominations we serve," she says. "I find joy through seeing many of my students exercise courageous leadership during their internships as they take risks in their commitments to social justice."

After September 11, 2001, Rev. Docampo, along with four other women, founded and led the Dallas Women's Interfaith Dialogue group for five years. "The most magnificent thing was to sit in a room, to be in relationship, to hear each other's stories," she recalls. "I ended meetings saying, 'The Divine Feminine has been with us tonight,' and they would all agree. These were Muslim, Christian, and Jewish women from conservative to liberal." With deep passion in her voice, Isabel elaborates on this kind of dialogue group as her vision for the future of the Divine Feminine in changing the church and the world. "If we could be unafraid to truly be in relationship with the Great Other and with the 'other,' whoever that may be—women, poor people, different races—and stay connected and do that kind of work where you really listen, the church will become less of an institution that has to have programs and become a place where there's healing because the stories are told and received, and every person is transformed."

All her life Rev. Isabel Docampo has indeed been preaching and practicing the same sermon—one of justice, of peace, and of transformation.

Dr. Mary E. Hunt

*Cofounder and Codirector, Women's Alliance for
Theology, Ethics, and Ritual*

Seeing Everyone in the Divine Image

"More than two decades after women-church began,
the movement is mature enough to let the needs of the
world, not the failings of the institutional church, guide it.
Women-church has never been a reform movement trying
to change a recalcitrant kyriarchal church. It has always
been a constructive feminist force that tries to embody
what it envisions. Members keep the justice focus sharp
by prodding one another to explore hard issues including
racism, reproductive choice, homosexuality, and economic
justice. . . . Leadership in house churches tends to rotate
among participants. Empowering lots of people to be
involved is a goal in women-church."[4]

Dr. Mary E. Hunt is active in the egalitarian women-church movement, describing it as "an outgrowth of both the refusal by the
Roman Catholic kyriarchal church to ordain women and the deeply felt
need by Catholic women to act publicly as moral and religious agents
despite exclusion from official church positions." She further states that
this very exclusion of women "has highlighted how inadequate church
structures are for men as well as women, in that they are antithetical to
gospel values of inclusivity and equality."[5] Local women-church communities have come together in large gatherings for activism, inspiration, and

education. One of these large gatherings "confronted the contradictions and challenges of racism and classism among women."[6]

Thirty years ago, Mary and Diann L. Neu (coauthors of *New Feminist Christianity*), along with a group of a dozen women, cofounded Women's Alliance for Theology, Ethics, and Ritual (WATER) "in response to the need for theological, ethical, and liturgical development for and by women." WATER is "a feminist educational center and network of justice-seekers."[7] Dr. Hunt comments on her joining with Dr. Neu to create WATER: "We two were white Catholic women well trained in theology, but as out lesbians who were publicly pro-choice, we were absolutely unwelcome in our own house. So we decided to use our skills and privilege to create new space where women could do their feminist religious work—teaching, writing, counseling, organizing—unfettered by the demands of the university or the church. WATER is the happy result."

Mary celebrates some of the accomplishments and the ongoing work of WATER. "In our first thirty years we have tried to expand the space and deepen the impact of feminists in religion," she says. "Our more than forty-five interns tell the story best as they take on leadership in many organizations around the world. Likewise, our various programs, projects, and publications have been aimed at amplifying women's voices and encouraging ever more participation. That work continues to unfold."

Through her teaching and writing, Dr. Hunt has also had a major impact on feminism in religion. With a master of divinity degree from the Jesuit School of Theology at Berkeley, a master of theological studies degree from Harvard Divinity School, and a PhD from the Graduate Theological Union, she has taught at Georgetown University, Iliff School of Theology, Pacific School of Religion, and Lancaster Theological Seminary. Dr. Hunt is the editor of *A Guide for Women in Religion: Making Your Way from A to Z* and coeditor of *Good Sex: Feminist Perspectives from the World's Religions*.[8] She authored *Fierce Tenderness: A Feminist Theology of Friendship* and edited *From Woman-Pain to Woman-Vision: Writings in Feminist Theology*.[9] Among her many other publications are articles in the *Journal of Feminist Studies in Religion*, *Concilium*, *Conscience*, and *Mandragora*; and chapters in books such as *Feminist Theologies, Heterosexism in Contemporary World Religion, Feminist Theological Ethics*, and *Sexual Diversity and Catholicism*.[10]

Mary states that her "earliest, deepest religious roots" are in the Catholic tradition. "Catholic is a language I speak, a symbol and sacramental system that I understand. In many ways the institutional church, what Elisabeth Schüssler Fiorenza has helpfully called 'kyriarchy,' has left me insofar as its structures and doctrines are anathema to so many things I hold dear. On the other hand, I feel a responsibility to do justice in and through my tradition, so I have not left it in any formal sense. I have never been tempted to join other Christian denominations, which I think of as marginally better on the surface but perhaps rather like Catholicism underneath it all. I feel a special responsibility to work in my own setting. That the Roman Catholic Church wields so much power in the world motivates me to pay attention to it in a primary way."

Although Mary feels she has little access to institutional churches and "no place" in her own Catholic denomination, her work at WATER models the changes in language and symbolism that she feels are vital to changing church and society. "In our work at WATER we have been careful to use inclusive/expansive language in liturgies, lectures, and publications to model just how easy and elegant it can be," she explains. "Language and symbolism are the coins of the realm in religion. They are how we articulate what is most dear to us, what is ultimately important. Both are deeply connected to the social order; neither is ever innocent. We learned the hard way that 'God Father Lord Ruler King' is a linguistic marker that gives men license to take more power than belongs to them. Mary Daly made this clear on gender terms; Anne McGrew Bennett pioneered ways of thinking about political power, especially war, as connected with language about the Divine. Following their lead, I have always been attentive to the use and abuse of language in this regard."

Including female language for Deity "does not guarantee feminist results," Dr. Hunt says. "But where feminist ideas have accompanied such language, the result has been the empowering and enlivening of those involved." In all her feminist writings, she uses inclusive language for the Divine. "God Laughing Out Loud" is one creative, enlivening example:

> In the beginning God enjoyed herself. She laughed out loud and laughed some more because it was good. She sat back and smiled. She clapped her hands in glee and imagined her sisters dancing. She did nothing but enjoy and it was everything.

God knew that there was work to be done—a world to create, people to form and a whole cosmos to plan. She even glimpsed the fact that creation would include meetings and that there would be injustice to right, and still she laughed, knowing that in the end it was all about pleasure.

She explained to no one in particular that enjoyment is what she intended life to be about: pleasure is the first principle. She knew that other would-be divinities stressed work and obligation. She reasoned quite astutely that if joy were the goal, then everyone could rest and relax, at least some of the time. Just thinking about this made her grin.

Light years later, when creation came into being and people began to toil and sweat their way, she noticed that her first principle had been replaced by work and pain. So she sent a reminder of her legacy. She gave it several names: celebration, recreation, fun, potluck dinners, fellowship. Some thought it was a vestige of days gone by. But God knew that it was the real thing. She called it salvation.[11]

Inclusive language for Deity makes a difference in the way we see ourselves, others, and the world, Dr. Hunt asserts. "It is important for people to see themselves in the image of the Divine. That men have long had this possibility is reflected in their sense of entitlement in the world. For women and children, it is a new experience. Hopefully, it will have a positive impact on self-image, social life, and global community. I am concerned that language reflect racial and class inclusion, attention to issues of sexual diversity, and clear analysis of the ways in which ableism functions to make certain bodies normative and other bodies exceptional. All of this is language-related."

Inclusive language, leadership, and symbolism in church will also contribute to change in the wider culture, Mary believes. "If the Divine is the greatest thing we can conceive (à la Anselm), then including many genders in the names of the Divine reflects the fact that many genders (I am wary of two-gender approaches) are fully human/divine," she says. "The hard part is that lifting up only male-gender people, styles, roles, and so on in religion gives implicit permission for people in other realms to act in similarly limited ways. To bring about peace and equality, justice and cooperation is a team effort for which having people from a range of backgrounds is necessary."

In addition to including many genders in language for Deity, Dr. Hunt uses genderless names. "I think of inclusive and expansive ways of conceiving of the Divine—numinous, Friends, Spirit, and Force among others—that express genderless notions."

Dr. Hunt feels that taking risks and meeting resistance come with her role as a theologian. "I think it is important to call it like one sees it, and risk is a minor consideration," she says. "I don't worry about pleasing the masses, or being acceptable in official circles. I am interested in creating theology that does justice beginning with the most marginalized. Of course, the world resists change and those in power resist mightily. So many of the efforts I have supported in this regard have come to naught. Most Sunday worship services in U.S. Christian churches are fraught with exclusive language. Conservative theologians try to make the case for such discourse. Mostly I see it as a matter of theo-politics, a matter of power. The resistance is often a measure of how deeply our work is getting into the mainstream."

Challenging the theology and politics in her Catholic tradition, Dr. Hunt raises questions about the election of Pope Francis. While she welcomes his simple lifestyle, she wonders if he will make more substantive theological changes that contribute to social justice. She wrote an article titled "Theology Has Consequences: What Policies Will Pope Francis Champion?" Here are some excerpts:

> Progressive Catholics had low expectations of the conclave since only what went in would come out, only hand-picked conservative, toe-the-party-line types were electors. Moreover, the process was flawed on the face of it by the lack of women, young people, and lay people. It was flawed by a dearth of democracy. Not even the seagull that sat on the chimney awaiting the decision was enough to persuade that the Holy Spirit was really in charge.
>
> Structural changes in the kyriarchal model of church are needed so that many voices can be heard and many people can participate in decision-making in base communities, parishes, regions, and indeed in global conversations among the more than one billion Catholics. Short of this, no amount of cleaning up the curia or leading by personal asceticism, which are both expected of Pope Francis, will suffice for more than cosmetic changes. Leaving aside the ermine-lined

cloak that his predecessor favored is symbolically notable but not institution changing....

The election of a doctrinally conservative pope, even one with the winning simplicity of his namesake, is especially dangerous in today's media-saturated world where image too often trumps substance. It is easy to rejoice in the lack of gross glitter that has come to characterize the institutional church while being distracted from how theological positions deepen and entrench social injustice.[12]

Mary finds inspiration and strength for her prophetic ministry from the most marginalized groups and individuals who struggle against oppression. "Survivors of sexual abuse, people whose governments oppress them, those who are made poor by global greed and uncontrolled capitalism, those who live under racist and colonialist oppression, women struggling for reproductive justice, LGBTIQ[13] people making the world safe for difference, among others, are all sources of inspiration for me," she says. "When I see their efforts, the risks and consequences for them and their children, I think my own efforts are tame by comparison. White, class, national, and other forms of privilege that I enjoy are a buffer against the worst of challenges."

In her work as a theologian and as codirector of WATER, Mary has had many rewarding experiences, which she celebrates. "Seeing so many of WATER's interns and visiting scholars doing important work in the world is very rewarding. I realize that I have made a place for them without which they would not be as able to do what they feel called to do. I also find it rewarding to see that positions I staked out decades ago are now quite commonly held—for example, on feminist ministry, same-sex loving relationships, and the like."

Dr. Hunt articulates a hopeful, expansive vision for the future. "I imagine that in time—perhaps not in my lifetime, but I realize that— feminist understandings of power, divinity, ministry, and indeed expansive understandings of religion as a human right and quest will be common. Then, many names of the Divine will resound among many communities that struggle to understand one another's perspectives and to embrace one another's visions as a part of their own. Human community and our connection to the natural order are in the balance. That is why this work is so vital."

Rev. Dr. Gail Anderson Ricciuti

Associate Professor of Homiletics, Colgate Rochester Crozer Divinity School

Bearing Her Life in the World

Because the mystery of your being, Holy One, destroys our safe
  assumptions and shakes the foundations of our religiosity like a
  mighty earthquake,
Jesus Christ, Sophia, have mercy on us.
Because our hearts are unaccustomed to your intimacy with our
  lives,
Jesus Christ, Sophia, have mercy on us.
Because our heritage has been bound by our own acquiescence to a
  tradition that has limited you to maleness,
Jesus Christ, Sophia, have mercy on us.

*(Here there is a time of silent meditation. Worshipers are then invited
to voice their own confessions, with each followed by the corporate response, "Jesus Christ, Sophia, have mercy on us.")*

Christ, our Sophia, is not imprisoned by the limitations of our
willingness or understanding. "In every generation She passes
into holy souls and makes them friends of God." And so, I tell
you the truth: In Her tender mercy is our liberation![14]

G ail Anderson Ricciuti provides creative worship resources (such as
  the litany above) in *Birthings and Blessings: Liberating Worship Services
for the Inclusive Church*, an alternative to traditional worship that limits
the Holy One to maleness. Rev. Ricciuti connects this male-dominated

tradition with other injustices. "Sexism, racism, classism, heterosexism—all of these are rooted in the same ground and built upon the
same assumptions: that one gender or class or race of human beings is
superior to others by Divine Right and should therefore be accorded
privilege unavailable to lesser people," she says. "Until all of those lies
are debunked, until all of those superficially constructed chains are
broken, no one has true equity or access in any *other* dimension! Even
when they look very different, there is an intimate connection between
one form of oppression and all the others."

In her preaching, teaching, and writing, Rev. Ricciuti challenges the
status quo to help overcome these interlocking injustices. "Anything that
unsettles the status quo about our common assumptions about the nature
of humanity or of God or of 'how things are supposed to be' is helpful
in breaking open further and truer understanding: in facilitating the in-
breaking of God's realm," she says. "Gender- and racial-inclusive leadership, language, and theology are not just optional, but critical to living a
faithful Christian life in a community of justice and peace; it's become my
conviction that anything less constitutes idolatry: substituting a part for
the whole and/or substituting a lie for the truth. To give little boys and
little girls the tacit impression that God is identified with one gender
and not the other, or that the characteristics of the Holy One are male
and Caucasian, is to lie about who they are and about who God is."

Commenting on the power of language and biblical interpretation,
Gail gives Virginia Ramey Mollenkott credit for helping her expand
beyond the literal to deeper meanings. At a gathering of Evangelical
& Ecumenical Women's Caucus–Christian Feminism Today (EEWC-
CFT), Dr. Mollenkott gave a presentation in which she interprets three
of Jesus's parables about workers in light of current economic injustices
that serve the interests of the 1 percent.[15] Rev. Ricciuti also sees this
deeper meaning of justice in another of Jesus's stories. "So our hermeneutics—the way we express, and hear, for instance, Jesus's teaching
about the widow's mite[16] and the tools we use and the depth at which
we interpret it—can make all the difference in whether we hear Jesus's
real meaning or distort the story into something that supports our prior
assumptions about economic justice," she says.

Preaching at an EEWC-CFT Gathering, Rev. Ricciuti illuminates
two of Jesus's parables that unsettle the status quo. Her inspiring sermon,

titled "A Quotidian Faith: Stories Sacred, Subversive, and Small," focuses on two parables in which Jesus images God as a woman: a woman searching for a lost coin and a woman baking bread.[17] Rev. Ricciuti calls God "She" throughout her creative sermon, in keeping with Jesus's female divine imagery. In her interpretation of the parable of the lost coin, she points out that Jesus images God as a poor woman: "Her house is dark. Otherwise, there would have been no need for her to light a lamp for this search. So we know that she was poor, with one of those peasant-class homes built around the tax code that dictated a certain taxation according to the number of windows and the height of the door frame. If you were poor, you'd forgo windows altogether and light and airiness. She has ten *drachmae*; and that's all she has, and lucky to have even that—twenty days' wages for a woman laborer who could earn only 50 percent of what the men around her earned even doing the same job. And we know that story too, don't we? Her story tells us that the God of the poor watches, searches, looks around, and listens for us."

Interpreting the parable of the baker woman, Rev. Ricciuti proclaims that the bread the woman bakes was "not status-quo bread," but "justice bread," bringing joy. The yeast that the woman uses was in that culture "a substance detested by the religiously observant." She mixes "this little bit of old, yeasty leaven in more than thirty-nine liters, that is almost nine gallons, of flour, three measures," enough to feed one hundred people. "The Spirit that is holy keeps persistently seeking the lost to keep company with Her and using the least to infuse the earth with abundance and glory and the aroma of rising bread. When we care enough to turn the house or the world upside down, seeking those missing and absent from the feast, and then bake up a surprising amount of bread to feed indiscriminately all who will join in, those familiar, subversive, and small quotidian acts are holy work."[18]

Gail grew up in a community church in Longview, Washington, a church that she says was "moderate to conservative theologically and socially." Her parents gave her and her younger sister the clear message that they were "no better than anyone else, but just as good as anyone else," and that they could be whatever they wanted to be. "In the pre-feminism climate of the fifties and early sixties, that was a message that taught us much more than I think my mother, in particular, was aware she was conveying," Gail says. "So it was also more extraordinary than

I knew at the time, when midway through college I began, after a long, secret period of discernment, to articulate to people in my home church my strong sense of being called to ministry, and was greeted only with supportive encouragement."

It never occurred to Gail that anyone would object to her call to ministry until she arrived at Princeton Theological Seminary. "I discovered to my great astonishment that there were people—*many* people, and most of them men my age—who actually believed that ordained ministry was not appropriate for females," she recalls. "I was astonished and incensed at what seemed to me bald-faced idiocy from supposedly educated people, and have often joked that it took me less than twenty-four hours to become a raving feminist! Looking back now, I see that it was nothing short of miraculous that as a child of the fifties and sixties, I had lived such a 'charmed' life and encountered countless beloved mentors, teachers, and pastors who were somehow already enlightened enough to perceive, respect, and celebrate God's calling in a young female life."

Growing up, Gail had no female clergy role models except one associate pastor in the United Church of Canada, whom she heard preach when her university band went on spring tour to British Columbia. Then a month before she graduated from seminary, she experienced a woman minister officiating at a communion service. "The power of that experience—and what it symbolized about God, about women, and about myself—was so overwhelming that I couldn't stop sobbing throughout the service," she says. "While I had already by then come to a theological understanding of the radical inclusiveness of God's creation and God's realm as proclaimed by Jesus, the inclusive proclamation of that evening's service was undoubtedly a large factor in the decision my husband and I made a year or two later to seek a copastoral position together—partly for what the message copastoring (then a revolutionary and almost unheard-of notion) would convey about male/female equality, and about God Herself."

After graduating from seminary and being ordained by the Presbyterian Church, Rev. Ricciuti served for twenty-five years as a parish pastor, twenty-three of those pioneering in copastoral models with her husband. For nearly twenty years, she has served as associate professor of homiletics at Colgate Rochester Crozer Divinity School in Rochester, New York. She is coauthor of two volumes of *Birthings and Blessings*, and is currently collaborating with an art professor on a book about what preachers might learn from artists.[19] In addition, she has written for *Feasting on the Word* and *Feasting on the Gospels*, and other homiletics commentaries.[20] At the divinity school, she teaches courses in preaching, liturgy, worship, critical theological thinking, Presbyterian polity, and church administration.

In her work with seminarians, Rev. Dr. Ricciuti tries to "stretch the boundaries of biblical and theological assumptions they bring with them from diverse denominational backgrounds." In worship classes she encourages students to expand their divine images. "I challenge them to use different names for God in their own prayers than have ever occurred to them before—even if this causes some discomfort—and to examine how prayer feels, how it 'works,' when the image of God is allowed to expand; and then to notice, scripturally, how many images and names exist there for the Divine that we have often ignored."

Believing in the importance of gender-inclusive leadership as well as language in the church, Rev. Ricciuti participates in the ecumenical, multicultural Equity for Women in the Church Community. "It seems to me incumbent upon those of us who had to 'fight' for our right to answer God's call to ministry to offer support to those coming after us," she says. "For those young women who may already have reaped the benefits of their foremothers' work, and who wonder 'what the problem is' (although such ease of entering ministry is still rare for women in many denominations), it is our responsibility to educate, to pass on a conscious legacy that prevents a new generation from falling asleep and inadvertently losing ground they had taken for granted. My hope is that we will keep awareness of these issues alive, and make clear how the 'ism' injustices are interrelated: one pulled thread unravels other rights as well."

In working for justice, Gail has taken prophetic stands that involve risks. "We women entering ministry forty years ago knew that simply stepping into the pulpit, before we ever preached a word, was already a visual image pushing people's boundaries and taking them out beyond their accustomed horizons," she says. "In the early days, it felt like simply being myself, not trying to fill the image of a male pastor, was itself risky. In more recent decades, the biggest risks in changing the theological assumptions and symbolism of Christianity have revolved around the work of opening church and ministry to gay and lesbian brothers and sisters.

The basic day-to-day work of 'reimagining' the breadth of God's embrace, of preaching justice and welcome and acceptance in the church, began to emerge as riskier than we had imagined. Some twenty years ago I discovered a hand-lettered death threat addressed to me that had been delivered to our home mailbox during the night. It was a vivid reminder that language, symbols, and theological imagination have always been riskier to challenge than we have sometimes acknowledged."

In her seminary teaching, Rev. Dr. Ricciuti continues to meet resistance to gender-inclusive leadership and language. She says that some students, both male and female, maintain that "Jesus chose only male disciples" or "Jesus only called God 'Father' and so that's the name we should use." She enjoys "messing with a few heads," pointing out "that Jesus also only chose Jews as disciples" and exploring "how revolutionary it was in Jesus's day to characterize the God of Israel as 'Abba'—'Daddy'!"

Experience of a woman pastor can also make a big difference in opening minds, Gail says. "I do believe, passionately, that all it takes for minds and hearts in the pew to begin changing radically is exposure to the ministry of a woman pastor. While there will always be those isolated, critical voices not about to change their minds in the face of new experience, nevertheless time after time I have seen theoretical opposition melt away in the light of the actual human experience of a woman's approach to leadership, preaching, and pastoral care," she explains. "I will forever cherish the decades-long friendship of Edwin, an older member of a church I served for just six months as supply preacher. He had never known a clergywoman, and was at the outset quite suspicious about how useful one would be; but very quickly, he became my greatest encourager and 'believer.'"

The Mennonite congregation with whom she currently worships shapes her vision of the future church. Gail says, "They are, intentionally, a genuine community of mutual care and welcome as well as of outreach for justice. Every member takes responsibility for the life of the church in diverse ways." In so doing, they embody one of Rev. Ricciuti's beautiful blessings:

> In the darkness as in light, may the Holy One seek and call us to
> bear Her life in the world.
> **In darkness as in light, may we hear, and bear, and bear each
> other up.**[21]

Rev. Dr. Cheryl F. Dudley

Global Religions Director, Arcus Foundation

Changing Our Default Settings

"All of us have a tendency to imagine our lives within the frames of what is familiar. We often begin by looking at traditional models of church and traditional models of leadership, and wonder if substituting a woman in the traditional male role of pastor will bring about transformation and eradicate the discriminatory energies of sexism, racism, and classism. Our prejudgments of who would be a good fit for *our* church defaults to the predominant make-up of a given congregation. An 'elite' church is often looking for an 'elite' pastor who mimics the pastors who have served the church in the past. We have to be aware and change our default settings. The best pastor for a given church may not be male, or the same race, or from the same socioeconomic background as once was customary for a congregation. When an alternative voice or leader appears, rather than rejoicing in the gift that has been sent, there is sometimes a lament of what may be lost in changing the model. I think that is faithlessness. Like Lot's wife, churches can crystallize and freeze their salt for looking back rather than becoming the salt the community now needs to experience God's presence anew. We need to find ways to encourage churches to be surprised by who God may be sending to shepherd them."

The interlocking injustices of sexism, racism, and classism pose a challenge for many clergywomen. Rev. Dr. Cheryl F. Dudley believes, however, that women pastors have the gifts to eliminate these "discriminatory energies" and create inclusive, multiethnic, multicultural churches. "Women pastors can be great catalysts for cultivating cross-cultural competence—sensitivity, awareness, and so on, in congregants. It doesn't just happen on its own; cross-cultural competence happens through planting and tending the seeds in growing a diverse community of faith."

In her various leadership roles, Rev. Dr. Dudley has made significant contributions to diversity in the church and to social justice. She has contributed to economic justice through serving as program manager and then executive director of Peoria Friendship House of Christian Service, a community-based ecumenical antipoverty organization, and through serving on the Homeless Youth Task Force and on the Fair Employment and Housing Commission. In Peoria, Illinois, she also served as acting director of African American Studies at Bradley University. As associate executive director of Church in Community Transformation with American Baptist Mission Societies, she developed resources to increase effectiveness of communities with growing diversity. In her current position as global religions director of Arcus Foundation, she identifies and cultivates religious partnerships to accomplish the social justice work of the foundation. Rev. Dudley preaches, teaches, and leads seminars in churches and in denominational, ecumenical, and interfaith events in the United States and around the world.

Because of her outstanding, creative leadership in these diverse settings, the ecumenical, multicultural Equity for Women in the Church Community invited Rev. Dr. Dudley to facilitate their Access and Equity for Women Clergy Conference. This historic gathering developed strategies to fulfill the big vision of equal representation of clergywomen as pastors of multicultural churches in order to transform church and society. Cheryl says that she accepted this invitation because she "connected with the vision of the conference" that Rev. Sheila Sholes-Ross, cochair of the Equity Community, passionately shared with her.

Personal experiences contribute to Cheryl's desire to increase opportunities for women ministers of all ethnicities. She says that when she was a child, some of her "most profound spiritual teachers were women as well as men," and that "this continues to be true."

Cheryl's parents instilled in her and her sisters "that nothing was impossible" to them, even though they might experience sexism and racism. "We were also warned that we would need to work hard and that hard work might not be enough because of inherent resistance and abject discrimination in the world. Despite this, we were encouraged and sometimes shown ways to cross thresholds of resistance in order to be faithful to the vision God has planted within. I came to realize that 'they wouldn't let me' was not an acceptable excuse. I was accountable to God, so that pushed me to look in unusual places: more often than not, those unusual places were where the most profound treasures were found. To be told 'you can't do that' was a counter motivation to go ahead and prove that the barrier declared was a false one."

Since childhood, Cheryl has had friends from many faith traditions. The older sister of one of her best childhood friends became a rabbi. "I have also met beautiful Muslims, Hindus, and Sikhs," Cheryl says. "In meeting and being impacted by persons of other faith traditions, I have found continuing clarity about why I believe what I believe, and about how I am able to connect to others who have similar values but different faith expressions."

While appreciating gifts she's received from diverse faith traditions, Rev. Dudley celebrates her own Baptist heritage. "I am a dyed-in-the-wool Baptist," she says. "I continue to claim our sometimes odd and diverse clan even when we have fallen short of the glory of God. Our love of story, both scriptural and personal stories, as a narrative of our faith continues to draw. Prayer, song, and warm *koinonia* (community) that bring together intellect and emotion fuel our faith and keep us true. I like to actively remember the good things about what it means to be a Baptist and discard the hurtful practices as not being authentically Baptist. I guess I am a selective Baptist in some ways." As a Baptist though, she has always sought out ecumenical alliances and friendships in order to experience a fuller view of the Christian faith. "I've been fascinated and perplexed by the distinctions within the Christian family, and have been led at times to explore these distinctions and employ them in my own practice of faith if I have found them meaningful," she says.

In her practice of faith, Cheryl has found that inclusive images of the Divine are needed to affirm the divine image in everyone. "Many of the images of Christ found in churches I have attended over the years have been beautiful and tender artists' renderings, but I think we recognized that these symbols are markers or shadows of the real truth of God's fullness," she says. "It is important for each of us to be able to identify herself in the Divine; otherwise, God's Spirit may fail to speak to us in connective and enduring ways. I appreciate the gift of recognizing God's image in a variety of cultural and gender forms. It's exciting to recognize the beauty of God's holiness within the diversity of the human experience."

Inclusive worship language and pastoral leadership are thus important, Rev. Dudley asserts. "God is inclusive and revealed in many forms, faces, words, and acts. The God of all creation invites us into relationship with Her and celebrates with us during those moments of recognition of grace and glory; this brings healing and reconciliation to us as individuals, as well as to the communities in which we live, work, and worship."

Rev. Dr. Dudley believes that including women pastors from diverse cultures and multicultural female divine names and images in worship will change the church and the wider culture. "I believe the inclusion of diverse gifts helps us recognize and receive rather than reject and repel sisters and brothers within and outside of our faith community who are different from us and who too are longing for acceptance and community," she says. "When one experiences an ethnically and sexually diverse church, it becomes the new normal. Once a church becomes diverse, it won't seem natural to go back to former monocultural experiences in worship and *koinonia*. Churches and communities who are used to having gender and ethnic diversities within their leadership or membership become practitioners of social justice and peace, no longer experienced in the theoretical or as an ethic or an intellectual idea, but lived out in the day-to-day practice of faith. It is in learning how to do 'the diversity thing' with less self-consciousness and self-congratulation, and unapologetically, that we will be 'called the children of God.'"

Women pastors from diverse cultures will also contribute to changing the hierarchical church structures to egalitarian ones, Rev. Dudley hopes. "I hate it when I see women pastors who default and adopt so-called male models of leadership," she says. "Women pastors more often than not have to juggle other active roles and responsibilities in their lives, such as being a spouse, partner, mother, caretaker of aging parents. They live out these roles, as well as, I pray, doing some self-care so they will flourish. I believe they can do these other roles better when freed from the stranglehold of hierarchical leadership. Ego and control are killers of the Spirit and of the person. The active expression of gifts from among the laity, rather than just the pastor herself, is a gift to the church. I think the use of effective leadership roles is a challenge for all pastors regardless of gender identity."

In advocating for gender, racial, and economic justice, Rev. Dudley takes risks. But she says that the greater risk would be in *not* advocating for justice. "When one doesn't risk, she forfeits her spirit and identity, and her salt is trampled under foot. When making a decision in my current call to advocate for sexual orientation and gender identity justice, I said to myself, 'If I do this, there may be no going back.' I felt the Spirit utter back, 'There is no going back, daughter; there is only going forward.' I breathed the sigh of peace in those moments of reckoning and receiving the opportunity to live my call out in another setting. Hey, we can't do any ministry without God. We rely on God's leading and listen for the still small voice to affirm the leading. We are reliant on God for the purpose, wisdom, and tenacity beyond our own ability so we are able to serve with courage, power, and a sound mind."

Living out her prophetic call, Rev. Dudley has met plenty of resistance. "But you shake the dust off your feet and move on to the next town, so to speak," she says. She also offers advice on what to do when people affirm the work of social justice instead of engaging in it themselves. "There will always be others who are interested and proud that you are doing the heavy lifting they are unable to do. These others want to live vicariously through you, and they do. Let them! You find strength in others supporting you in active and in tacit ways."

Rev. Dr. Cheryl Dudley articulates a hopeful, dynamic vision for the future of the church. "I think that vision is unfolding. I think the church will thrive, but not necessarily in the forms that we now know best. Technology and mobility have changed the world significantly over the past few decades. Despite rapid changes, people continue to yearn for meaning and connection. We will find new ways, maybe better ways to do it. My vision for the church is that the mystic and activist gifts of faith will intertwine and feed each other. There is a lot to do, and we need the strength to do it well."

Part 5

Wisdom's Works of Caring for Creation

The whole creation suffers from male-dominated theology that has at its foundation an exclusively masculine naming and imaging of Deity. References to the earth are traditionally feminine, but the feminine is not given sacred value in our worship. Like females, the earth continues to be devalued, exploited, assaulted, and abused.

Including female divine names and images in our worship connects the revaluing of females to the revaluing of the earth, contributing to overcoming sexism and exploitation of the earth. Ecofeminism works against the interconnected oppressions of gender, race, class, and nature.

Female names and images of the Divine affirm the sacred value of females and all creation, inspiring spirituality and activism for a sustainable world. Biblical female images of Deity, such as *Ruah* ("Spirit") giving birth to creation and nurturing creation and *Sophia* ("Wisdom") guiding us to care for creation, provide powerful support for our involvement in ecology.

Female images of the Divine give greater value to the role of peaceful preservation and nurturing of life, traditionally assigned to women. *Ruah*, Wisdom, and other female personifications of the Divine inspire our work of caring for all creation.

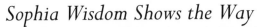

Sophia Wisdom Shows the Way

(Sung to the tune of "America the Beautiful")

Sophia Wisdom shows the way to liberating life,
to caring for creation now, so Earth will long survive.
Awake to work and advocate to save Earth's treasures rare,
protecting all the living ones, all nature everywhere.

The land is scarred and fractured deep; pollution fills the air,
and poisoned oceans threaten life; it's time to show we care.
Sophia Wisdom calls to us, to stop destructive ways,
to work with Her in saving life, to act without delay.

Sophia Wisdom still creates new beauty every day,
the golden trees, the dancing deer, the flowers' wild display.
Come, join Sophia, nurturing Her precious gifts for all;
conserving life in every form fulfills our sacred call.[1]

Words © 2012 Jann Aldredge-Clanton   MATERNA

Rev. Dr. Genny Rowley

Pastoral Theologian; Religious Environmentalist

Neighbors in the Whole Community of Creation

Farm Blessing

We gather with eyes open wide,
Creative Presence connecting with the generative soil beneath our
  feet.
This is a place of life, green and growing,
And complexity: some things live well here, and some things
  struggle.
And mystery: who can say what tomorrow will bring?

So we gather this day: hoping to bless this land, and how it reminds
  us to live:
mindful and aware of our neighbors, the people and plants and bees,
thankful and active in our vocations and communities,
justly and kindly in our comings and goings
open to the stirrings of Spirit of Life, who is always making things
  new.

Through creative worship resources (such as the "Farm Blessing" above), social activism, and academic research, Rev. Dr. Genny Rowley invites care of all creation. In an article in the *Huffington Post*, she connects her faith to advocacy for the natural environment:

Christianity envisions people gathered around a table as one of its central symbols: We come together through breaking bread and drinking from a common cup. These are practical symbols, pointing to our interdependence in creation, in each other and in God. Asking those that represent us in government to act for our values is an effort worth making. It requires the belief that we are called to participate in stewardship of the land and water on which we depend and to help create a society that promotes human health. To hope for a world where we share a table together, supported by a blessed garden in a circle of abundant life, is faith worth acting upon.[2]

Genny earned a PhD in pastoral theology and pastoral care at Brite Divinity School with a research focus on "congregational groups who are doing ecological justice work as acts of care for the wider earth community," and is completing a book form of her dissertation that focuses on hope and courage in the face of ecological crises. Dr. Rowley serves as the Alliance of Baptists liaison to the National Council of Churches eco-justice program, participates in the interfaith GreenFaith program that provides training and community for religious environmentalists, works with Interfaith Power & Light to promote care of creation, creates liturgy for faith communities, and writes about environmental activism for online journals and on her website.[3] She celebrates her "wonderful and busy call" that combines "changing the way human beings relate to the natural world, advocating for more just and caring relationships between people, and keeping a constant dialogue going with the Christian tradition and its participants."

Genny grew up in nondenominational evangelical churches that were very conservative theologically. Her training as a social worker led her to question this theology. "I hit the limits of that kind of theology through caring deeply about social justice," she says. "One question about why fighting for people's full humanity matters led to another, and before I knew it, I was in seminary."

While studying at McAfee School of Theology of Mercer University, Genny found support for theological exploration and expansion. "I owe my professors a great deal. I was terribly frightened of how my worldview was changing, and their compassion and thoughtfulness enabled me to be honest with myself and search deeply for what mattered to me in my free-church tradition," she recalls. "As my vision of just love expanded, I couldn't ignore the ways we human beings treat creation like an object for our use, rather than a partner in the community of life."

To further explore this vision, Genny focused her doctoral research on faith communities who are trying to change their relationship with creation at the grassroots level. For two years she researched and wrote about religious environmentalists working from their local congregations. "The synergy between engaging the issues affecting their local communities and tapping into an existing network of community, dialogue, and wisdom seems to create a wellspring for sustained activism," she says. "I am inspired by the congregations I've studied. These communities are really transforming the churches they are involved with, creating language bridges between their love of nature and their faith traditions, making connections between social and environmental justice, and highlighting all of the 'green spaces' in the Christian tradition. In my work as a scholar, I'm trying to shift our understanding of humanity toward being part of a sacred web of life, all of which is sacred and part of God's being-in-the-world. Without valuing our connectedness to creation, we miss part of God's expression."

Ecofeminist scholars have helped Genny understand the connections between women and the natural world and the connections between the oppression of women and the oppression of the natural world. "Changing our relationship with the earth from one of mastery over something to one of kinship and respect is vital if we are to flourish spiritually, and if we are to physically survive as a species," she says. "Moving from relationships of acquisition, where we have to possess something to be happy, toward relationships of presence, where we seek to genuinely connect to those beyond ourselves—human and otherwise—is a central task of ecofeminist worship."

Inclusive language, Genny believes, is vital to this worship. "In my work as a pastoral counselor and chaplain, I've seen over and over again how our language plays such a huge role in creating our worldviews and self-identity," she says. "I recall the first time I read the NRSV translation of the Bible in my teenage years; I didn't know why exactly, but I felt like the text spoke to me in ways that other translations I owned didn't. Looking back, I realized that was my first experience with the power of inclusive language, and I have since been an advocate for radically inclusive and expansive language in worship: offering a rich variety of names and images for the Divine is an act of radical hospitality that can connect unique individuals to the mystery we call God."

Here is one of Genny Rowley's beautiful prayers, demonstrating her belief in the power of an expansive divine imagery.

Responsive Advent Invocation

> She comes to us like fresh air in a stifled room:
> **Signaling our hearts to prepare for the unexpected, the subversive, the truly joyful, and deeply thoughtful.**
> This candle reminds us of the light of hope.
> **In the stillness of our worship here, we light this candle, and we affirm once again that we are a people of God.**
> Let us remember that without hope, people struggle to find their way.
> **May this flame stay bright within us, now and in the days to come, as chances to partner with Hope make their way into our everyday lives.**

In her liturgies that include female names and images of the Divine, Rev. Rowley affirms all people in the divine image. She also affirms all creation in the divine image. Although traditional Christian theology holds that humanity alone bears the *imago Dei*, or image of God, she views the entire world as created in the divine image: "A variety of theological interpretations invite us to view human beings as participants with the whole community of creation, focusing on the immanence of God throughout the created world," she writes in an article for *Unbound: An Interactive Journal of Christian Social Justice*.

> This interconnected, relational theology creates an ethical pull to care for the entirety of creation, because the *imago Dei* is the mutual, indwelling love that is present in all that God has made. For religious environmentalists, interpretations like this one help debunk the myth of human exceptionalism through the realization that the suffering befalling creation also befalls all who have been created. If the Christian tradition invites us toward active neighbor love, religious environmentalism invites us to broaden our understanding of

neighbor to include the whole community of life that God created and blessed as good.[4]

It took a while for Genny to see this connection between human beings and the natural world. "For a long time, caring for people and caring for creation seemed like two separate things to me," she explains. "About a year into my doctoral program, I began to wonder about this assumption. In my own life and in the lives of the people consulting with me through Brite's counseling center, the ways our minds, bodies, and spirits are connected to the physical world we inhabit became increasingly noticeable. Basic ecology holds that everything is connected to everything else. Inviting health and wholeness into one area of life seems to open doors into other areas in need of care and attention."

Rev. Dr. Rowley's passion for environmental justice continues to grow from her ministry as a pastoral counselor, chaplain, theologian, and teacher. "I've spent a lot of time caring for people in different ways," she says. "I've come to believe that you can't care well for people if you don't also care for our planet! We, too, are a part of nature—not separate from it. We breathe air, eat food, and drink water each day in order to live, and the pain of the environment is also our own. This can show up through sadness when a favorite stand of trees is paved over for a shopping center, through the soaring childhood asthma rates in urban areas, through the obesity epidemic plaguing our nation as a result of overconsumption of processed foods, and through the need to heat and cool our inside air in the increasingly extreme weather we experience as a result of climate change."

In her academic research and her work with interfaith environmental groups, Rev. Dr. Rowley affirms the importance of faith communities in caring for creation. "Religious environmentalism is one way that people of faith are responding to the need to care for creation," she says. "This means connecting the values of one's faith tradition to ecological issues. In my own Christian tradition, the value of neighbor love motivates me to consider both who I understand my neighbor to be, and how I can express this love in a time full of environmental challenges."

Even though church has been an "edge-place" for Genny and she has thought often about leaving, two things keep her coming back: "connections to genuine, interesting, and thoughtful people; and hope that things never stay the way they are forever." She realizes that for change to happen, she has "to step up and participate."

Through her prophetic ministry Genny does participate in changing churches in many ways, including how they talk about the Divine. "The idea of the Divine is primarily mystery for me, and most church experiences I've had talk about what we 'know' about God. I'd much rather talk about what we don't know! Our human experience is so small and so sacred—putting our experiences in conversation with our living faith traditions gives me hope that they can change as we change, through Divine Wisdom breathing us forward into the future."

Including female divine language and women pastors in worship will also open possibilities for changing churches and the wider culture, Genny says. "It's my hope that gender-inclusive leadership, language, and theology will create space for authentic and fulfilling relationships between people of all genders, sexualities, races, classes, ages, and abilities. Changing the way we talk about the Divine and one another helps open up possibilities for creative love and kinship between all people, removing an unhealthy level of competition and insecurity that comes with being an object on a hierarchical scale. I think it expands our idea of hope and possibility when we see that Love and leadership have so many forms and faces."

Genny articulates a hopeful, expansive vision for the future: "I hope for a day when the idea of Mother-Sister-Daughter God is a comforting norm for people of faith, instead of something people fear, and for a day when acting in the interest of the whole community of earth is second nature," she says. "I hope for a time when dominant notes in our faith traditions ring out all the ways people do justice, love kindness, and walk in genuine humility together. I pray for a day when our idea of heaven is bread for all who are hungry, clean water for all who thirst, and a place at the table for every member of the community of life on this planet. I dream of no less than heaven on earth, because I have seen glimpses of it in the here and now—in stands of old-growth forests, in the community gardens feeding hungry families, in the delight of children as they discover something new and wonderful. I hope quite stubbornly that if we dream passionately and act faithfully, She creates this future with and through us."

Rev. Dr. Rebecca L. Kiser

Intentional Interim Pastor, Presbyterian Church (USA)

God as Gender-full

"Our Bible contains lots more images and metaphors for
God than the official, orthodox Trinitarian formula. God
is indefinable in human thought and language, so we end
up using many names to try and capture the hugeness,
the awesome enormity, the variety of experiences that
make up our story with God. In the text we read from
Proverbs, you'll notice in your Bibles that 'Wisdom' is
capitalized as a name, and Wisdom is pictured as a woman
calling out to people to come to Her. We call several
books of the Protestant Bible the Wisdom books—Job,
Psalms, Proverbs. In the Catholic Bible there is also a book
called the Wisdom of Solomon. People who study world
religions often talk about the 'wisdom tradition' within
various religions. The figure of Woman Wisdom, or Lady
Wisdom—or in Greek, *Sophia*—is a part of this. Folks
who have studied Holy Wisdom in both Proverbs and the
Wisdom of Solomon have noticed a great correlation
between what is said of Her and what is said of Christ,
especially in the book of John. Much of what is said in
John's prologue about the Word was taken from what
is said in other places about Holy Wisdom. It's neat to
read about Holy Wisdom on Trinity Sunday, because
this name emphasizes that God can't be captured by any
one definition, one experience, one perspective, one
interpretation. Rather, God comes to each of us in the way
we need in order to hear, to respond."

131

Rev. Dr. Rebecca L. Kiser proclaims the power of divine names and images and expands people's theology through biblical preaching and teaching (such as in the sermon excerpt above). She describes her style as "like a bridge" as she explores experiences and interpretations and then finds "ways to bring them back to the church and bridge them."

Rev. Kiser encourages experience of the Divine not only through human images, both female and male, but also through nature. In another prophetic sermon she applies incarnational theology to all of creation:

> My soul soars when the garden is lush, and flowers are blooming, the bean plants are up, the tomato cages full of leafy plants, rows of red radishes, purple eggplants, dark burgundy hollyhocks, sunflowers—I love all of them. I hadn't made the connection to incarnation until I read Hildegard of Bingen. I thought incarnation just referred to Jesus. But you see, Hildegard makes that mystical leap that sees Jesus, wholly God and wholly human, as teaching us a deeply incarnational truth of reality—that God is here with us, Immanuel, that the material, the human flesh, the "matter" of life is interpenetrated with God. Spirit and matter are not separate things. Spirit moves around, among, and within us. We have not looked at this creation that God calls "good" in the very first chapters of our book of faith and seen God, and therefore we have not cared for it, been stewards of it, but rather have been users and exploiters of its gifts. We've made religion and salvation matters of the inner life and a future, nonearthly heaven—and here we sit when the world God made, and the world God sent the Christ to save is at the brink of ecological suicide. Perhaps it is to us that the vision of Hildegard, of that greening power of the One who is life itself, of that deep view of incarnation—perhaps her words, rediscovered in this day and age, are those words we need to hear and live for the world to be literally saved.

For many years, Rebecca has been caring for creation. She has been gardening since her seminary days, and loves to dig and play in the dirt and "go home tired, with the smell of soil" on her hands. Her doctor of ministry project and dissertation, titled "The Other Day in the Garden," describes her work with the civic league, city council, and area businesses in Norfolk, Virginia, in starting an organic community garden. She chose this project, she says, because of her passion for ecotheology, "creation spirituality's awe and love of creation." She designed this community garden with "a central commons area that would invite the public in" and with "freeform beds and not straight paths because curving paths invite more meditation." A year after the creation of the garden, Rebecca and her team received an award for environmental responsibility from the city government.

When she served as pastor of First Presbyterian Church in West Plains, Missouri, Rev. Kiser also participated in a community garden. "Environmental issues have been on my mind and heart since I started doing the work for the community garden in Norfolk," she says. "I've read a lot about ecospirituality or 'ecofeminism,' as some call it. That's a big issue for me." In the community garden in West Plains, she used one plot to grow produce for a local food pantry. She also challenged church members to take a plot for hunger relief.

Rebecca grew up in an independent fundamentalist church in Washington, D.C. Through experiences in college and in seminary and then as a Presbyterian pastor, her faith expanded. She writes, "I've described my faith life as like one of those funnel gadgets, being raised in the extremely narrow end of fundamentalism, then moving into the gradually widening scope of the evangelical, through orthodox Reformed theology, and now probably more progressive."[5]

Because Louisville Presbyterian Theological Seminary was open to women in ministry, Rebecca chose to go there. She thought it would also be progressive on the use of inclusive language, but she met resistance when she worked on a task force that published an inclusive-language worship resource for use in the chapel. "Inclusive language about people was a given by that time, but inclusive language about God was the cutting edge," she says. "At one point I got into a really big discussion with a systematic theology professor about language for God. We were trying to say 'Creator, Redeemer, Sustainer,' and he just went ballistic. He got really red-faced and said that if you weren't baptized in the name of the 'Father, Son, and Holy Spirit,' those exact words, it was not a Christian baptism and didn't count. There was some real resistance to the language change. Some people were really invested in the maleness of the language. Words have power."

During the time when she was healing from the traumatic loss of her baby daughter Emma, Rev. Kiser expanded her divine images to include the feminine. She writes:

> As I began sorting out and dealing with my anger and grief, images of God in the feminine arose in my prayer and became agents of healing and restoration. This was surprising to me because, at the time, I was not comfortable using feminine pronouns or imaging God in the feminine. I had talked of seeing God in the people who came to be with us, bringing dinners and fruit baskets and desserts as well as their love and care. Yet I had difficulty accepting this image or feeling any comfort from it. Suddenly, I remembered that old picture from my Sunday school days, where Jesus is standing at the heart's door and knocking—only when I pictured it now, Jesus was carrying a covered casserole. The image captured me, so I decided to sculpt it. The form that emerged from under my hands was a woman, like so many of the people who had come to my door. She carried a 9x13 pan of either lasagna or chicken and rice; I couldn't decide. She became a focal point of all my ambivalent feelings, for I felt gratitude and comfort from her presence at the same time that I experienced a raging anger that she didn't do more. I raged at her, and still she stayed, her face concerned, her gift in her hand. She was not put off by my anger; she didn't take her gifts and go home. I came finally to realize that she is who she is, and the anger was mine, the expectations were mine, the desires for protection and security were mine, the disappointment that came from a false image of God was mine. She is who she has always been: compassionate, strong, present, passionate, truth, connected from the womb, unafraid, encompassing, mysterious. Encountering God this way made me reevaluate the notion of God as beyond gender and see God as encompassing both genders—gender-*full* rather than genderless. I look on the growth of spirit and creativity I have experienced as gifts from my daughter Emma and think it is somehow appropriate that it was she who, through her brief time on earth, introduced me to the Great Mother in God.[6]

A Re-Imagining Conference gave Rev. Kiser another powerful experience of the Female Divine. "The language throughout the whole conference was inclusive," she recalls. "We could sing without changing words under our breath, and they called Christ 'Sophia.' They used the name 'Christ-Sophia,' and they called God 'She' for the whole three days. It was delightful!" Even though she caught flak and lost job opportunities for attending this conference, Rebecca celebrates this transforming experience. "For the first time, I heard God addressed in female pronouns for three days straight, in worship and in sermon," she writes. "It was a turning point in my own appreciation of the feminine, as well as a turning point in claiming my own point of view as I returned to a presbytery holding hearings and town meetings about a conference they considered heresy and even blasphemy."[7]

Rev. Kiser laments that the church does not lead the way on social justice issues. "I hate it that the church is often the last to see something that seems to me so obviously a Christian expression. We're the last ones to get on the bandwagon. And then people call us 'politically correct,' like it's not really a theological issue. It was hard at first to give my experience of discrimination as a woman the same kind of credence I'd been giving the experience of African Americans in our country. That was an obvious issue to me, but to apply that to women was hard. Once I began to see the women's issue as a similar thing, suddenly all these other groups demanded my empathy as well—LGBT persons, other minorities, battered women, disabled people. I'd like the church to be proactive on some justice issue. I wish we'd taken the lead on the gay and lesbian issue. Our churches are really a part of our culture, and we don't stand apart and criticize it really well or speak God's word to it. Learning to talk feminist or womanist theology opens up a lot of doors." Currently, Rev. Kiser's justice ministry includes participation in the ecumenical, multicultural Equity for Women in the Church Community with the purpose of opening doors for all clergywomen.

In the Presbyterian Church and in all denominations clergywomen still have difficulty in fulfilling their call to serve as pastors, Rev. Kiser acknowledges. For the fiftieth anniversary of women's ordination in the Presbyterian Church, she organized a celebration. She contacted all the women of her presbytery to find out when they were ordained and where they had served. "We published that and read it at the celebration," she recalls. "We had the ones who were there stand up. As we went down the list of names, it became obvious how many had gone into social work, how many had become counselors, how many were members at large. There were only four or five who had church positions. People came up afterward and said they had no idea we had that many women in our presbytery and that so many of them couldn't find church jobs. For example, my friend Rev. Susan Haugh went into social work because she couldn't get a second call. When she retired, she asked me to speak at the presbytery meeting about her ministry. She was one of the first one hundred Presbyterian Church (USA) clergywomen. She led the way, and has been a real encouragement and mentor to me and others. After I spoke about Susan, she was invited to comment. At the same meeting we took two young women under care to go to seminary and to become pastors. Susan said, 'I hope you all hear out of all this that when you make these promises to these young women, you need to be ready for their gifts.'"

Rev. Dr. Kiser envisions a future church inclusive of clergywomen's gifts and the gifts of all people. "It would be a widely inclusive group of people who have learned to be together, despite all kinds of dissimilarities, that ideal of unity in the midst of diversity," she says. "I love to see people do creative worship and bring all kinds of gifts into it, all kinds of people and all kinds of imagery. When we can welcome those different from ourselves, we discover more about the fullness of humanity and the fullness of God. It means we've moved beyond living in fear, and are learning to live in a bigger picture where we trust a God who is all in all. It means we've entered the welcome of the table, where God says that people will come from north and south and east and west and sit together at table. I have this ideal, and I would like to work toward it." Through her gardening, preaching, writing, and advocacy, Rebecca joins Wisdom's work of making this ideal a reality.

Rev. Daniel Charles Damon

Composer; Pastor, First United Methodist Church, Richmond, California

The Amazing Diversity of Creation

Pray for the Wilderness

Pray for the wilderness,
vanishing fast,
pray for the rain forest,
open and vast;
pray for the people who live in the trees,
pray for the planet brought down by degrees.

Learn from the elephant,
eagle and whale,
learn from the dragonfly,
spider and snail;
learn from the people in neighboring lands,
learn from the children who play in their sands.

Work for the justice created things need,
work for the health of each plant and seed;
work for the creatures abuse has betrayed,
work for the garden God's wisdom once made.

Pray for the atmosphere,
pray for the sea,
learn from the river,
the rock and the tree;

work till Shalom in full harmony rings,
trust the connection of all living things.[8]

An internationally published writer of hymn texts and tunes and a United Methodist pastor for many years, Rev. Daniel Charles Damon calls for care of creation through hymns like "Pray for the Wilderness" and many others with ecology and other social justice themes. Rev. Damon also serves as adjunct faculty in church music at Pacific School of Religion in Berkeley, California, and plays piano in clubs in the San Francisco Bay Area. This multitalented minister has published many hymn collections, anthems, and articles; contributed hymn texts and tunes to numerous hymnals and supplements; written hymn translations from Vietnamese, Portuguese, and Shona languages; with Patrick Matsikenyiri edited *Njalo, A Collection of 16 Hymns in the African Tradition*; released three recordings of hymns, carols, traditional songs, and a solo piano recording of jazz standards; and toured Zimbabwe with the Jubilate Choir from the Pacific Northwest Conference of the United Methodist Church.[9]

Dan grew up in the Evangelical Free Church in Rapid City, South Dakota, where he says he learned to value his "relationship with God, scripture, and congregational song." In his early twenties Dan moved to Berkeley, California, and a few years later enrolled in Pacific School of Religion, an ecumenical seminary. He tells people that he has "a conservative upbringing and a liberal education." Dan writes about a personal experience that opened his mind to inclusive language while he was in seminary:

> After traveling all the way from North Dakota to Ohio for a summer master's program, my sister was refused entry into a preaching course because she was a woman. As a first-year student at Pacific School of Religion, I had been bucking inclusive language; but my sister's experience helped bring justice for women into focus as a concern for me. Before I left seminary, I was writing my first inclusive language hymns.[10]

Dan says that he continued to put the variety of divine images he learned in seminary into his hymns. "Using this variety gives power to social justice work. In scripture we find many images and names for God. Even the Trinity gives us the divine mystery as three-in-one. I believe our tradition has at times reduced the images of scripture to a 'men's club' of images. An all-male clergy also impoverishes the church. I believe we need to use balanced imagery in order to create social justice in our world. As Paul Tillich said, 'Never say "only a symbol."' He knew the power of the symbol."

Including female divine imagery in worship, Dan believes, contributes to changing churches so that they become receptive to women clergy. "Many denominations now have women clergy. I think the variety of imagery for God is helping this to happen."

Rev. Damon has written a number of hymn texts using female divine imagery, including "Goddess of Love," "Holy Mother of All Living," and "Wisdom Watches as We Pray."[11] He wrote the words and the music for "Goddess of Love," published in his collection *Garden of Joy*. In this hymn and in many others, Dan calls for inclusion of everyone in the church. His focus on female images of the Divine gives a theological foundation for this inclusiveness.

Goddess of love, we want to worship
not as outsiders waiting for crumbs,
but as your children—part of your body,
we long to praise you—part of your church.

Goddess of joy, your name is wondrous,
your thoughts are holy—deeper than ours,
yours is one body, many the members,
Goddess, embrace us, make your church one.

Goddess of peace, we give you honor
when we harm no one, seeking the good.
Who is an outcast? Who will decide this?
All those excluded are welcome here.

Goddess of hope, we want to worship,
not with dull sameness, but in new ways,
till all your people feel their inclusion,
hear their name spoken—one of your own.

As Rev. Damon has worked to change the church, taking pro-phetic stands on gender and other social justice issues, he has ex-perienced some opposition. "Not everyone likes these changes," he says. "I have learned to be patient, to accept people where they are. I don't go into a parish and change everything. I do use new hymns when they fit a theme. Over time my churches change toward the balance of imagery. We recently had a study session on language issues."

Rev. Damon believes in the importance of staying within the church to change the church and the wider culture. "I like the 'work within' model of leadership," he says. "I think it is the best way to make lasting change."

In his many years as pastor of First United Methodist Church in Richmond, California, Rev. Damon says he has "fostered a spirit of exploration." From the "Welcome" on the church's website, it is ap-parent that he has also nurtured a spirit of inclusiveness: "The people of Richmond First UMC are called to share God's love as we minister with and to all persons in Point Richmond and beyond, providing worship, nurture, fellowship, and service. Our welcome knows no boundaries of age, race, ethnicity, culture, gender, sexual orientation, economic condition, physical or mental ability. We embrace and seek to preserve the beautiful, amazing diversity of God's creation. We cooperate in ministry with other local churches and groups of God's people as we participate in Christ's mission of peace and unconditional love."[12]

Rev. Damon is grateful also that this church is receptive to his hymns with expansive imagery. In various churches through the years, he has also used inclusive, varied imagery in his preaching. In some churches he previously pastored that were more conservative, he says he was "less skillful at presenting new ideas."

No matter what challenges he has faced, Rev. Damon has affirmed the power of inclusive language to change the church and the wider culture. "As we speak, so we become. As we change the church, so we change society."

Hymn writing is Dan's favorite vehicle for changing church and so-ciety. "I find sharing my faith through my hymn writing to be the most rewarding part of my work. I love the challenge of putting simple, fresh ideas to a strong, singable tune."

Through all his creative ministries, Rev. Damon expresses his passion for justice. In an article titled "A Cry for Justice in Hymnody," Dan writes:

> Justice is not a peripheral issue in scripture. Justice is not in the margins. It is a central theme. The way we treat people, the planet, and ourselves is important. Our faith makes a positive difference in the world when we "do justice." The words we sing inside and outside of our places of worship can be powerful agents of change. How are we currently singing about justice? What have we failed to write about, publish, select, and sing? If you are like me, you will sing the truth before you say it.[13]

Rev. Damon articulates a hopeful vision for the future of the Divine Feminine in what we sing and in all that we do in the church. "I think the Divine Feminine will, in time, balance with the Divine Masculine," he says. "I think our language will come to reflect the truth that the Divine includes female and male and transcends them. The Holy Mystery deepens with study, prayer, and experience."

Rev. Connie L. Tuttle

Pastor, Circle of Grace Community Church, Atlanta, Georgia

Justice for Earth and All Creation

"Godde's word, God's justice, will not be silenced, because
even if we are stove-up with fear, all of creation will speak
out! I am reminded of how right now the earth is speaking
to us out of deep anguish for justice. Calling us to justice
in voices of the wind and oceans, farmlands and glaciers.…
We must stand and speak our truth and demand respect,
justice and compassion for all people—for people of
all races and nationalities, all spiritual paths, all classes,
genders, sexual orientations, all abilities—and for the
planet and all the creatures that dwell on the planet, on
earth and in the oceans and streams and in the air."[14]

Rev. Connie L. Tuttle issues a prophetic call for justice for all creation in a sermon titled "The Silence of Good People," preached
at Atlanta's Circle of Grace Community Church, which she founded
more than twenty years ago, serving as the pastor of the church ever
since. The church's website includes this mission statement:

Circle of Grace Community Church is an inclusive feminist Christian
worshiping community. We are nondoctrinal and seek to reimagine
understandings of language and stories, symbols and metaphors.
Our commitment is to inclusivity. We honor each one's truth
and each one's journey and feel called into community as a way of
faithful response. We offer a safe place to be on a spiritual journey
while challenging the assumptions of our culture. We welcome all

persons regardless of race, gender, sexuality, ability, class, culture, age, and religious background. We use inclusive language in our reference to God and humanity. We understand feminism to be a critique of power. We feel called to embody God's holy community and hold a vision of a sacred future. For us, it means a table that is filled with women and men, children and older people, people of color and white people, gay men, lesbians, bisexual people, transgender people, heterosexual people, and people with disabilities. We call ourselves radically inclusive, antiracist, pro–all the hues and textures of humanity, ecofeminist and, yes, Christian.[15]

In weekly worship services, this progressive, feminist, Christian worshiping community transforms traditional liturgy, including confession and words of assurance. "At Circle of Grace we come to confession as truth-telling," Rev. Tuttle explains. "We believe that speaking the truth is the beginning of all healing and transformation. We are invited to speak the truth to ourselves, to one another, and to Godde that we might begin that journey." Here are examples of words of assurance that she wrote for Circle of Grace:

> Those who come to Godde in genuine regret for the barriers they have met or helped erect in order to build Godde's household to suit human design, She compassionately forgives. We are the household of freedom, the home of the Holy One. May all who enter find welcome and find a home.

> The good news is that Godde accepts us as we are and keeps on offering us new life. By the grace of Sophia Christ, we are forgiven.

> One fact remains unchanging—Godde has loved you. She will always love you. That is the good news that brings us new life!

Rev. Tuttle affirms her commitment to gender-inclusive worship. "I bring theology to Circle of Grace inclusive of the Divine Feminine in language, images, metaphors, stories, prayer, and liturgy—though not to the exclusion of male imagery," she says. "We use the word 'Godde' (pronounced the same way as 'God') in worship to express the presence of both the feminine and the masculine within the term. It is one word we use to encompass the idea, especially in written liturgies used antiphonally. The visual reinforces our underlying shared assumptions."

Connie grew up as an "army brat" in a "church without the boundaries of denominations." She says that her spirituality was thus "formed by chaplains of many and diverse denominations," leading her "to understand Godde outside denominational boxes and dogma." Another formational experience as she matured on her spiritual journey was praying to Godde as Mother when she was in a time of crisis as a young adult. "I had not been exposed to the concept of the Divine Feminine; it was not part of theological dialogue at that time, but I reached out to Godde and met Her from my need."

When she was twenty-five, Connie felt called to ministry. As an elder at Clifton Presbyterian Church in Atlanta, she became active in the church's program for underprivileged neighborhood children, supported the church's declaration of sanctuary and participation in the Underground Railroad for political refugees from Nicaragua, and helped begin Clifton Night Hospitality, a night shelter for sick and aging men, that Circle of Grace now participates in. Connie comments on her experiences: "Faith and social justice were always inextricably intertwined. As my understandings and experiences of the Divine expanded, the call to peace and justice widened to include women; people with disabilities; lesbian, gay, and transgender folk—and the earth itself."

Working her way through Agnes Scott College as a carpenter and painter and as a sitter with the ill and dying, Connie earned a degree in Bible and religion and then went to Columbia Theological Seminary, affiliated with the Presbyterian Church (USA). However, at that time the Presbyterian Church did not allow openly practicing homosexual people to be ministers. "After graduating from seminary I was *persona non grata* in the Presbyterian Church (USA) because I was openly lesbian," Connie says. "I left the Presbyterian Church because there was no place for me. Would I have lied about who I was to stay? It was the one option I was presented. My answer was no."

Connie taught classes titled "Feminist Christian Theology and Spirituality" when she was discerning the shape her call to ministry would take. "Out of those classes emerged a group who said, 'We want to do church this way.' And so we did, muddling through what it meant to begin a church that was progressive, ecumenical, and feminist." The first worship service of Circle of Grace Community Church was held in 1993. "The community ordained me to ministry, and we have been dancing and stumbling along ever since," Rev. Tuttle says.

In forming this progressive church, Rev. Tuttle and Circle of Grace members agreed on inclusive worship language as foundational to justice. "The power of language is one thing feminist theologians have addressed from the beginning, and the issues are as true now as they were then," she says. "Language constructs our reality. Exclusion implies both the powerlessness and worthlessness of the excluded. And then there is the issue of how and who we see ourselves and others to be. What and who reflect the Divine? From where does our wisdom come? Our authority? All the people of the church must have their voices heard if we are to reflect the rich diversity of the Sacred. And if all are sacred, then we must work to make the world safe and just for all."

Inclusive leadership and language are important in changing the church as well as the wider culture, Rev. Tuttle believes. "Including women pastors and feminine divine names and images in worship changes the church and the world primarily because it shifts the power dynamic and opens one door to a better understanding of partnership in leadership, relationships, politics," she says. "In the wider culture it offers or *can* offer a concrete vision of a different kind of authority. Gender equality invites sexual equality. Including women pastors and female divine images in church challenges the status quo of the culture. We are all challenged by change. Opening images, metaphors, and symbols invites a freshness, unexpected insights, and challenges to rote ways of thinking. For children, it encourages wilder sacred imagination!"

Rev. Tuttle expresses gratitude for her church community's encouragement to take risks with language, ideas, and symbolism, and to continue to expand language about the Divine. "At Circle of Grace we call ourselves a gracious heresy," she says. "Pushing my own theological edges challenges me."

Many challenges and questions come to Rev. Tuttle as she builds a community that seeks to include the differences of race, gender, sexuality, ability, class, culture, age, and religious backgrounds. "How do you create worship that is inclusive of many traditions? That allows for many understandings? That includes many perspectives and experiences? And that explores the theologically and experientially unfamiliar?" she asks. "We are fortunate to celebrate the richness of our diversity with constant vigilance to the questions: Is everyone's voice being heard? And who is not at the table? As feminists, we are committed to honoring each one's truth. That is the value we keep returning to. We are not alike. We do not seek to be alike. So how can we travel together? Those questions are always open and before us. The folks who stay are willing to live with occasional discomfort, to be challenged and to find and make way for the Spirit to work. That means we talk frankly about race, sexuality, and the varieties of theological histories and spiritual experiences. We have found two things to be true: the pain of rigid patriarchy, no matter what form it takes, is universal; and we have to keep talking, even when it is difficult."

In meeting these challenges Rev. Tuttle draws from many spiritual resources. "My relationship with Godde and my spiritual practices help me through times of criticism and setbacks," she says. "Working with my spiritual director keeps me steady when I feel off-kilter. I get inspiration and strength from the people with whom I make community—from those who wrestle with the challenges of severe mental illness to scholars worshiping with us who push the edges of theologies of disability or feminist/womanist theologies."

Rev. Tuttle is changing the church and the wider culture through creating a radically inclusive, feminist church. As she creates liturgy inclusive of female and male and more, she has found reimagining Eucharist and baptism to be especially meaningful and rewarding. "I don't know what is likely or what will happen in the church universal," she says. "Will there be a growing openness to the Divine Feminine? I hope and pray so. At Circle of Grace we are at a place where we must be mindful not to be exclusive of the Divine Masculine. A wonderful problem, isn't it?"

Rev. Connie Tuttle's ministry increases my belief that there will be a growing openness to the Divine Feminine to provide balance to the Divine Masculine, which still predominates in the church universal and in our culture. The prophetic, creative work of Rev. Tuttle and Circle of Grace Community Church contributes to increasing openness to Wisdom and to the transformation that flows from Her.

Part 6

Wisdom's Works of Nonviolence

"**H**appy are those who find wisdom, and those who get understanding.... Her ways are ways of pleasantness, and all her paths are peace."[1] Wisdom's ways bring peace. She works to end all violence.

Violence inflicted routinely on women and girls in much of the world is one of the "paramount human rights problems of this century," write Nicholas D. Kristof and Sheryl WuDunn in *Half the Sky*.[2] In the United States alone, every nine seconds a woman is battered or assaulted.[3] Nearly one in five American women has been raped in her lifetime, and almost half of female victims experience their first rape before age eighteen.[4] One in three women in the world experiences some kind of abuse in her lifetime.[5] Worldwide, an estimated four million women and girls each year are bought and sold into prostitution, slavery, or marriage.[6] As noted in *Half the Sky*, "More girls have been killed in the last fifty years, precisely because they were girls, than people were killed in all the battles of the twentieth century. More girls are killed in this routine 'gendercide' in any one decade than people were slaughtered in all the genocides of the twentieth century."[7] Exclusively masculine divine language and imagery in most worship services lay a foundation for this worldwide violence against women and girls by devaluing them through exclusion.

This patriarchal worship that gives greatest value to straight males also contributes to violence against LGBTQ people. In the United States alone, 54 percent of LGBTQ people express concern that they will be victims of hate crime.[8] Reports of violence against LGBTQ people continue to rise, and two out of three hate crimes go unreported.[9] Transgender women and racial minorities in the LGBTQ community are most often targeted.[10]

Clearly, our world is in desperate need of Wisdom's works of peace. We give deep value to Her peaceful ways when we include Her in our worship. Wisdom and other female personifications of the Divine inspire our work of nonviolence.

Awake to Work for Peace on Earth
(Sung to the tune of "O Sing a Song of Bethlehem")

Awake to work for peace on earth through Holy Wisdom's power;
come, join together, give our all in this most urgent hour.
For ages long has Wisdom cried with message strong and clear;
so many people have refused Her call throughout the years.

Still Wisdom calls to everyone to join Her work of peace;
now let us rise to follow Her so justice may increase.
We all are broken from the wounds that violence brings to earth;
we all are longing for the day our wholeness is rebirthed.

Rejoice, for Holy Wisdom comes with guidance for each day;
She lives within us and above to show the peaceful way.
Rejoice, for Wisdom blesses life with gifts beyond compare;
then let us cocreate with Her a world so free and fair.[11]

  KINGSFOLD

Rev. Judith Liro

Priest, St. Hildegard's Community, St. George's Episcopal Church, Austin, Texas

Weaving Our Lives Together with Sophia-Spirit

"I yearned deeply to believe in nonviolence, but I kept thinking that it was impossible, that nonviolence couldn't be effective because that wasn't the way the world was made. I was converted to nonviolence through reading Walter Wink's *Engaging the Powers*, which helped me see that the 'principalities and powers' had cast their spell on all of us, had us in a trance thinking that the only thing that would work was violence.[12] It helped my mind catch up with my heart."

For many years Rev. Liro has been teaching nonviolence through transforming the language and symbols of the church. This reserved, soft-spoken minister does not like the conflict this has caused. "I'm aware of some people who are cut out to be prophets; they enjoy stirring up trouble," she says. "I'm not like that."

But beginning when she was at Episcopal Theological Seminary of the Southwest, Judith caused a stir by suggesting that the seminary do an inclusive-language liturgy that she had experienced at the denomination's General Convention. "It created this huge uproar," she recalls. "My suggestion was for a onetime liturgy with something under consideration in our own church. A woman who had been one of my closest friends never spoke to me again after that. One of my best-loved professors was also strangely opposed. I discovered that there were prayer book fundamentalists."

In her seminary homiletics class, Judith preached a sermon on the importance of inclusive language in which she proclaimed: "Some say that the issue of language is trivial, even cosmetic. I would heartily disagree. It is about as inconsequential as the air we breathe because it shapes who we are and affects how we think. If the words we use to pray and worship exclude persons even when we have no desire to be exclusive, then I believe we are faced with a fundamental danger. If you would tell me of the great difficulties involved in changing language and conclude that nothing can be done, then I would counter that the difficulties run as deep as human sin and that our restoration is dependent upon God."

When she was serving as one of the priests at St. George's Episcopal Church in Austin, Texas, Rev. Liro preached a sermon on inclusive language. "All hell broke loose," she recalls. "I think people were angry because the sermon touches on what holds patriarchy in place. It attempts to uncover patriarchy and identify the core of this whole system that is basically evil and that we all participate in and don't even know that it's there. I think that's why it's so hard to get people to even be aware of the need for inclusive language. It's so tied into everything. Without patriarchy, we couldn't keep wars going. The economy would be changed. Language is the sacrament, the visible part. And if we start messing with that, it might make everything else unravel. I think that people are not conscious of it, but I think there's the sense that we can't go there."

Around this time Rev. Liro's bishop gave an address at Diocesan Council that was supportive of the Persian Gulf War, and there was a "Courtesy Resolution" for the delegates to accept his address. "I felt trapped, like I couldn't vote against it," Judith says. "But voting for it was like voting that I supported the war. I was horrified by it. I felt like this was not my church. Where was Jesus in the war and political power?"

A few years later at St. George's Episcopal Church, Rev. Liro preached a sermon on nonviolence in a worship service commemorating the fiftieth anniversary of Hiroshima. "It was a service that tore the parish apart," she recalls. "I was really careful to express nonviolence in

a way that wasn't polarizing. I tried to connect nonviolence to the kind
of sacrifices that had been made in World War II, that were important
in the lives of some of the parishioners. But I didn't succeed, at least
not with everybody. It wasn't just the sermon, but the prayers and the
whole service. It was like an earthquake that changed the landscape, and
my journey turned dramatically in a particular direction."

Soon Rev. Liro felt a call to begin a new community within St.
George's. With the generous support of Rector David Hoster, she and
other members of the church created this new community committed to inclusive language and drawing from insights they had gained
in the Servant Leadership School of the Church of the Saviour in
Washington, D.C. St. Hildegard's Community began on an Epiphany
Sunday with a creative service blessing both the new community and
the traditional community of St. George's.[13]

Years later I had the joy of worshiping with St. Hildegard's
Community. Seated in a large circle with members of the Community,
Rev. Liro led this prayer she created:

> Ancient Love, Vibrant Life-giver,
> Stir compassion in us,
> Longings in our heart and action:
> for our own bodies and for all bodies,
> for the Earth fallen prey to robbers,
> for Half-the-sky passed by.

Rev. Liro and several lay members of the community, wearing albs
covered with flowing lime green chasubles, led the liturgy from within
the circle. We sang "This Ancient Love," including these words: "Long
before She laid her arm of colors 'cross the sky, there was a love, this
ancient love was born."[14] The offertory hymn, "O Beautiful Gaia,"
images the Divine as "Ancient Sophia."[15] After the Eucharist, we sang
"Ground of All Being," which balances the images of "Mother of life"
and "Father of the universe."[16]

In her sermon that day, based on Jesus's parable of the Good
Samaritan, Rev. Liro picked up the image of "Half-the-sky" from her
prayer, alluding to the title of a book of the same name by Nicholas
Kristof and Sheryl WuDunn.[17] Rev. Liro uses "Half-the-sky" as a symbol
for the women of the world. According to a Chinese proverb, "women

hold up half the sky." In Rev. Liro's creative interpretation of the Good Samaritan parable, the injured one represents the women of the world, as well as the earth and our own bodies. "My three examples—our bodies, the earth, and women of the world—are connected," she says. "It is patriarchal ordering and values that have demeaned them all, setting them up for exploitation. Jesus didn't know the word 'patriarchy,' but his parable shows that he was well aware of the brokenness to the human family when artificial lines of value, domination, and exclusion are drawn. He calls us to kinship and friendship and community with ourselves and with each other, with Divine Love and the web of Life."

After the liturgy, Judith tells me she has tried to bring the power of *Half the Sky* into conversation with scripture in a way that addresses the deadly imbalance in our world. "For me, feminism is about a healthy balance of feminine and masculine and is not anti-male," she says. "It encourages all of us to embrace our wholeness, to know full humanity that comes from living in deep connection with God's wholeness. Liberating God from narrow metaphors opens up new possibilities for Divine-human relationship. I believe that 'Half-the-sky passed by' applies to our naming of the Divine as well. God is the injured One imprisoned in the narrowness of our naming and understanding. Often St. Hildegard's uses diverse divine images that are gender-neutral. At other times we intentionally pray with feminine names such as 'Sophia' to balance the male images that most of us carry around already. We experience tremendous vitality brought by this wholeness."

Even as a child, Judith had a social justice conscience and what she describes as a "sense of the Holy." When she was twelve, she initiated worship at home with her family. In her high school years she was active in a Presbyterian church in her hometown of San Antonio, Texas, serving as president of the youth group and preaching on Youth Sunday. "By the time I was about to graduate, I wanted to go to seminary in Christian education," she says. "It didn't occur to me about wanting to be ordained. I was still firmly in my role, what was permitted as female. I'm sure the way I thought about God was male." When Judith was in high school, the civil rights movement also became important to her. "Because of Jesus's teachings, I was beginning to have different ideas about civil rights than my family of origin," she says. "Desegregation was being implemented in San Antonio schools. My heart thrilled with the courage of civil rights activists. I felt set free to love beyond my own family and to experience a caring that could stretch out to the world."

Judith's call to ministry continued to unfold after she graduated from Colorado College, married, and moved to Austin, Texas. She became active in All Saints' Episcopal Church, and then studied theology at Episcopal Theological Seminary of the Southwest. After graduation, she was ordained deacon and a year later became the first woman ordained an Episcopal priest in Austin. After she had served many years as a priest at St. George's Episcopal Church, her call to re-create the church led her to initiate the new community of St. Hildegard's.

Commitment to inclusive language proved to be the most challenging for St. Hildegard's Community in relationship to the institutional church. In an article in the newsletter of the Evangelical & Ecumenical Women's Caucus, Rev. Liro writes about this commitment:

> In the years leading up to the birth of our community, we had become more convinced that the dominance of male imagery in the language of the liturgy was undermining the possibilities for women to experience ourselves as beloved, gifted, and responsible beings. With the sacred feminine devalued, the shadow side of the masculine supported violence and dehumanization. What sense did it make for some of us to counsel women who were survivors of domestic abuse and rape and fail to see the church's role in weaving the subtle underpinnings of this culture? How could those of us who worked to prevent war or heal its wounded fail to see the way words in our worship unconsciously played a supporting role in its justification? St. Hildegard's longed to be a place where the wholeness of God and humanity could be experienced as much as possible. When we chose to be a Eucharistic community, we entered into a carefully guarded domain—the sacred core identity of the Anglican tradition. In order to incarnate these transforming changes, we had to find a way to compromise with integrity. I believe that Sophia showed us the way.[18]

In her advocacy for inclusion of female divine images in the language of liturgy to support justice and healing, Rev. Liro uses this powerful metaphor: "I like the useful metaphor of several factories that are built on a river and pollute the water of a village downstream. A hospital is built to treat the illnesses that result, but there is still a need to track down the source of the pollution and to clean up the water itself. Many organizations, including the church, do the important work of the hospital. Yet I have also come to realize that the church is one of the factories that contributes to the problem. Our liturgical language with its current heavily masculine content supports a patriarchal hierarchical ordering. Most are simply unaware of the power of language. The status quo, which includes the exploitation of the earth, poverty, racism, sexism, heterosexism, and militarism, is held in place by a deep symbolic imbalance, and we are unwitting participants in it." Rev. Liro says that she is grateful for those working in the Episcopal Church to write and adopt expansive language resources and hopes that St. Hildegard's creations can contribute to these resources for wider use.

On a pilgrimage to the island of Iona, Judith received a message. "I was being communicated with that the Sacred Feminine is emerging, that somehow I'm a part of that," she says. "I'm hoping that what I'm doing in a small way will begin to come in a larger way." Judith's vision for the future of the Sacred Feminine includes an interfaith dimension so that people look beyond differences for "commonality" and "appreciation of diversity."

The prophetic, expansive ministry of Rev. Liro and St. Hildegard's Community inspires hope for the church as a part of New Creation in the world. Judith affirms Sophia's hand in her call to re-create the church: "St. Hildegard's Community has come about through Sophia's grace. Sophia-Spirit is creating a welcoming, healing, justice-nurturing place as She dances with us and weaves our lives together. Our life is in God's hands, and we live sustained by Her breath and energy."[19]

Marg Herder

Writer; Musician; Director of Public Information,
Evangelical & Ecumenical Women's Caucus—Christian Feminism Today

Knowing Her, Loving All People

"I've never owned a gun, nor will I. No one will ever be
able to steal my gun and use it to kill someone else. I
will never need a gun. Because I believe something this
guy named Jesus said, 'But I tell you, do not resist an evil
person. If anyone slaps you on the right cheek, turn to
them the other cheek also.'[20] If someone is going to shoot
me, I will be shot. I will never need a gun. When people
talk about killing people in a video game, I don't act like
it's cool. I say that it seems pretty messed up when killing
people, even virtually, is entertaining to someone."

Marg Herder wrote this passionate challenge the day after the awful
tragedy at Sandy Hook Elementary School in Newtown, Connecticut,
where gun violence killed twenty little children and six teachers:

I realize that even spending my dollars supporting movies or TV
shows that involve lots of gun violence is a tacit endorsement.
Today I can't keep my mouth shut about war any longer either.
It's all related. We need to address gun violence on an individual,
family, and societal level. I pray that we finally admit our permissive
gun laws, our virtual glorification of gun violence, and our active
denial of what is really happening in war led us to where we are
today, weeping for dead first graders and their teachers. I pray that
we realize our denial, our failure to even try to create change, our

unwillingness to take a public stand, implicates us personally when things like this happen. And I pray that we stop being too lazy, or too afraid, or too damn comfortable with the status quo, to do something about it.[21]

Four months later, after the terrible tragedy at the Boston Marathon, where bombs killed and injured people, Marg continued her plea for nonviolence:

> Will we make the difficult decision to respond with love, searching for ways to connect with each other as a people and support those affected, perhaps even directing our attention to creating a world of peace and equality where violence is never considered necessary to achieve an end? I will choose love. I pray for love and healing to wash over all of those who are suffering as a result of the tragedy in Boston. And I pray for the fullness of Divine love and healing to pour down on those who initiated the Boston explosions so that they will never again feel the need to cause the suffering of others. I hope you will all join me in praying that our nation will be swept up in a great and miraculous current of love, refusing to meet violence with violence.[22]

For many years Marg has been choosing love even for those who have hurt her. When organizers of an Indianapolis Gay Pride Celebration planned to prevent several antigay Christian churches from renting booth space, Marg suggested a different response:

> I know the spiritual damage similar Christian groups are doing and have done to our people. Intolerant Christians nearly ended me thirty years ago. But times are changing and we must carefully consider if adversarial action is still as necessary as we once felt it to be. I want to propose to you that we, LGBT people, now find ourselves in the position to either live into the peaceful, loving, tolerant, and diverse society we have been advocating for the last fifty years, or adopt the same exclusive, judgmental, and abusive outlook that has caused us so much anguish in the past.[23]

It hasn't always been easy for Marg to follow this peaceful path. Growing up in Indianapolis, Marg was very active in her Presbyterian church. Her grandmother, who played piano for the Sunday school, and her mother, who worked with the children's choirs, groomed

Marg to be a church musician. Marg sang in the choirs and worked with younger children. She says that when she was young, the church was the only place she felt she belonged. Then in her teens, Marg became aware of her lesbianism and told a minister in her church. He told her that he would no longer allow her to work with the children. Slowly Marg realized that her life with the church was over. "No loss has ever been so painful," she says. "I found myself torn open, like a tortoise whose shell had been ripped off. I was a part of the church, I thought my life would always be in the church, and once I admitted I was homosexual I was told I was no longer worthy of participating in the church. This rejection was so consuming, and so confusing, that it is impossible to describe. In the end, it was easier for me to walk away from the church, from all I thought I would be, than it was to walk away from the truth of my gender identity and sexual orientation."

In her twenties, Marg played in an all-female rock and roll band, "Software," and majored in religious studies at Indiana University–Purdue University Indianapolis. She says that she is still very grateful that her family never shut her out, as the families of most of her lesbian friends did. Also, she is gratified that her parents helped start the first support groups for friends and parents of gays and lesbians at their church.

For many years Marg worked hard and did what she could to keep herself from feeling. "The societal view of lesbianism led me to internalize a lot of self-loathing and despair," she says. "I put a lot of effort into trying to escape these feelings, using drugs and alcohol, working a lot, generally doing my best, but really just skimming the surface of life."

Marg says she finally realized that her painful experience with the church had caused her to ignore her spirituality. "I quit drinking and started taking better care of myself, physically and emotionally, and began to find my way back to Spirit. I feel that I move toward Spirit when I am in my studio creating music, walking around with my camera, participating in ritual with trusted friends, or off in the woods backpacking and being alone in nature."

A writer, musician, photographer, and sound artist interested in the exploration of the intersection between incarnation and divinity, Marg also currently serves as the director of public information for Evangelical & Ecumenical Women's Caucus–Christian Feminism Today (EEWC-CFT). Her website includes some of her creative work, and she writes the *Christian Feminism Today* blog "Where She Is."[24] The blog title plays on words, referring to the Divine as "She" and to where Marg is also.

One of the first people I meet when I arrive at a recent EEWC-CFT Gathering in Indianapolis is Marg Herder. She scurries around the meeting room, setting up the sound system, keyboard, PowerPoint, and other equipment. In cyberland, I had come to appreciate Marg as the codesigner of the awesome EEWC-CFT website. In person, she is gracious, kind, witty, and loving. During the conference, her talents continue to unfold as she balances creative gifts and technical and analytical skills.

For most of her songs, Marg writes the words and the music as well as performing and recording them. Here are the lyrics to one of her songs:

A Name

A name …
What you like me to be? Sum it up so we all can see.
Let's just call it a name. Let's just make it a righteous game.

So you can know me better.
So you can know me well.

"Patriarchy has had control over discursive expression. So it has been a misogynist culture that has determined what words get entered in the dictionaries."

Hey!

"… as she who controls the language controls the politics."[25]

A name …
Now that you've got me down you can start trying to turn me 'round.
Now you've figured me out you can help me to learn what it's all about.

So I can fit in better.
So I can fit in well.[26]

Commenting on "A Name," Marg further elucidates the power of language when she writes:

It's all in the language, and the language was created by patriarchy. Think it doesn't matter that God is referred to almost exclusively as He? Sure, you're enlightened enough to think of God as a force, or a presence, or as Spirit. But when you need a pronoun, what pronoun do you reach for? It matters. It is huge. Try calling God by female pronouns in almost any Christian church sometime. See how that goes over. Try referring to God as She in your own speech. Feel weird? Feel kinda like you're breaking a rule, being bad? If you were raised in mainstream culture here in the United States or any other Western country, you were socialized to think of God as He. Where does that leave all us female people? With the prevailing consensus that God is other. Men are "made in the image of God." Women, well, we're just the afterthought. A helper for the people who were created by God to be just like Him.[27]

Continuing to unfold the meaning of "A Name," Marg shows how labeling people also contributes to their devaluation and exclusion:

So to a lot of people I'm a lesbian, a feminist, a liberal. And because they label me that way it means they don't have to listen to anything I say, they don't have to empathize with me, they don't have to think of me as equal to them. Because of those labels I become other and less-than. They don't have to investigate my existence, learn about me as an individual. Because they have named me. And once I am named as other, all that remains is for society to induce me to change so I become more acceptable, standardized. If I refuse to change, I am punished by exclusion from mainstream society.[28]

Through her creative work, Marg illuminates a spirituality of love and nonviolence, a spirituality that all people can share as equals. Her female references to the Divine contribute to her message that all people are created equally in the divine image. "I'm trying to wrap my head around the perfect way to understand and communicate how we, as a species, can become more kind and generous and peaceful," she says. "I am still holding on to a belief that we don't have to be killers, we don't have to judge and condemn others, we can be merciful, we can be beautiful, we can be loving. All of us. I'm always trying to deepen my understanding of Spirit. How She moves in this world, why She gave birth to all that is, why She put us right here, right now. I'm always trying to communicate to the person sitting across from me, or listening to my recordings, or looking at my pictures, or reading my words, 'Please let this experience be meaningful. Please feel Her in this moment.' I like to think that She in Her grace is actually all of creation in the act of creating Herself, so when I fully open myself to the motion of Her creation, I can create truthfully."

In her song "We Can Know Her," Marg challenges people who wound others with destructive speech and behavior to come to know this Creative Spirit and Her inclusive love.

> How can we hope to survive if our souls ain't alive
> And how can we ever escape if you're sealin' our fate
> How your children must fear, to see your love disappear
>
> You don't know Her
>
> You tell us what you know but you can't bring yourself to look in
> our eyes
> We don't see what you're gonna lose by thinking everyone could
> walk in Her light
> You say the Passion was real, so what did Her Son reveal
>
> Well it sure isn't what you're sayin' now, that we're somehow
> unworthy to share in true fellowship with you. If you think that,
> you don't know Her. So if your time really is tickin' away like
> you say you'd better come to know Her.
>
> We can know you.
> You can know us.
> We can know Her.[29]

In her comments on this song, Marg expresses hope that "love and forgiveness will dissolve" the fear of judgmental people. "Eventually judgmental and wounding Christians (and those of other religions) will not be able to turn their backs on Her. Eventually they will come to know Her and in doing so they will finally be able to love all people."[30] Through all her prophetic, creative work, Marg joins Divine Wisdom's work of love, peace, healing, and justice.

Rev. Dr. Monica A. Coleman

Associate Professor of Constructive Theology and
African American Religions, Claremont School of Theology

Knowing a Savior by What She Does

"The Dinah Project organized a church response to sexual violence through worship, community education, and counseling. The Dinah Project has been my own saving grace for the mere fact that it made the difference between a vacuous spiritual life and including God in my healing process. It made the difference between a growing skepticism for churches and clergy, and a belief and understanding that the church can be a safe place for those who have experienced sexual violence. The Dinah Project helped me to see beyond my own experience and pains to the larger community that also desires healing, compassion, and safety."[31]

Rev. Dr. Monica A. Coleman created the Dinah Project after her traumatic experience of sexual violence. "It was almost three years after accepting my call to the ministry and nearly one year into my studies in divinity school," she writes.

My commitment to both God and the church had just recently transformed from that of an active church member to that of a professional. I was still trying to figure out what that meant. In the middle of this process, I was raped by a man who was also a seminarian, and also clergy. And I didn't have much of anything to say to God. I had talked to God throughout the rape, pleading for intervention. Pleading that somehow, some way, God would stop this thing from happening to me. After the rape, there was no more pleading and no more praying. Honestly, I was absolutely disgusted that the same God to whom I prayed and whom I worshiped was the same God to whom my rapist would pray and worship. It was too much for me to handle.[32]

Monica found psychological, medical, and legal resources to help her. "But there was something missing," she writes. "I still struggled in my personal relationship with God. I didn't quite know how to pray anymore. I didn't know how to worship God anymore."[33] When she turned to churches for help, she found pastors who suggested that the rape was her fault or who minimized her trauma. Finally she found a church with a pastor who responded appropriately to her painful experience. There at Metropolitan Interdenominational Church in Nashville, Tennessee, Monica started the Dinah Project, which grew into a comprehensive ministry program to assist churches of all races and theological perspectives with healing responses to sexual violence. This project gets its name from the rape of the biblical character Dinah, daughter of Jacob and Leah.[34] The program spread to churches all over the country through Monica's book, which details methods for planning and implementing it.[35]

"The Dinah Project was the toughest thing I've ever done," Monica says. "It was emotionally painful, and we had no money. But there was nothing I did that was more rewarding than the Dinah Project. It was hard. But it was also really good, the work we did in the community. I knew that this was what God had called me to do and that God would give me what I needed to do it."

Monica describes herself as a "born theologian" and a "church girl." She grew up in Bethel African Methodist Episcopal (AME) Church in Ann Arbor, Michigan. She also spent much time at Shiloh Baptist Church in Washington, D.C., when she visited her grandparents on Christmas and summer vacations. "We were always at church," she says. "Going to church was like brushing your teeth. It was not optional. I grew up in church—church hats, church dresses, gloves, and the whole nine yards!"

Growing up with messages about the importance of education as well as church, Monica entered Harvard University when she was only seventeen. "It wasn't till I went to college that I actually saw women clergy," she recalls. "I didn't think about being a minister, but now women clergy seemed more normal." When Monica felt a call to ministry, she at first responded, "No, no thank you, God. I don't want to do this." She didn't like public speaking, and didn't want to preach.

Not long after, Monica was in Atlanta attending a National Black Women's Health Project Conference, where Rev. Dr. Renita Weems was preaching. While listening to her, Monica started thinking again about her call to ministry. She then met Renita and for the first time said out loud, "I'm going to preach." Renita responded, "Well, good for you!"

After graduating magna cum laude with honors from Harvard University with a degree in African American studies, Monica entered Vanderbilt School of Divinity. There she also had professors she describes as "amazing" and "progressive," who "had really great feminist and social justice approaches to religion." Monica had better experiences in the academic world than in the church, though. "The AME denomination in Michigan wasn't used to women clergy, and they weren't used to young clergy," she says. She had challenging experiences when she met with ordination committees. "They would ask me these totally sexist questions like, 'What if you marry a Baptist?'" Monica recalls. "I said, 'I'm nineteen. I'm not thinking about marriage.' I know they weren't asking guys that. I had this radical idea about equity, and people could see that."

Monica recounts a conversation she had with one pastor before a worship service in which she participated:

> "Are you going to change clothes?" the pastor asked.
> "Why would I change clothes?" Monica replied.
> "You're wearing pants."
> "Well, *you're* wearing pants."
> "I told you that you need to wear a suit."
> "This is a suit. It's a pantsuit."

A year after graduating from Vanderbilt Divinity School with a master of divinity degree, Monica was ordained as an elder in the African Methodist Episcopal Church. She describes her ordination process as challenging partly because she was direct in saying that she didn't want to be treated any differently from men. But when it came time for her ordination examination, one of the ministers on the ordination council redirected the conversation, asking the presiding bishop if he had seen her article in the *AME Journal* on clergy sexual misconduct and her article in *Essence* about the work she was doing in the area of sexual violence. Then when the bishop asked Monica what she wanted to do, she said that she wanted to be a professor. He replied, "Good. Go be one of the church's great scholars."

That is just what Rev. Dr. Coleman has done. After receiving her doctorate in philosophy of religion and theology from Claremont Graduate University, she became the founding director of Womanist Religious Studies at Bennett College for Women in Greensboro, North Carolina, the first undergraduate religious studies program to focus on the spiritual experiences of women of African descent. She has taught systematic theology at Lutheran School of Theology in Chicago, and currently serves as associate professor of constructive theology and African American religions at Claremont School of Theology. She has become well known as a womanist theologian and a process theologian.[36]

In *Making a Way Out of No Way*, Dr. Coleman creatively connects womanist and process theologies to develop a postmodern womanist theology that addresses the evils of violence and injustice. "Postmodern womanist theology focuses on the teaching and healing communities that learn from the past in order to creatively transform the world," she writes. "Womanist theologies of salvation state that Jesus Christ can be seen as a black woman. Postmodern womanist theology argues that a black woman is often Christ. The Savior may be a teenager, a person living with a disability, a lesbian woman."[37]

In the womanist tradition of engaging black women's literature, Monica gives an illustration of a Savior from *Parable of the Sower*, a science fiction novel by Octavia E. Butler.[38] Lauren Oya Olamina, the African American teenage protagonist of the novel, walks north from a fictional suburb of Los Angeles when in a not-too-distant future her neighborhood enclave and family are destroyed. Other refugees join her journey, and she teaches them her "God-is-Change" theology. "Lauren emerges as a Savior because she courageously uses her abilities to creatively transform," Dr. Coleman writes. "Nevertheless, Lauren is an unlikely Savior. Because Lauren is young, black, and female, her leadership is questioned by the larger world."[39]

Making a Way Out of No Way gives another example of a Savior: Rev. Dr. Kathi Elaine Martin, founder of God, Self, and Neighbor (GSN) Ministries in Atlanta, Georgia, offering religious community to people who experience racism and heterosexism in both Christian communities and the wider society. Monica writes:

> As an openly black lesbian woman with mental health challenges and multiple sclerosis, Martin does not appear to have the characteristics of a Savior. Yet as a theologian, teacher, preacher, and activist, Martin proves to be a worthy Savior.... Like postmodern womanist theology, GSN understands the Savior as one who puts forth a theology of love and justice while generating greater awareness and health in the community.... A Savior is known by what she does. She leads a community that makes a way out of no way.[40]

In third-wave postmodern womanist theology "no one is left out, and no one is left behind," Rev. Dr. Coleman proclaims at a Faith and Feminism, Womanist, Mujerista Conference at Ebenezer/herchurch Lutheran in San Francisco. She elaborates on the "open hands" of third-wave womanist theology, which engages black women's religious experiences as it draws from Christian and other religious traditions as well as from black women's literature. The goals are "justice, survival, quality of life, equality, acceptance, and inclusion."

Diverse leadership and symbolism in church make a difference, Monica says. "It was so important for me to see women clergy. Those who identify as feminists are especially helpful because they preach differently. Some preachers are women but there's nothing different about how they look at things. Feminists look for the underside of the texts. Racially diverse images in worship are so important, too. I think you should be able to see yourself."

In teaching theology students, Dr. Coleman finds receptivity to expansive divine imagery. "That's why I like training ministers, because I get to expose them to liberation and feminist and womanist theologies," she says. "It's exciting to teach this new information to people who are preparing to be ministers and leaders. When I teach *imago Dei* (image of God), I use the example of transgender children. When we work on language for God, my students don't always dig this female language. So I have them rewrite the twenty-third Psalm, using images I give them, like 'God is my Mother' or 'God is my Counselor,' instead of 'the Lord is my Shepherd.' I say, 'What do we know about sheep? We live in L.A.! What do we know about shepherds?'"

Inclusive leadership, language, and theology are inseparable from social justice, Monica says. "In many ways this inclusiveness is part of the social justice movement within the church. The fact that people rail so much against female language for God shows how important it is. It's just amazing to me how much people are attached to God's being a man. Some in the leadership of the church are actually happy with gender inequity, even if they're not saying women can't preach anymore, which of course some churches do say. Many churches have women preachers, but then they don't treat them the same. There's so much sexual harassment that goes on and that's tolerated and covered up. And then women, even if they have more education than men, get smaller churches that don't sustain them financially. All that still happens. So to take any steps toward gender equity within the church— that's a social justice movement within the church. If you're able to see injustices in the church, then you're usually able to see injustices in other places, too, and understand that part of the divine calling is to resist injustice wherever it's found. But some churches can see race all day long and not see gender, and vice versa, which I just don't get. Or they can see gender and race but not sexuality; it's all the same stuff!"

Through her prophetic writing, teaching, preaching, and activism, Rev. Dr. Coleman contributes to healing these interlocking injustices. She articulates her vision for the transformation of the church. "It's a feminist church. It looks like Ebenezer/herchurch in San Francisco and like Circle of Grace in Atlanta. Of course, woman images of the Divine are in these inclusive churches. They're not dogmatic, but very welcoming to people of all faiths." Monica envisions a national organization of these inclusive feminist churches and a website to help people find them. Her vision for the future of womanist theology is that "it would be as expansive and diverse as black women are in all ways" and that it would help all women "to assert our own authority."

Dr. Virginia Ramey Mollenkott

Author; English Professor Emeritus, William Paterson University

Radicalized by the Bible

"If we teach ourselves to value roles traditionally associated with the female on a truly equal level with those associated with the male, the result will be the enrichment of all humanity. Inclusive God-language is a step in the direction of that enrichment.... Whereas many religious leaders lament their inability to do more to alleviate world hunger, the nuclear threat, and other economic and racial inequities, their own language is something they could control almost immediately. By recognizing the female presence in their grammatical choices, and by utilizing biblical references to God as female, they could demonstrate the sincerity of their commitment to human justice, peace, and love."[41]

Dr. Virginia Ramey Mollenkott's prophetic book *The Divine Feminine: The Biblical Imagery of God as Female* includes Holy Wisdom among the biblical female divine images contributing to peace, justice, and love.

The Bible equates justice with Wisdom and Wisdom with the Christ. So in our minds there can be no division between individual, privatized righteousness and the attempt to correct the societal, structural forms of justice. In the Hebrew Scriptures, personal and social renewal was accomplished by Holy Lady Wisdom; in the Christian Scriptures, it is Lord Christ who makes all things new.

The combination of Wisdom/Christ leads to a healthy blend of
male and female imagery that empowers everyone and works beau-
tifully to symbolize the One God who is neither male nor female
and yet both male and female.... Letting this symbol unfold within
us, we can live with less fear and therefore more love.[42]

Extending love even to those who respond to her with anger and hos-
tility, Virginia embodies Wisdom's work of nonviolence. In an article
titled "Affirming Queer Spirituality in a Sometimes Hostile World," she
states: "If you hear suggestions that you should kill yourself or others,
or attack people, you can know for sure that the source is evil, not sacred. What is suggested by an agent of the Holy Spirit is always loving,
kind, reconciling, and peaceable."[43]

Virginia describes herself as a "progressive evangelical," who
was "raised in Protestant fundamentalism." Born into a working-class
Philadelphia family, she grew up in a Plymouth Brethren church, which
she attended with her family three times on Sunday and every Tuesday
evening. In her fundamentalist family and church she says that "women
could not ask questions during a Bible study, let alone teach anything
to other participants" and that "God was male, and therefore men were
the heads of home, church, and society."

For about the first thirty years of her life, this fundamentalism
stifled Virginia but also gave her the biblical knowledge that would later
bring freedom. She writes:

> The Christianity I learned from my Protestant fundamentalist fam-
> ily was enough to strangulate my desire to celebrate my own par-
> ticularities and thus to embody God in just the way She had created
> me to do. But during those same years, the keys to my eventual
> liberation were also being provided. Although many right-wing
> Christians despise what I have done with the keys they put into
> my hands, the fact is that the same Bible that deeply oppressed me
> has also been the most vital element in setting me free. It is not an
> overstatement to claim that I have been radicalized by the Bible.[44]

Studying literature led Virginia to her discovery of female names and
images of God in the Bible. She recalls feeling "terrified," however,
when she first tried to call God "She." With a PhD in literature, Dr.

Mollenkott then began writing articles on biblical female divine imagery for the Christian feminist journal *Daughters of Sarah*.[45] These articles eventually became her book *The Divine Feminine: The Biblical Imagery of God as Female*. In the introduction, Dr. Mollenkott writes:

> It seems natural to assume that Christian people, eager to transmit the Good News that the Creator loves each human being equally and unconditionally, would be right in the vanguard of those who utilize inclusive language. Yet a visit to almost any church on Sunday morning indicates that alas, it is not happening that way. Whereas a "secular" publisher like McGraw-Hill has insisted on inclusive language for almost a decade, the language of Christian preaching, prayer, and hymnody is still laden with exclusive-sounding references to men, man, brothers, sons, and the God of Abraham, Isaac, and Jacob. And the pronoun for that God is "he." As if to assure us that the lopsidedly masculine language is intentional, the leadership in local congregations and national church organizations is also lopsidedly male. Despite the fact that many women and men have already exited from Christianity (and Judaism) because of such gender and sexual imbalance, the exclusiveness continues.[46]

Shortly after the publication of *The Divine Feminine*, Dr. Mollenkott received an angry letter from a woman who wrote, "How dare you refer to God as female! Don't you know that God is HOLY?" Virginia asked the woman to consider what she was saying about herself and about women in general: "If we are made in the image of a God who is holy, are we not also holy?" Others have tried to discount Dr. Mollenkott's work on inclusive language. "Various women and men have told me how 'trivial' the language issue is, but their flushed faces tell a different story."

Since the early 1970s, Dr. Mollenkott has been challenging the church to use inclusive language. She served on the translation committee of the National Council of Churches' Inclusive Language Lectionary and was a stylistic consultant for the New International Version of the Bible (NIV). She says that she did what she could on the NIV "to lighten the male God and human focus," but that she couldn't do much because of the translators' conservatism.

For more than forty years Dr. Mollenkott has been changing church and the wider culture through her writing and teaching about human equality, not only in her college classrooms but also in church conferences, seminaries, and guest lectureships. She has authored or co-authored thirteen books, including *Women, Men, and the Bible*; *The Divine Feminine*; *Godding: Human Responsibility and the Bible*; *Is the Homosexual My Neighbor? A Positive Christian Response*; *Sensuous Spirituality: Out from Fundamentalism*; *Omnigender*; and *Transgender Journeys*.[47]

Dr. Mollenkott's prophetic work for justice and equality has at times brought angry, violent threats. While serving on the Inclusive Language Lectionary Committee, she and other members of the committee received death threats. Bob Jones University, where she earned her undergraduate degree, calls her a "'demon' whom they hope God will 'destroy.'" Bob Jones University's hatred, she suspects, "is more about my lesbianism than my God-language, but they are interrelated since both undercut male supremacy."

Undaunted by threats and angry attacks, Dr. Mollenkott continues her work as a powerful voice for inclusive language as foundational to human equality and nonviolence. "We do not even grasp our own experience until we have language for it," she says. "For instance, I did not understand my own discomfort in wearing a skirt or dress until I learned the term 'transgender.' As long as our references to God are always to male or else to neutral imagery like 'rock,' men will continue to seem more in God's image than women. And worldwide abuses of women and girls will continue because females will be viewed as less god-like and less human than males."

Virginia gives specific, helpful suggestions for bringing language inclusive of all genders to the church. "Make no mistake: gender-neutral language for God does *not* dislocate assumptions about male primacy. It takes overt feminine pronouns and female or transgender metaphors for God to shock the mind into seeing the Holy One as anything but male, since the word 'God' is male-gender in the first place. Simply using the masculine term 'God' with the feminine pronoun 'She' already includes people who consider themselves neither entirely male/masculine nor entirely female/feminine but somewhere in between." She continues, "It is also important to point out the biblical fact that Adam was both male and female before Eve was divided off from 'his' side, and that God made both male and female in Her/His image and appointed both of them to be caretakers in charge of creation. When speaking of human beings, it is important to say 'people' rather than 'men and women'; but if you want to use the latter, you should say 'women and men and in-betweens,' or 'women and men and transgender people.' Alternating male and female God-imagery is the best we can do. And while the humanly divine Jesus is rightly referred to as 'he,' once Jesus has ascended and becomes the Christ within the Godhead, 'she' becomes appropriate as an aspect of the Divine Feminine. We women are part of Christ's Body just as much as men are, and our language should reflect that."

Gender-diverse language for the Divine brings many beneficial changes to the church, Dr. Mollenkott believes. "In the few places where diverse God-language is used regularly, women and transgender people are empowered to become more active leaders, and men are empowered to express their emotions and act on their generous desires to serve others. So everything looks and feels more Christ-like." This diverse language, she says, will also "tend to break down either-or hierarchies such as clergy versus laity."

Many gifts come through expanding our understanding of humanity as well as divinity, Virginia believes. "By revealing the dazzling diversity of creation's sex/gender continuum, the transgender movement is changing society's concept of what nature is, who or what God is, and what authentic human experience looks like."[48] She explains that those "who do not or cannot conform to society's false gender roles and rules are reclaiming 'queer' as a word about diversity that was previously used as a slur," and she names other gifts that queer people share with the world. She writes:

> By the circumstances of our queerness we have been forced to do a lot of introspection about the interconnectedness of sex, gender, justice, and spirituality. One of our greatest queer gifts to society is to help people overcome the gender stereotypes that alienate men from women, alienate almost everyone from their own bodies, and oppress women and girls all over the world. As the somewhat masculine mother of a son whom I dearly love, I resent that boys are still told that "real men don't cry" and "real men are always in control of every situation." What nonsense! And I grieve over the fact that around the world, women perform most of the hard labor but often

receive only whatever food is left after the men have eaten. In Africa, thousands of women are dying of AIDS because they have no right to refuse unprotected sex with husbands who are HIV positive. Such facts reveal that the binary gender construct does not merely differentiate men from women, but also elevates men above women. But because we queer people combine male and female traits in a multitude of ways, we offer society some visual and embodied assistance in putting aside such unjust perceptions and practices.[49]

Continuing to challenge our perceptions and expand our experiences, Dr. Mollenkott gives this expansive definition of "transgender": "most liberated people, heterosexual or otherwise, are transgender because they do not match society's traditional expectations for men and women."[50] In *Transgender Journeys* she writes: "The deepest oppression I have known stemmed not simply from being female, nor even from being lesbian, but from being a gender transgressor," meaning that as a "masculine woman" she "undercuts society's binary gender construct."[51]

Gender inclusiveness is closely connected to peace and social justice, Virginia asserts. "Only people who are at peace with themselves and their community can truly contribute to world peace and justice. But by being divisive in its language and policies, the church has (inadvertently?) become one of the most unjust and discord-producing aspects of modern society."

Because she "cannot stand the exclusively male God-language," Dr. Mollenkott does not attend church regularly. Instead, she finds her faith community in Evangelical & Ecumenical Women's Caucus (EEWC) and through other conferences and workshops. She says that her "greatest ongoing experience of community" has come from EEWC.[52] She also affirms, "I consider myself a member of the universal church of Christ's Body, in whom I live and move and have my being."

Dr. Mollenkott envisions a hopeful future for inclusion of the Divine Feminine and all genders within the church. "The future looks bright, but it may be a long time getting here. Our work is to keep on sharing what we have learned without letting ourselves get too attached to immediate results." Virginia is doing just that as she keeps on sharing in Divine Wisdom's work of equality, justice, and nonviolence.

Rev. Marcia C. Fleischman

Pastor, Broadway Church, Kansas City, Missouri

Holy Mama's Peaceful Vision

Inside Mother God lies a deep question.
Why are my women being rejected?
Why is the Feminine being repressed?
Who are the brave ones who will address
Why women are constantly being abused?
Why is equality being refused?...
Where are the bold ones who will play my song,
Which from the beginning I wanted all along?
Male and female dancing together,
Joined by love, respect and not a tether.
A grand symphony of musical light
Playing, displaying throughout the night.
The love of the creation with which I flow,
To join the chorus of joyous glow.
Who are the people who will hear my song?
With Mother God you always belong.
Within the Feminine you can't go wrong.
The balance so divinely choreographed,
The steps, the swaying—Glory at last!
Love always and forever,
Mom[53]

On the cover of Rev. Marcia C. Fleischman's empowering book *Wild Woman Theology: In the Arms of Loving Mother God* is an image of Mother God, a robust African American woman, holding the world in her hands and wearing a lime green T-shirt with infinity signs on it. Rev. Fleischman, who created this image and all the images in the book, describes her Mother God image: "The infinity designs speak of her infinite essence. Her face is only partially revealed to express the fact that God is always somewhat hidden. Her charm bracelet includes the symbols of major religions of the world. All these symbolize her loving creative energy from which all things are born. The sun and the moon rise over her shoulders."[54]

Female images of the Divine contribute to nonviolence and healing, Rev. Fleischman believes. "I think the Divine Feminine would help eliminate abuse," she says. "If people saw God as feminine, could they abuse women? I think the whole dynamic would change. The beginning of Genesis says that male and female are created in the divine image. To me, that's just basic. The Divine Feminine is very healing, and especially powerful for women. I'm an intelligent, well-educated person, and I struggle with self-esteem and equality issues. I think of the women who aren't as blessed as I am or as encouraged as I am and the women who are abused and beaten and have such a horrible time. To see that they are made in God's image is healing and empowering. Like in *The Secret Life of Bees*, the women find such a deep connection with the Black Madonna whom they worship."[55]

Marcia knows firsthand how healing the Divine Feminine is. When she was trying to recover from the abuse she had suffered from her boyfriend's and dad's messages about the second-class status of women, she had a mystical experience of the Female Divine. She was questioning whether or not she was really created in the divine image, and she heard Mother God say to her, "Just as your daughter looks like you, you look like me."

Growing up in a Presbyterian church in Lexington, Missouri, Marcia says she searched for the meaning of religious symbols. When she was twelve, she attended communicants' class that met every Saturday for a year. In the class each student had the opportunity to teach a lesson. As Marcia taught about a hymn she liked, "Sweet Hour of Prayer," she felt an energy flowing through her. Afterward, the minister said to her, "That was really inspired." At that time Marcia had no idea what he meant, but looking back on that experience, she says, "I think the presence of the Spirit was in what I was saying."

In college Marcia became involved in Campus Crusade for Christ. She soon felt conflicted because the people in Campus Crusade seemed to experience God so powerfully and yet they held the belief that "women were second class and had to obey men." For a while she thought she had "to buy these rules because these were the people who had Jesus."

After graduating from DePauw University, Marcia earned a master of education degree from the University of Missouri–Columbia. In her first teaching job in Bell City, Missouri, she also experienced gender discrimination. She learned that a man, who did not have a master's degree, had been offered the same job at the Bell City school for higher pay. When she confronted the school superintendent, he said that the man was offered a higher salary because he had a wife and child to support.

In the church Marcia also pushed for equality. At Broadway Baptist Church in Kansas City, she advocated for equal treatment of a woman hired as youth minister. When Marcia became one of the ministers at the church, she again raised the question of equality for women. "What is this I'm hearing that you guys get because you're ordained? You get housing allowance, and it's a big tax break. Women deserve the same thing." Soon after, the church ordained Marcia.

But then, the Kansas City Baptist Association threatened to oust Broadway Baptist Church for ordaining women. The Association met at First Baptist Church in Raytown, a suburb of Kansas City, to vote on whether or not Broadway would have to leave. The pastor of the Raytown church had been in Marcia's practicum class at seminary. He had asked the only other woman in the class about her ministry goals. She told him she wanted to be a missionary nurse, and he told her that was fine because she wouldn't need to be ordained. Also, he told her that he "just loved that cute little outfit she had on and that nail polish, that she looked so good." Marcia said she felt like vomiting. "It was just awful. He didn't even ask me what my ministry goals were."

At the Association meeting at the Raytown church, Rev. Fleischman sat in the front row with two other women ministers from Broadway. "It felt horrible to be sitting there like in a witch trial," she recalls. "We were being told we were 'less than' because we were ordained and we were women." The vote was taken, and Broadway stayed in the Association by four votes.

Not long after, when Broadway Baptist Church voted to become welcoming and affirming of LGBTQ persons, the Kansas City Baptist Association and the Southern Baptist Convention did oust the church. The church took "Baptist" out of its name, and it became "Broadway Church." Before this action, the church had become divided over the homosexuality issue, and Rev. Fleischman almost lost her job because of her prophetic stand for LGBTQ equality.

During this time, Marcia began experiencing shortness of breath. She learned that she had advanced primary pulmonary hypertension and would need a double lung transplant to survive. During the months of her rehabilitation from the transplant, she began to discover her artistic talent. "I started getting these visions of angels and drawing them and then painting them," she says. "Then I had an exhibit and sold the paintings and raised $5,000 for the church kitchen remodeling fund. I painted from 5:30 in the morning till midnight. I was high on prednisone and so energized." Some of her angel paintings remain on exhibit at the church. Before the Sunday morning worship service I attended at Broadway Church, Rev. Fleischman took me into the foyer of the church to show me these paintings. Amazed, I looked up at the magnificent angel paintings, ranging from six to twelve feet tall, in vibrant colors of purple, emerald, scarlet, violet, teal, gold, blue, and pink. The angel images represent diversity in race and gender, and have titles such as *Cloud of Witnesses, The Message Is Love, Faith,* and *Hope.*[56]

Because of her belief in the power of divine images to shape our actions, Rev. Fleischman is working on another book titled *What Does God Look Like?* "If we have a judgmental, punishing God, we become judgmental and punishing," she says. "If we have a kind and loving God, it's easier for us to be kind and loving." When I interviewed Marcia at Broadway Church, she showed me some of the pictures she's created for this book. One is of Mother God with Her head on a cloud like a pillow and Her feet on the earth. Ursa Major, the Great Bear constellation, is pulling a blanket of stars over Her as she dreams the solar system into existence. Some of the images come from the parables of Jesus: the loving Father, watching the prodigal son coming home; the Woman finding the lost coin; the Mother Hen with chicks. Marcia shows me her pictures of people worshiping, of the homeless in a soup kitchen, of a newborn baby, of nature experienced by a man out fishing, of a grandfather reading to his grandchild, of a loving mother holding her child, of the burning bush, of a woman looking in a mirror, of the infinite universe—all images of the Divine. It is vital to include female divine images to affirm the equal value of all people in the divine image, Rev. Fleischman believes. "If we could increase the image of Mother God, people could experience healing."

Increasing female divine names and images caused controversy at Broadway Church, and some people left the church. During this time in a Sunday worship service, people spontaneously began to change the words of one of the songs, replacing "He" with "She." With tears in her eyes Marcia says, "You could hear it across the whole congregation. They were singing about God as 'She.' It was a moment of joy. It was wonderful because it had been painful to go through that change. Now we could call God 'She' in worship services and be more open to embrace female images of God."

The Female Divine for Marcia is a deeply spiritual issue, as well as a social justice issue. "The first time the church sang 'In the Garden' with 'She' references, the Spirit touched me," Marcia says. "When we sang 'She,' I was bowled over, I started crying, and I couldn't stop. That image of 'She' being in the garden with me reminded me of my mother, who loved raising roses. The Divine Feminine has healing and empowering possibilities for women and for men. For our church the Divine Feminine has been a doorway opening us up to a larger vision, to seeing things in a larger way."

A mystical feminist, Rev. Fleischman talks freely about hearing from the Spirit and seeing visions. Her vision for the future of the Divine Feminine reaches from the church to encompass the whole world. Marcia envisions a Black Madonna, surrounded by rays of light, embracing the earth. "She is affecting all these different situations for women around the world. I see the images of all the abused girls being empowered. You can already see it happening through this whole thing called 'The Girl Effect.'[57] Girls and women who are educated give back to their communities. People are beginning to see how important it is to deal with women's issues."

Marcia's vision of the Black Madonna holding the earth recalls the picture on the cover of her book *Wild Woman Theology*. At the beginning of the book, "Holy Mama" proclaims a healing, peaceful vision:

No longer will my child live in defeat,
But always victorious
Always glorious
Coming always closer
To hear my heart beat.
Throbbing with life
And happiness always,
I will dry their tears,
Erase their fears,
For I am always near,
A loving mother,
A holy other,
A Holy Mama,
We know each other,
One another.[58]

In Her love letter at the end of the book, Mother God calls people to "create a cooperative global community." That is just what Rev. Marcia Fleischman is doing.

Part 7

Wisdom's Works of Expanding Spiritual Experience

Our Milky Way Galaxy contains more than a hundred billion stars. The Milky Way is just one of hundreds of billions of galaxies in the universe. Why would we ever try to limit the Maker of so vast a universe to a single gender? The majority of churches do, however, still limit Deity to a small set of male names and images, such as "Father," "King," and "Son." This exclusively male language obscures the fullness of the Divine.

Divine Mystery exceeds all our thoughts and words. All our language for divinity must then be metaphorical. We can never fully express Divine Reality in words or concepts. But we can begin with the wide variety of metaphors for Deity in scripture. Biblical revelation gives a multiplicity of divine images, female as well as male and nonhuman, to suggest the vastness and all-inclusiveness of our Maker. Including in our worship this wide variety of biblical images will expand and deepen our spiritual life.

Viewing Deity as including male and female and more releases all people to discover new power and to experience a deeper spirituality. Language that does not limit Deity opens our minds and spirits to new spiritual experiences. Our praying and meditating and creating expand into new dimensions. When we balance female and male images of the Divine, we come to a fuller understanding of who we are and experience greater freedom to fulfill our potential in the divine image. As we include Wisdom and other female personifications of the Divine, we open ourselves to the fullness of the Creative Spirit within us.

Star of Wonder, Star of Wisdom
(Sung to the tune of "O God Beyond All Praising")

Star of Wonder, Star of Wisdom, guide us to find Your way;
shine upon us with Your vision of bright and peaceful days.
Lead us forward through each challenge, helping all be fair and free,
as together we're creating a new reality.
All our gifts and graces blossom, fulfilling hopes and dreams;
then we marvel as the whole world alive with beauty gleams.

Star of Wonder, Star of Wisdom, illumine minds and hearts;
guide us on Your healing mission; Your radiant life impart.
Light new pathways for our journey, leading to creation new;
send Your truth expanding always to show a wider view.
Then all heaven and earth will open with possibility,
A whole universe before us, far more than we can see.[1]

Words © 2009 Jann Aldredge-Clanton   THAXTED

Deborah Hall

Lay Theologian; Founder of Sophia Sisters, Chandler, Arizona

Mother God Nurturing My Soul

"As a result of continued study and reading of works by feminist theologians, I realized that my lifelong struggle with low self-esteem stemmed from being raised in the church where men's stories were the ones written about in scripture and men were given leadership roles in the church. Connecting with the Divine Feminine allowed me to go deep within where I discovered my original goodness and unconditional love for myself."

Deborah Hall deepened her spiritual experience through discovering female divine images and women's stories in scripture. In religious studies courses at Arizona State University she had become aware of how women are "oppressed in the church and society." Later, her work as a counselor also helped her understand the impact of this oppression on her spirituality and that of other women.

Growing up in church, Deborah came to believe that "God the Father" was in charge of her life and the entire world. "I believed if I prayed to God, 'He' would answer my prayer because I was a faithful believer," she says. "This belief began to unravel when my mother died when I was twenty-three. She suffered from rheumatoid arthritis and was scheduled for joint replacement surgery that we prayed would help her walk again. Instead, she died of complications from the surgery. I struggled with the notion that the 'God in charge' would allow my mother to die."

Eight years later, Deborah suffered another tragic loss that also challenged her belief system. "Our infant son died a few days after his birth," she relates. "Again, we had cried out to God to save our baby. Where was God in all of this? As I searched for answers, my spiritual understanding deepened, leading to a 'revisioning' of God as 'One Who Is with Us in Our Suffering'—a nurturing God who suffers along with us."

After these difficult experiences, Deborah returned to college and took courses in communication studies and religious studies, including critical inquiry and gender inequity. She earned two degrees from Arizona State University: a bachelor of arts degree in communication studies and a master of counseling degree. Currently, she serves as an outpatient therapist at Mountain Health and Wellness in Apache Junction, Arizona.

As her spirituality continued to expand, Deborah dialogued with others about imagining the Divine as both female and male. "People would agree with me that God is not solely male," she recalls; "however, when I would suggest that we use feminine words such as 'Her' and 'She' in addition to male pronouns for God, they would say, 'Well, it isn't right to use male or female pronouns for God because God is really Spirit.'" Deborah spoke with her pastor about including female words for the Divine. She says that although he agreed that there is "feminine as well as masculine imagery for God in the Bible," he preached only one or two sermons a year with this feminine imagery. And the songs used in worship services "overwhelmingly contained masculine terms for God, including 'He,' 'His,' and 'Him,' as well as words such as 'King' and 'Ruler,' traditionally male terms."

Desiring to explore female divine names and images, Deborah began Sophia Sisters in her church. The group first studied the book *Learning a New Language: Speech about Women and God*, by Beverly Jane Phillips, who co-led the book study with Deborah.[2] Deborah describes how the group moved from the church to her home and changed to include worship: "Interestingly, when I approached church leadership about doing the book group, the book had to be 'reviewed' by the pastor, and I was cautioned that this group should not be a 'male-bashing' group," she recalls. "After we finished the book study, we wanted to continue meeting, so we now meet in my home. Others have joined us, and we now include a worship time with our book study. I yearned for worship using feminine pronouns and imagery for God, so I plan and lead the worship portion for our group. Our worship is based on the season of the year or what we are discussing from our book study and includes responsive readings, inclusive hymns, prayer, guided meditation, and communion." Here is an excerpt from "Celebration of Peace," a liturgy Deborah created for Sophia Sisters:

Call to Communion

Leader: Sisters in Christ-Sophia and women of peace, we commune together this evening remembering the words of Wisdom, Sophia, "Peace I leave you." In Ruah (Spirit), we work for peace in this world. As we eat this bread and drink this cup, may we walk in peace with one another.

Acts of Communion

(Each one takes a piece of bread.) "Take, eat the bread of new life." *(As the grape juice is passed around, dip the bread in the cup.)* "Drink the cup of the risen Christ-Sophia."

Leader: Through this communion ritual, Christ-Sophia offers us the gift of peace. Let the spirit of Wisdom rise up in each of us as we do justice, love kindness, and walk humbly with our God.

Deborah finally left her church but has not found another local church with inclusive worship. "Currently, I am not affiliated with a church locally. Although I tried to bring change to my local church, I grew weary of the patriarchal structure and language that permeate the church culture. I loved singing in the church choir; however, the language used in so many of the songs was patriarchal, and it became painful for me to sing them."

Now, in addition to worshiping with Sophia Sisters, Deborah is one of the long-distance members of Ebenezer/herchurch Lutheran in San Francisco. She says she joined Ebenezer/herchurch because of their emphasis on the Divine Feminine in worship. "When I worship there, I experience healing as the community offers 'a witness of holy nurture and inclusive justice.'"

Deborah elaborates on the importance of including female names and images of the Divine in worship: "The language and symbolism we use for God, or the Divine, defines for us who can be God-like or who can represent the Divine or divinity to others," she says. "When I was growing up, only men could do 'great things' for God, such as become pastors or hold an office in the church. If we speak of God using exclusively male imagery, females cannot identify this divine experience as belonging to us. As Mary Daly stated, 'If God is male, then male is God. The divine patriarch castrates women as long as He is allowed to live on in the human imagination.'"

Including the Divine Feminine in worship, Deborah asserts, will bring beneficial change to the church and the wider culture. "When we imagine God as Mother, for example, I believe we will be less inclined to send our young people off to war. We may be more inclined to dialogue ways to bring peace and understanding among people and nations."

In a "Meditation on Diversity," which she wrote for a Sophia Sisters worship service, Deborah elaborates on the benefits of gender-inclusive images of the Divine: "Patriarchy not only creates hierarchies, but at the same time attempts to consolidate and oppose difference and diversity. As feminists we need to embrace diversity … in nature, in each other, and in our beliefs. We can see a prime example with the current political scene. There is so much debate on who is a true Republican or Democrat and 'who toes the party line.' There is so much energy and money wasted. What would happen if more time were devoted to celebrating the uniqueness of each individual as a divine child of Christ-Sophia? I think of a mother who has two children and says, 'I love both of you just the same.' A mother knows that her children are very different from one another; however, she can love them both equally. This image of Mother God nurtures my soul!"

Expansive divine language and imagery, Deborah believes, will empower all people to "use their unique gifts to work for justice in society instead of being restricted by what is traditionally 'masculine' or 'feminine.'" Including female divine imagery will also give children the message "that females have abilities to lead and to be 'God-like,' and it is acceptable for males to support women in leadership."

It felt risky to start the Sophia Sisters group and to leave her local church, Deborah says. "It also seems risky to share my story with others because I fear being rejected. Many people I meet are so entrenched in patriarchy that in the beginning it is more about introducing the idea of the Divine Feminine and then inviting them to our group," she explains. "When I take the approach of dialoguing about inclusive symbolism, people are open to discussion; however, some do not come when invited."

At times Deborah becomes discouraged by the slowness of the education and "awakening" process. "I feel strongly, however, that there are many women who, like me, feel as though they do not 'fit' in the traditional church and are looking for something else. This convinces me that I must continue."

Deborah has found resources to meet the resistance and challenges that she faces as she transforms the language and symbolism of Christianity. "Spending time in meditation and prayer brings me inspiration and strength," she says. "I find that lighting candles and listening to music helps me connect to the Divine Feminine. My Sophia Sisters give me strength and encouragement through the struggle. Each time we meet I feel inspired to carry on. One of my gifts is being able to create and pull together worship based on a theme or topic of the week. Certain hymns, prayers, and scriptures come to mind that culminate in our celebration time."

Also rewarding to Deborah is that members from another group, called "Sophia Sisters Roundtable," join Sophia Sisters for a combined worship service every three months. "Many of the women have been hurt by patriarchy and have given up on organized church," she says. "Our time together brings healing and a renewed sense of empowerment 'to do justice, to love kindness, and to walk humbly with our God.'"

Deborah articulates her vision of the transformation the Divine Feminine will bring to the church. "My vision for the future of the Divine Feminine within the church is that it will be a diverse community where love, in the form of acceptance and understanding, is emphasized. When the institutional church was established some four hundred years after Christ's death, creeds and dogmas were established as a way to unify and consolidate beliefs. My hope is that this new movement of the Divine Feminine will be one in which the uniqueness of each person and her or his *experience* will be valued and celebrated." Deborah continues to use her creative, prophetic gifts to join Sophia Wisdom in making this inclusive, expansive vision a reality.

Rev. Larry E. Schultz

Composer; Minister of Music, Pullen Memorial Baptist Church,
Raleigh, North Carolina

Singing the Gospel of the Divine Feminine

"One of my passions is that expansive theology spreads and grows because of the benefits. It gives me purpose and meaning to have discovered the Divine Feminine and other theologies of inclusion. This is the Good News message for me now, a liberating message. The Divine Feminine opens up so much more in our imaging Mystery. There are ways of singing about the Divine that we haven't explored, like with transgender images. And what are the divine images on other planets? Perhaps there's a third gender out there, or four or five genders. It's very important for me now to balance images, to help interpret the feminine that was lost when patriarchy took over. And now string theory, the concept of all the particles of life being vibrating strings, opens new possibilities for music ministry. If we discovered what it means for us all to be musical beings, vibrating sound waves, how would that connect us with the universe?"

Rev. Larry E. Schultz's mission is expanding theology and spiritual-ity by creating music that includes female images of the Divine. "For me, the gospel to share is the Divine Feminine and expanding imagery and theology because of all the benefits for all people," he says. "For a long time I've known about abuse of women and girls.

My mother has been very involved with a battered women's shelter in Tulsa, Oklahoma, and I've heard her talking about that. I want to provide music resources that include female and male divine images so that all children grow up to know they're valued."

In providing this inclusive music, Rev. Schultz ventures where few ministers of music will go, altering the words of some well-loved familiar hymns that are not under copyright. For example, Larry modified "Wonderful Words of Life," to include Sophia Wisdom language:

> Wisdom graciously gives to all wonderful words of life;
> listen now to Her loving call, wonderful words of life.
> All so freely given, moving us to heaven;
> beautiful words, wonderful words, wonderful words of life.
>
> Sweetly echo Sophia's call, wonderful words of life;
> offer justice and peace to all, wonderful words of life.
> Wisdom-Guide and Savior, worship now and forever;
> beautiful words, wonderful words, wonderful words of life.[3]

Rev. Schultz even changed the "Gloria Patri" to the "Gloria Matri" and references to God as "He" to "She" in an anthem with regal images. "Many churches will just substitute 'God' for the word 'He' in an anthem or hymn," he says. "I've found that you end up singing such a guttural word, 'God, God, God,' back to back, and it's just not pleasing poetry. And the word 'God' has male connotations. So a wonderful thing we've done, out of a sense of balance, is not to change 'He' to 'God,' but to change 'He' to 'She.' In this entire anthem I changed every 'He' to 'She.' It was an anthem that used psalm-like words: 'Worship God in majesty,' and 'Worship God who rides on the wings of the wind.' I thought, 'That's Mother Eagle who rides on the wings of the wind.' So it made utmost sense to sing 'She': 'She rides on the wings of the wind'; 'She reigns in glory and in majesty.' We ended with the 'Gloria Matri': 'Glory be to the Mother and to the Christ and to the Holy Spirit; as it was in the beginning, is now and ever shall be, world without end.'"

Larry's story begins quite literally in church. He was born on a Sunday night when his three sisters were attending the worship service at their church, Phoenix Avenue Baptist in Tulsa, Oklahoma. "My mother and father were at the hospital," Larry says. "My sisters tell the story that right as the service was coming to an end, the phone rang. Everyone in the church could hear the phone ring, because it was in the pastor's study, which was behind the sanctuary off the foyer. The pastor asked the person who prayed the longest closing prayers to pray so that he could run back to the phone during the benediction. My sisters knew that call had to be from the hospital, so they were anxiously sitting there, and the man was praying and praying his lengthy prayer. As soon as he said, 'Amen,' from the back of the church the pastor yelled out, 'It's a boy!'" Larry laughs and says, "And I've been in the church ever since."

Although a deacon in their church, his father worked more behind the scenes than up front. Larry describes him as a "very diligent, gentle, patient person," working as a stationary engineer in various buildings in downtown Tulsa and then for American Airlines, and as a volunteer doing handyman jobs for people in the church. Larry saw his mother as a "leader, a very organized, upfront person" in the church and community. "I did not grow up in a church that had a woman on the staff as a minister," he says. "My mother is probably the first woman I saw in the pulpit, because she was the director of the Vacation Bible School for years. My mother is a very strong woman." These experiences of his mother and father influence the way Larry images the Divine: "Now as we think about creating hymn texts that speak of God in male terms as very gentle and in female terms as very strong, I have this picture in my home."

A theme in Larry's story is that he has always been ahead of his time and advanced for his age. When Larry was only thirteen, he made a commitment to church music ministry and began leading revivals for churches throughout Oklahoma. When he was just sixteen, he became part-time minister of music at Phoenix Avenue Baptist Church and was ordained to ministry. While he was high school, Larry won his first music composition contest.

In addition to his family, professors at Oklahoma Baptist University and Southern Baptist Theological Seminary influenced Larry's openness to women as pastors and to inclusive divine imagery. One of his seminary professors was Dr. Molly Marshall, who was later forced to resign when fundamentalists took over the seminary and objected to her as an ordained pastor. "I think what formed me most at Southern Seminary was the fundamentalist takeover of the Southern Baptist Convention," Larry says. "The Bible was being used as a weapon to hurt others, and those I saw being hurt were women professors, like Dr. Molly Marshall. My support of women in ministry connected also with my upbringing in my family, knowing that women were strong leaders in the church. I think that would eventually connect with my supporting worship of the Divine Feminine."

Another formative experience for Larry in seminary was studying the distinction between the Jesus of history and the Christ of faith. "We studied Albert Schweitzer's book, *The Quest of the Historical Jesus*," Larry recalls.[4] "My Christology began to change. Most of the hymns I sang growing up equated Jesus to God. Now I've come to the place where I say the 'God in Jesus.' It's helpful to me when we want to sing of God as 'She' or as *Ruah* or with other female names, that Christian worship doesn't have to be tied up in the male Jesus of history, but the God in Jesus, which is the God in us, expressed in so many ways."

At Southern Seminary Larry met his future wife, Cindy. "I was in awe of Cindy for many reasons, especially for her gifts," he says. "We have shared a partnership in ministry and in life. So I could easily love a Divine Feminine God, loving Cindy as I do. And then later when I came to understand parenthood, I could see God as Parent. And the image of God as Friend comes to life for me, because Cindy and I have always been best friends. Cindy and my children, Ryan and Kelly, instill in me the importance of balancing male and female divine images."

Many ministers of music are even more resistant to inclusive language than pastors because of the difficult tasks of finding inclusive anthems and hymns, of changing existing exclusive words, and of creating new hymn texts. Also, ministers of music often face copyright issues when trying to change words in more recent music as well as the resistance of choir members and congregations to singing new words. "You have to be brave enough and find ways to bring inclusive music to worship," Larry says.

At First Baptist Church in Walterboro, South Carolina, Rev. Schultz began by selecting hymns with gender-neutral language and highlighting the few female images in the hymnal. At First Baptist Church in Greenwood, South Carolina, he used Brian Wren's "Bring Many Names" and other hymns that incorporated some female divine imagery. Larry got complaints that he was "just trying to be politically correct." He says that some people didn't understand that his "emphasis on language in hymns was for reasons of theology and more expansive worship."

While minister of music at the Greenwood church, Rev. Schultz became more active in the Cooperative Baptist Fellowship (CBF), one of the groups that broke away from the Southern Baptist Convention. But when the CBF voted to exclude LGBTQ people, Larry left CBF. "I remember being almost physically sick because that's how the Southern Baptist Convention had been treating people," he recalls. "At the end of that meeting, I stood up and recited the passage that in Christ there is 'neither male nor female, Jew nor Greek, slave nor free,' adding 'in Christ there's neither heterosexual nor homosexual, for we are all one in Christ Jesus.'"

A year later, Rev. Schultz became minister of music at Pullen Memorial Baptist Church. Larry was delighted that Pullen had taken a stand, ten years earlier, to endorse acceptance of LGBTQ people and their full participation in the life and work of the church. Because of that stand, Pullen was ousted from the Raleigh Baptist Association, the Baptist State Convention of North Carolina, and the Southern Baptist Convention. At Pullen Larry has also found openness to inclusion of female images of the Divine in worship. He finds fulfillment in creating new music for Pullen and for a wider audience through his publications. "It's fulfilling to spread the good word, to bring the Divine Feminine and other expansive imagery to people," Larry says. "We remember words we sing more easily than words we hear or speak. That's one reason I've gravitated toward writing for children." Indeed, an experience with his own children reinforced Larry's determination to provide children female and male divine images to sing. Larry, Kelly, and Ryan were riding in the car, listening to a musical setting of *Old Turtle*, in which various animals and elements of nature argue about who God is.[5]

"She is a great tree!" sang the willow tree.

"That's my part!" Kelly, three years old at the time, joyfully exclaimed.

Ryan, who was seven, responded to the description of God as a growling male bear.

"When she was only three, my daughter had identified with a feminine image of God, and it made her exuberant," Larry says. "This experience with my daughter and son affirmed that children delight in the realization that God is like them and that they are made in the divine image. This understanding gives each child a deep sense of self-worth. Kelly and Ryan related to images of God whose gender matched their own, while learning that the divine image was also in others different from them."

About a year later, Larry jumped at the opportunity to write a children's musical that included female and male divine images. "*Imagine God!* has been one of the most fulfilling creations to get out there, and Choristers Guild is such a highly respected publisher," he says.[6] "I believe it's important not just for adults to include the Divine Feminine and other expansive imagery, but that we bless our children with it, instill in them at the earliest ages. Then it becomes a natural and meaningful expression for them. One of the reasons for our *Sing and Dance and Play with Joy! Inclusive Songs for Young Children* is that I've not found any other music resources for that age group with the Divine Feminine and other open, inclusive theologies."[7]

Rev. Schultz blesses children and adults through his prophetic, creative works and through the artistry and passion with which he conducts choirs and congregations. He affirms his continued openness to expanding his creativity and spirituality. "The Divine Feminine opened up a whole new world, and I realized that God is more than just a grandfatherly figure rocking up there in the clouds somewhere. Now I wonder, 'Who is the God we worship in Her/His fullness?' I've stuck with my initial calling to music ministry, but I've had to keep finding new expressions of it to have it be authentic. I keep discovering these new paths, and the Divine Feminine has been a very big part of that."

Rev. Beverly Jane Phillips

Presbyterian Minister; Author

Learning a New Language for the Divine

"Nothing we can say about God will ever be adequate to describe the burning mystery which is the Divine. But opening up our vocabulary to include feminine names and pronouns will bring a dimension to our understanding of God that has been tragically neglected. The idea of SHE WHO IS brings to bear all the loving, care-giving, wisdom-supplying richness of the female created in God's image. The feminine in God is a reality we must accept if justice for all is to prevail in the world. We must learn a new language."[8]

Rev. Beverly Jane Phillips challenges us to expand our spiritual understanding through including female names for the Divine. She states that her purpose for writing her book *Learning a New Language* was "to bring theology inclusive of the Divine Feminine to the church and to the wider culture." She explains the book's title:

Thinking and speaking of God using inclusive words and metaphors is akin to learning a new language. New words must be learned and used. Old words must be used in new ways. This is an emotional as well as an intellectual activity. Learning and using these new words is difficult even for people who believe it is high time we acknowledge that the flourishing of women, and thereby the flourishing of men, children and creation, depends upon the inclusion of women in the naming of God and in all other ways as equal in value with men.[9]

Growing up in First Presbyterian Church of Hastings, Nebraska, Beverly describes her spiritual background as "rich and open." Two years after the Presbyterian Church decided to ordain women, Beverly told her pastor that God had called her to the ministry. He responded, "If God has called you to the ministry, far be it from me to stand in your way." This pastor, her dad, and two youth pastors were strong supporters as she followed her call to ministry.

Beverly found this same openness at Hastings College, a Christian liberal arts school, and at San Francisco Theological Seminary. She was the only woman in her class in seminary and was one of the first women at the seminary to receive a bachelor of divinity degree, later called a master of divinity degree. She recalls that at first most of the men in her seminary class were "a little amused" by her presence there, but they soon learned that she "meant business." In seminary she met her future husband, Norm, now a retired Presbyterian pastor. She celebrates that he has become one of her strongest supporters "in using feminine images for God and in calling God 'She.'"

After graduating from seminary, Beverly could not be ordained because she did not have a call to a church position. So she served as the minister's wife in churches Norm pastored in Nebraska and Kansas. It was not until twenty-eight years after she graduated from seminary that Beverly was ordained as a Minister of Word and Sacrament in the Presbyterian Church (USA) to be the Hunger Action Enabler for the Presbytery of Chicago. An activist on issues of hunger and poverty, Rev. Phillips later served in the position of regional organizer for Bread for the World for Illinois, Indiana, and Missouri.

"The years of raising our two adopted children enriched my spiritual journey not only because they were a gift of God to us, but also because of their chronic diseases," Beverly says. "We discovered Jim's asthma when he was two years old, and Nancy's type 1 diabetes manifested when she was eight. As my prayers to God for their healing went unanswered, I began to write daily in a prayer journal. My book *From Heaven to My Heart* not only contains prayers from almost forty years of daily journaling but also shows the movement of my faith experience.[10]

It illustrates how a woman who fell to her knees to beg a male God for favors changed to a woman who feels the very presence of Sophia God in her heart."

This dramatic change began when Rev. Phillips discovered Elizabeth Johnson's *She Who Is: The Mystery of God in Feminist Theological Discourse*.[11] "My very spirit was transformed by her theology of the Divine Feminine," Beverly recalls. "As I was reading, the thought kept coming to me that all women whom I had led in retreats and classes *needed* to think about these truths."

So Rev. Phillips decided to make *She Who Is* more accessible to laypeople. "I wrote to Elizabeth Johnson and asked if she would give me permission to write a paraphrase of her book," Beverly explains. "Dr. Johnson was delighted! She said there is a desperate need for interpreters between academia and people in the pews. She gave me permission to write a book about her book. I soon discovered that paraphrase was not only unworkable, but not helpful." In *Learning a New Language* Beverly includes the main ideas from each chapter of *She Who Is*, along with her own insights and experiences. She summarizes some of the main points in *Learning a New Language*: "It emphasizes the fact that the names we call God not only convey the kind of God we worship but in turn define how we act. I not only define feminist theology but also describe the theology that has made an idol of maleness. Any names we use for God are metaphors; human beings can never find or create a word that describes God in Her wholeness. Scripture and classical theology can be legitimately understood as descriptive of a feminine God as much as a male God. God does not cause our suffering for some reason unknown to us, but She suffers through our hard times with us."

The study of *Learning a New Language* led to the formation of two Sophia Sisters groups in Arizona—one in Phoenix and one in Chandler. The Phoenix group continues to discuss feminist theology books, and the Chandler group, founded by Deborah Hall (see page 181), also includes worship services. Beverly participates in both groups. The two groups have met together for worship and plan to continue these joint worship services.

Rev. Phillips also brings language inclusive of the Female Divine into her leadership of Bible studies and worship services for Presbyterian

Women in her congregation and in the Presbytery of Grand Canyon. And she was successful in encouraging her pastor to address prayers to "Mother/Father God" in worship services. "I am always on the lookout for women and men who will study *Learning a New Language* together and discuss the ideas in it," she says. "They are hard to find, but I know there are women especially who have a longing in their spirit for the Divine Feminine. I think most of them don't even know such a thing is possible."

In writing and promoting *Learning a New Language*, Rev. Phillips has taken risks and met resistance. At Christian conferences some people want to argue with her, she says, but "most ignore me and my book." She finds inspiration and strength for the challenges through her practice of daily prayer. *From Heaven to My Heart*, drawn from her prayer journals, includes prayers with expansive language for the Divine, such as these:

Dear Lord our God Sophia and Precious Mother, Christ Sophia,
Spirit Sophia, you are so great! How great You are
and Your greatness is unsearchable!
You are love. You are love shared!
Love connecting!
Love growing!
Love creating!
Love amazing!
Love blessing!
Love elating!
Love discovering!
Love unending!
Love abounding!
Love prevailing![12]

Christ-Sophia, Nowhere I go does anyone talk feminist theology. Everyone is trying to put forth ideas that will save the church and save the world, but none of them are feminist ideas. When I see starving children I regret that I am no longer doing anything to help them. And then I think that You are calling me to preach and proclaim that Your nature is male and female. I believe that is the way the church and the world will be saved.[13]

Learning a new language that includes female names for the Divine is vital to justice and peace as well as to expanding spirituality, Rev. Phillips believes. "Language and symbolism are important enough to go to all the effort to change two thousand years of church tradition because the world and all its peoples and creatures and natural beauties would be treated better if our language about God affirmed the fact that God cannot be named by masculine names alone," she says. "Whatever religion we adhere to, naming God is the most important activity we engage in. However we name God, that name affects our behavior. Thus, when God is always and only masculine, we treat all things masculine as superior not only to women but to all of nature as well. That gives males power to subordinate women and all things to their own will. When God is seen as feminine, the playing field is evened out and abuse of women, children, and nature is lessened. If feminine images as well as male can be used for God, all of creation would flourish in ways that are not possible when God is only male. Regarding God exclusively as male sets up a hierarchy of importance and power. Mary Daly said it best, 'If God is male, then the male is God.' That very concept makes it legitimate for men to rule with an iron fist over women, children, and all creation. What the Godlike male deems right is what is right, from denying women the right to choice about their bodies to clear cutting of trees in order to mine precious metals, from using children as laborers to polluting the air and water of the whole earth. Using feminine divine images would make God's good creation flourish."

Including female names and images of the Divine will make a big difference for all people and all creation, Rev. Phillips writes:

> Being able to speak of God with feminine names can have long-term benefits not only for women but for children and men and all of creation. It is true for us as it has been for all people of all ages that how we refer to God sets the standard for our behavior. The standard that is set by using masculine names exclusively for God sets up a hierarchy in which men are more privileged than women, because when God is always "he" men are seen as more Godlike. In this hierarchy, women, children, and nature are subject to men and all the rest of creation is subject to men. This arrangement needs to be changed if people and creation are to live in peace and wholeness.[14]

Rev. Phillips articulates an expansive, hope-filled vision of the transformation that will come through the balance of female and male images of the Divine in worship. "Worshiping God in God's fullness as masculine and feminine would transform the world into a place where no one is at the top and no one is at the bottom because the idea and practice of hierarchy would not exist; women would rule, study, and work with men in equity because the value of each would be recognized; each child would be treated like the angel spirit she is because Mother God cherishes each one of Her children; there would be no wars because Mother God would send belligerent children to their rooms to talk it over before they hurt each other and innocents; there would be no hunger because Mother/Father God would insist that all the food be shared equally; there would be no prisons because She would see each person as an individual and provide for their spiritual needs; there would be no guns because no one would need to take anything away from anyone else; women's reproductive health would take precedence over rigid theological beliefs; mentally challenged people would be cherished; there would be no rape and abuse of women and children; the beautiful places in nature would be preserved and treated as sacred," Beverly explains. "These results all come from the heart of a loving Mother. Over the generations people have had visions of utopias and tried to build them. None of them worked for very long at least partly because they were designed with a male God image in mind. My utopia would succeed because the values and actions would center on a Divine Parent, Mother/Father whose only concern would be to have a healthy, happy, thriving family."

Through her prophetic writing and teaching and advocacy, Rev. Phillips continues to join Sophia Wisdom in working to make this vision reality. "If I were an artist I would repaint the picture of Christ standing in the garden knocking at the door of the heart. It would depict me standing, knocking at the door of my heart. I need to be let into the place in my heart where Sophia already dwells and has always dwelt. I look forward with excitement and some holy fear as to where She is calling me."

Rev. Alice D. Martin

Healer, San Francisco, California

Divinity Within and Around All

"Including multicultural female divine imagery in church
offers people expanded symbolism, giving them a deeper
understanding of the divinity within themselves and
around them. I feel that wider varieties of divine symbols
and names give a greater access to people. Exposing
people to a multitude of images gives them a choice and
a way to connect to the Divine that feels appropriate for
them. It also helps in bringing up a dialogue of diversity
and understanding of different cultures. It is part of the
inclusiveness trait that is inherently connected to opening
oneself to the Feminine Divine and validating the feminine
energy that runs through each of us."

Rev. Alice D. Martin reclaims the power of multicultural female
divine images to deepen and expand spiritual experience. These
images, she says, have been suppressed and/or forgotten. "Worship of
the Feminine Divine was very much prevalent for 35,000 years or so
before Christianity emerged. A lot of the symbols and language used by
the early Gnostic Christians, and even by the ancient Israelites, included
the Feminine Divine. But as patriarchy fully took over, the inclusive and
enlightening language was dropped or changed."

Alice grew up in the Catholic Church until at the age of fourteen
she "renounced Christianity." She explains: "Because of the hypocritical nature of the church and its violent history, I grew despondent and
wary of the preaching from the male clergy." But she continued to

find the gospels of the Christian Scriptures inspiring. The inclusivity, tolerance, and forgiveness she found in Jesus's preaching and parables "resonated and spoke truth" to her. "As I got older, I remembered and admired those things about the Bible, while wanting nothing to do with a Christian church."

Four years ago Alice started feeling drawn to images of Mother Mary. "I didn't understand this as I felt I wasn't a part of the Christian religion anymore, but as things in my life became rougher I felt a yearning for a Mother image," she says. "Most of the time, I would ignore this calling, but every once in a while I would pause by a statue of Mary or pay more attention to Goddess imagery and information that came my way. When things got worse for me, I would have mental images pop up of the Mother holding me for comfort and healing."

Alice describes her healing from an "emotional breakdown" through female divine images in her meditation and through finding Ebenezer/herchurch Lutheran. "Images of the Feminine Divine grew stronger, and finally I went to a Goddess Rosary at herchurch," she recalls. "When I walked into the sanctuary for the first time, I could immediately feel a presence of 'mother' energy that was warm, nurturing, compassionate, and healing. Soon after that, I started attending herchurch on a regular basis and became an involved council member. Herchurch has been critical in providing me a place of worship of the Feminine Divine that still has a familiar structure of Christianity without the patriarchal baggage."

Her healing from an emotional breakdown began a "spiritual emergence," Alice says, that resulted in her completion of a two-year program at a meditation and healing school. The school included a ministers' workshop, as well as meditation workshops, that led to her ordination as a minister. Rev. Martin became an "intuitive healer" as she learned to "see energy" and to heal herself and "help facilitate the healing of others." She is pursuing an MA in philosophy and religion with an emphasis in women's spirituality at California Institute of Integral Studies (CIIS), and is considering going on to earn a doctorate. Her work at CIIS has revealed that her life path could lead to being a "teacher and healer in the area of social justice."

Rev. Martin finds deep reward in contributing her healing gifts to the church and beyond. At Ebenezer/herchurch Lutheran she brings creative energy to worship services through taking part in the drumming circle. "When I use my gifts and talents to help enhance the experience and growth of herchurch, there is a powerful sense of accomplishment and being a part of something bigger than myself," she says. "Also, when I perform a healing and I see the immediate shift in energy for that person. In a direct way, helping others heal themselves also helps heal me and gives me new insight to my connection with the universe."

While she knows that her healing ministry will take her to places and people not open to inclusion of female images of the Divine, Alice celebrates the freedom and inclusiveness of worship she now experiences at Ebenezer/herchurch Lutheran. "Although I feel I am in a cozy spot for my current practice, I know that eventually my life path will take me to places where openly worshiping the Feminine Divine is an anathema," she says.

Recently Alice wrote a critical essay on the systematic oppression and controlling of the Feminine Divine by patriarchal economic, religious, and social institutions. "When patriarchy was gaining a foothold, about five thousand years ago, there was resistance and rebellion in taking away the Mother Goddess," she states. "The image of the Feminine Divine seems so ingrained in humanity that even under the most brutal conditions of oppression She still manifests somehow in our collective consciousness. This is why Mother Mary, in the Christian religion, is so revered. It is a way to access Mother Goddess while under the thumb of patriarchy."

Including female names and images of the Divine in church will change the wider culture, Rev. Martin asserts. "Because the Feminine Divine is oppressed in this world, feminine energy—with traits of compassion, nurturing, creating, and community—is oppressed. Therefore everyone, including straight white men, suffers to some degree. Creating ways to allow a greater number of people access or a means to connect to the Feminine Divine and validate the Feminine Divine within each of us will consequently bring about a shift of consciousness to tolerance, social justice, and respect for the earth and her resources. In my opinion, it is already happening, but the stranglehold that patriarchy has on world power is tough to overcome."

Among the female divine names Rev. Martin cites that resonate with her are these:

Mother God—The word "God" has a lot of masculine energy around it with some oppressive connotations to it. Having the word "Mother" in front of "God" reclaims Her role as Creator while tempering and honoring the Masculine Divine.

Gaia—This is Mother Earth. Bringing this name into the mix, I feel, helps us remember She who physically nourishes us and helps us thrive.

Grandmother—I feel we need, as a society and spiritually, to relearn our respect for the Crone. The image of the Crone or Wise Woman has been severely damaged ever since the start of the witch burnings in the fifteenth century. The Crone has much wisdom and gifts and talents to share with us. We miss out on extreme healing and learning opportunities when we belittle her as too old and addled or evil and conniving.

Rev. Martin acknowledges that she will face resistance to her expansive, inclusive spirituality. "As I continue my studies and take advantage of opportunities, like this interview, to talk about the importance of validating and honoring the Feminine Divine, I know I will come up against resistance and intolerance," she says. "There are many spiritual leaders who are taking risks that are helping to lay down a stronger foundation for whatever risks and inroads I make in the future. Right now, I am in a place of gratitude and acknowledgment for those who have taken up the challenges of bringing the Feminine Divine into the church."

By providing a model for bringing multicultural female images of the Divine into the church, Ebenezer/herchurch Lutheran gives Alice a faith community conducive to her spiritual exploration and growth as a minister. "This church is a structured Christian framework that is fluid and open enough to allow me to explore my faith and grow in ways that are appropriate for me," she says. "Faith-wise, herchurch is my home. I think it is a model for allowing multicultural images of the Feminine Divine while keeping what I consider the best of Christian traditions, whether reclaimed from the Gnostics or highlighted from the Lutheran tradition. Herchurch is an incredibly nurturing environment that encourages exploration of the Feminine Divine at your own pace and in a way that is appropriate for you. When I do begin to branch out as teacher/healer/preacher, I hope to embody this same type of philosophy in my future interactions. My part right now has been to add my ability as an intuitive healer to our congregation. My hope is to help expand the self-awareness of others and provide access to another approach to healing and self-empowerment."

Strength and inspiration for her ministry also come from her training at the meditation school, where Alice learned to "ground, center, and validate" herself. "It sounds a bit simple, but feeling my connection to the planet and validating my permission to be here helped give me access to the presence of the Feminine Divine, which in turn gives me greater strength and nurturing," she says. "It is hard to accept and feel love and strength when you don't love yourself and feel you will fail. Going inward and being fully present with whatever is going on in the moment helps give me access to the Divine so that I can seize inspiration and opportunities that may not be present otherwise."

Rev. Martin envisions the healing that will come to the world through the Female Divine. "In my spiritual experience, Mother is the Creator and Source," she says. "And while I don't think that the Feminine Divine is greater than the Masculine, I would like to envision more of an emphasis placed on the Feminine Divine to help heal and bring greater awareness to compassion, forgiveness, and nonjudgment. The Feminine and Masculine Divine together equal our existence and our ability to evolve. They are yin and yang; one cannot exist without the other, and there is always a striving for balance. Right now in this age, we are out of balance with too much masculine energy (patriarchy); placing emphasis on the Feminine Divine will help bring our collective spiritual growth more into balance." Alice continues to contribute her creative, healing gifts to fulfill this vision.

Part 8

Wisdom's Works of Interfaith Collaboration

As Wisdom guides on ever-expanding paths, She calls people of diverse religious and spiritual traditions to work together for justice and peace. When we join Wisdom's work of taking down divisive walls, we discover our common values and the power of our combined efforts to transform our world. Working together, with our diverse gifts and traditions, we can do the work of Wisdom in ways far beyond what any religious group can do alone. In a world of wars and violence, oppression and brokenness, we can join together as sisters and brothers from many religions to bring peace and wholeness. Divine Wisdom unites us to work for justice for people of all races, genders, classes, sexual orientations, and abilities. She brings us together to care for the earth. Divine Wisdom unites us to bring healing to all people and all creation.

Wisdom and other female personifications of the Divine form a foundation for interfaith collaboration. Wisdom is an ancient divine image, common to many religious traditions. "Wisdom" is *Hokmah* in Hebrew, *Hikmah* in Arabic, and *Sophia* in Greek. She comes as Kwan Yin and Tara in Asian spiritual traditions, as the Black Madonna in Catholic traditions, and as Isis in Egyptian traditions.

Existing before all religions, Divine Wisdom took part in creation. The Hebrew Bible records Wisdom saying, "Ages ago I was set up, at the first, before the beginning of the earth."[1] She guides people of all spiritual traditions to work together to restore creation by the power of Sister-Brother Spirit within us.

We Long to Dwell in Unity

(Sung to the tune of "Though I May Speak with Bravest Fire")

We long to dwell in unity,
our varied gifts in harmony;
come, Sister-Brother Spirit, come,
and show the way to make us one.

The Spirit lives within us all,
and helps us claim our sacred call;
we join to heal divisive ways,
creating fair and peaceful days.

We shall go out in hope and peace;
our finest gifts will be released.
Together joyful songs we raise,
our Brother-Sister Spirit praise.[2]

Words © 2010 Jann Aldredge-Clanton   O WALY WALY

Dr. Chung Hyun Kyung

Lay Theologian of the Presbyterian Church of Korea;
Associate Professor of Ecumenical Studies, Union Theological Seminary

The Great Mother of All People

> "It is so easy to connect and collaborate with the Divine
> Feminine in my interfaith work because every deep
> spiritual tradition has their own Great Mother, the Divine
> Feminine. And Earth, Gaia, is our mother. We are all
> earthlings; we are sisters and brothers who came from one
> Great Mother."

Dr. Chung Hyun Kyung celebrates the contribution of female images of the Divine to interfaith collaboration.[3] She especially
sees the connection between the Holy Spirit and Kwan Yin as bridg-
ing Christianity and Asian religious traditions. In an address titled
"Welcome the Spirit; Hear Her Cries," delivered at a World Council
of Churches Assembly, Dr. Chung proclaims:

> For me the image of the Holy Spirit comes from the image of Kwan
> Yin. She is venerated as goddess of compassion and wisdom by East
> Asian women's popular religiosity. Her compassion for all suffering
> living beings makes Her stay in this world enabling other living be-
> ings to achieve enlightenment. Her compassionate wisdom heals all
> forms of life and empowers them to swim to the shore of Nirvana.
> She waits and waits until the whole universe—people, trees, birds,
> mountains, air, water—becomes enlightened. They can then go to
> Nirvana together where they can live collectively in eternal wisdom
> and compassion. Perhaps this might also be a feminine image of

the Christ who is the firstborn among us, one who goes before and brings others with her?[4]

She holds up a picture of Kwan Yin and says, "This is my Holy Spirit. The Holy Spirit hears the cries of people, exactly what Kwan Yin does."

After her address Dr. Chung responded to accusations of being a syncretist, of combining Christian teachings with elements of other faith traditions. In her response she challenged Western values imposed on the developing world:

> You are right, I am a syncretist, but so are you. I know I am a syncretist, but you don't know you are a syncretist because you have hegemonic power. Non-Christian cultures, when they try to interpret the gospel out of their life experience, they are syncretists! But they are just being true to their identity, history and culture. I think in order to really heal the world we need the "wisdom of darkness." This can be the Third World, dark people, women, or our "shadows"—all the things we do not want to confront within ourselves, so we project them onto others and call them terrorists. So, I think that we need "endarkenment" for a while, not enlightenment, to heal the world.[5]

Growing up in Korea, Hyun Kyung began to raise questions about economic justice that would later lead to her healing work. When she was ten years old, her father had to declare bankruptcy and move the family to a poor neighborhood. Through diligent study and determination, she did so well in school that she got into the most prestigious high school in Korea, where her good grades led her to an excellent college. In college Hyun Kyung became involved in the Korean student movement and for the first time "felt proud of coming from an economically deprived family."[6] In this movement she discovered some of the realities of the developing world. "I learned the nature of colonialism and neo-colonialism, which were the causes of the chronic suffering of our people. I began to realize that the poverty around me was not the result of bad luck or laziness but due to unequal power relationships among people, institutions, and nations."[7]

After earning BA and MA degrees from Ewha Women's University in Seoul, Hyun Kyung came to the United States to study theology. She earned an MDiv degree from the School of Theology at Claremont, a diploma from the Women's Theological Center in Boston, and a PhD from Union Theological Seminary in New York. Currently, in addition to serving as an associate professor of ecumenical studies at Union, Dr. Chung is a lay theologian of the Presbyterian Church of Korea and a Buddhist dharma teacher. She sees herself as an "intellectual, political, and spiritual shaman-artist" who tries "to express the Divine Feminine rather than explain about Her and Her power."

I heard Dr. Chung speak at a Faith and Feminism, Womanist, Mujerista Conference at Ebenezer/herchurch Lutheran in San Francisco. She fills the sanctuary with her gracious, compassionate, wise words and presence, embodying the Divine Feminine whom she describes. Hyun Kyung tells of a vision of the Divine Feminine that came to her when she was working toward her PhD at Union Theological Seminary. She had been deeply conflicted because she had wanted to write her dissertation on Asian feminist liberation theology, but felt she had to write it on "dead European men" in order to get the degree. The Holy Spirit, or "Kwan Yin," came to her in this time of crisis, helping her finish the dissertation in three months so that she could receive her PhD and then later write on Asian feminist liberation theology. "The Buddhist goddess of compassion came to this Christian theologian," Dr. Chung says. She explains that Kwan Yin gives her power in other life crises, telling her, "I am you, and you are me; there is no difference." Dr. Chung also connects the Divine Feminine with Divine Love, that "original Love, creating everything and making everything possible." She states that "people are longing for the Divine Feminine" to bring more peace and justice to the world. She sees hopeful signs of change by noting that people are turning away from "colonialism, imperialism, and American empire and sense of exceptionalism" and growing in awareness that the earth is not "an object to explore and exploit" but "the body of God, our mother, our friend, our teacher." The "rise of the Divine Feminine," Hyun Kyung says, is connected to ecological, peace, economic justice, and anti-imperialistic movements. She celebrates the "Divine Feminine dwelling in earth," bringing "ecojustice in the world."

Dr. Chung identifies herself as a feminist, an ecofeminist, and a "salimist," a Korean word that means "to make things alive, to give life, to nurture and care for life." She says that Asian women and women in all cultures need to define feminism for themselves:

> Every feminist movement must have its own interpretation—like movements for democracy. We don't want the hierarchy. But it manifests in different ways from culture to culture, and women in every culture have the right—and responsibility—to define what feminism is for them. The commonality is the belief that women do not have status equal to that of men—and the desire to do something about it. If you agree with these two points, then you are a feminist.[8]

Dr. Chung gained international recognition when she introduced Asian women's theology in her book *Struggle to Be the Sun Again*. The title of this book comes from the poem "The Hidden Sun" by a Japanese woman, Hiratsuka Raicho. "In her poem, she claims that 'originally, woman was the sun. She was an authentic person. But now woman is the moon.' That means once Asian women were self-defining women but now they have become dependent women defined by men in their lives," Dr. Chung explains. "Therefore Raicho perceives Asian women's struggle for liberation as 'Struggle to Be the Sun Again.' I think her poetic expression aptly shows Asian women's yearning for wholeness."[9] In the introduction to this book, Dr. Chung further explains her purpose:

> Doing theology is a personal and a political activity. As a Korean woman, I do theology in search of what it means to be fully human in my struggle for wholeness and in my people's concrete historical fight for freedom. By discerning the presence and the action of God in our midst, I want to empower my own liberation process as well as that of my community…. My theological questioning neither falls from the sky nor is derived primarily from the academy. Rather, it comes from my anger and hope as a Third World woman who refuses to be victimized by any kind of colonization. My theology is also inspired by my burning desire for self-determination, and it originates from a liberation-orientated, Third World interpretation of people's history.[10]

Dr. Chung also writes about the importance of including female divine images, based on the biblical teaching that Asian women use most frequently, "that men and women are created equally in God's image (Gen. 1:27, 28)."[11] She further states: "It is natural for Asian women to think of the Godhead as male and female because there are many male gods and female goddesses in Asian religious cultures.... Many Asian women believe that an inclusive image of God who has both male and female sides promotes equality and harmony between men and women."[12]

Among the female divine images Dr. Chung notes in Asian women's theologies are Life-Giving Spirit, Mother, Woman, and Shaman.

> The emerging generation of Asian women theologians emphasize God as a life-giving spirit they can encounter *within* themselves and *in* everything which fosters life. Many Asian women think God as a life-giving power can be naturally personified as mother and woman because woman gives birth to her children and her family members by nurturing them. In many Asian women's writings, God is portrayed as mother and woman.... When Asian women begin to imagine God as woman and mother, they also begin to accept their own bodies and their own womanhood in its fullness. The female God accepts us as we are more than the patriarchal male God. This female God is a vulnerable God who is willing to be changed and transformed in her interaction with Asian women in their everyday life experiences.... Many Asian women portray Jesus with the image of mother. They see Jesus as a compassionate one who feels the suffering of humanity deeply, suffers and weeps with them.... Another female image of Jesus comes from the image of the shaman.... As the Korean shaman has been a healer, comforter, and counselor for Korean women, Jesus Christ healed and comforted women in his ministry. In Korea the majority of shamans are women.[13]

In an interview, Dr. Chung talks about how her image of God has changed through the years to include the Female Divine. "As a theological student I always thought God is Spirit, that there is no image," she says. "But I really had an image of this white man with blue eyes and long hair and white robes. White man with big nose. It was my image of God. My intellectual side said God has no image because God is Spirit. But all my upbringing as a Christian in Korea, in the Korean church, which was founded by many Western missionaries, all my Sunday school education was based on this picture of God who looked like Moses in the movie *The Ten Commandments*. But through long personal struggle, I realized one day my image of God now is like a middle-aged Korean woman, looking like my mother, very warm and affirming, very available and strong and down-to-earth. When I prayed, she came to me. That image is my image of God. It's very liberating because before when I prayed to God who is white, who is old, who is man, it was difficult for me to be connected with him."[14]

As Dr. Chung affirms, this discovery of the Female Divine has provided a foundation for her interfaith work. Her teaching and research include Christian-Buddhist dialogue, interfaith peacemaking, Zen meditation, approaches to disease and healing in various religious traditions, goddesses and women's liberation in Asia, mysticism and revolutionary social change, and ecofeminist theologies and spiritualities from various countries. She is a founding member and councilor of the International Interfaith Peace Council, and she produced an award-winning, eight-part series, "The Power of Women in World Religions," for Korean Public Television. She has researched Muslim women's involvement with peacemaking efforts in sixteen Muslim nations, and hopes to use this knowledge to facilitate dialogue for Christian feminists with the Islamic world. In addition to *Struggle to be the Sun Again,* Dr. Chung's published works include *In the End, Beauty Will Save Us All: A Feminist Spiritual Pilgrimage*; *Letter from the Future: The Goddess-Spell According to Hyun Kyung*; and *Hyun Kyung and Alice's Fabulous Love Affair with God*, coauthored with Alice Walker.[15]

In the conclusion of her prophetic address at the World Council of Churches Assembly, Dr. Chung extends an invitation for unity in the work of renewing creation. "Dear sisters and brothers, with the energy of the Holy Spirit let us tear apart all walls of division and the culture of death which separate us," she says. "And let us participate in the Holy Spirit's political economy of life, fighting for our life on this earth in solidarity with all living beings and building communities for justice, peace, and the integrity of creation. Wild wind of the Holy Spirit, blow to us. Let us welcome Her, letting ourselves go in Her wild rhythm of life. Come Holy Spirit, renew the whole creation."[16]

ᘒᕽ

Lana Dalberg

Writer; Activist; Lay Theologian

Face-to-Face with the Mother

"Multicultural images of the Divine Feminine are vital. I intentionally expanded beyond my circle to include many women of different faiths and multicultural backgrounds because cultural perspectives different from our own offer us new vantage points and fresh insights."

Lana Dalberg interviews women from diverse cultural and religious backgrounds in her book *Birthing God: Women's Experiences of the Divine.*[17] When she had the idea of gathering women's spiritual stories, she at first wanted to focus exclusively on women "who specified Sophia or Divine Mother or Goddess." But as she reached out to women in various faith traditions, she says she decided not to limit the project. "I wanted it to be open to all women, however they characterized their spiritual experiences. I was surprised. Women who I thought wouldn't lift up the Divine Feminine because they seemed more traditional referred to God as 'Mother' or talked about experiences of the Divine that were similar to the women who identified themselves as Goddess worshipers. I felt blessed that so many women came forward to share their stories with me."

Lana grew up in a loving Lutheran family; her father was a Lutheran minister and her mother a church organist. From an early age she felt drawn to Native American spirituality. In college, she became involved with Central American peoples' struggles for liberation. With a desire to learn more about liberating theologies and to practice them, Lana began work toward her master's degree in theological studies at Pacific

Lutheran Theological Seminary. Feminist theology was not one of her interests at that time. "Through my twenties and thirties, I was all about empowering whole communities—men *and* women together working to transform poverty and injustice," she recalls. "As I entered my late thirties and early forties, I became more aware of women's oftentimes 'triple' oppression—gender, class, and race—and I became more sensitive to gender inequity in my own life."

During this period in her life Lana began meditating daily and experiencing visions of the Mother. "These visions were the beginning of my understanding of the Divine Feminine, and they came from within," she says. "My inner spirit opened itself to the larger Spirit, and I came face-to-face with God as Mother. Scenes unfurled on my inner eye in undulating landscapes, and she stepped into them. A tall African woman, the Mother was someone my heart recognized instantly, even though I had been raised with male images of God."[18] Lana continued to record her visions.

> Today I saw myself emerging from the water, clothed in buckskin and with long black braids. But as I emerged, I saw pieces of myself break off like shards—shards of me falling away, splashing into the water. I was afraid, and I reached toward the sun, my Mother. The sun voice said, "Behold, here is my daughter, with whom I am well pleased." And I was a woman's body again: curvy, voluptuous, pregnant, and, although pregnant, old. I walked with a cane. I carried age in my bones. The time came for me to bring forth the child in my womb. I gripped a pole, and my Mother Midwife soothed me, stroking my hair, patting my brow dry, feeding me water to drink, and whispering words of encouragement in my pain. My pain was the labor of birth but the pain of not knowing, too. I heaved and groaned through the pains, and I birthed an adult—an androgynous human being that was as big as me, that merged with me, swirling like the symbol of the yin and the yang. This was my birth, I realized. I searched for my Mother God, and I heard her say, "I am here: in the rain, in the sun, and in the earth. I will always be there for you."[19]

Several years later Lana wrote this poem, titled "Mother God":

God to me
Is my dark-haired mother,
Stroking my forehead
As she lullabies me to sleep.

My Mother is the earth
And all her creatures,
The web that brings us into relationship
With one another.

God to me
Is the Mother
Who spills Her essence into the world,
Creating and calling us to create
From the wombs of our being.

God to me
Is the Mother
Whose voice was drowned out
For most of history.

And yet,
I find Her in my deepest wisdom.
Alone, I feel Her touch
Upon my brow,
Mothering me still,
Mothering us all.[20]

It was through meditation that Lana came to understand the importance of including female divine images and female leadership in the church. "In meditation, immersed in the consciousness that unites all of us, I was broken open to see the damaging effects of a church that excludes and puts down many elements of this wondrous creation," she says. "Excluding some humans from full participation because they are female is damaging to everyone. It reduces everyone's wholeness."

To help transform the church so that it is contributes to wholeness, Lana actively participates in Ebenezer/herchurch Lutheran in San Francisco, a member of the mainstream Evangelical Lutheran Church of America. "I attend a church that focuses on uplifting the Divine Feminine," she says. "We are always re-envisioning the Divine. God as

Mother, as Baker-woman, as Midwife, is constantly kneading us, calling us to follow in Her image and to create anew. This birthing and creating anew has a ripple effect."

Lana's most recent publication is *Birthing God*. "A little over two years ago while at a Faith and Feminism conference sponsored by herchurch, I had the idea of gathering many women's stories of their spiritual experiences," Lana says. "I felt called to elicit women's spiritual stories and to lift them up for others to celebrate." These inspiring stories reveal culturally diverse experiences of the Divine, inviting openness to the Divine in all.

In the introduction of *Birthing God*, Lana explains her process in writing this book and celebrates what she learned:

> I made room in my professional and domestic life for a new project, asking women to share their stories with me. I started closest to home, in my church community, and broadened the circle to draw in others who were interested. Many of the women had been involved in courageous, compassionate work for years, and they were just now recognizing the injustices thrust upon the collective female soul. Some were creating women's circles, others were collaborating in ecofeminist ventures to safeguard the earth, and others were involved in healing and creative work to lift up the Divine Feminine. Instead of disparaging themselves, these women were embracing themselves as cherished and one with the Divine. I learned many things as I interviewed these women, but everything they shared reinforced one simple treasure: however we name Spirit, we receive it with deep-hearted openness. Our receptivity is active, recognizing the value we bring to relationship by trusting and honoring the God within; by experiencing Spirit as soul mate; by glimpsing the Divine all around us; and by allowing God to cradle and nourish us. At the same time, our spirituality is a process, unfolding and growing with each passing day. Our spiritual stories are full of missteps and unabashed celebration. They are narratives of suffering and of hope; lessons in shedding fear and learning to love ourselves. Ours are embodied stories that begin with emptying so that we can glimpse the Holy Other, this Light who appears in ways unplanned, unexpected, and unsettling. Our lives are the surprise that begins with the response, "Let it be."[21]

From her experience at Ebenezer/herchurch Lutheran, Lana affirms the power of multicultural female divine images to bring gender equality and justice: "At herchurch, we are changing the culture. Former council president, Susan Solstice, says that it's important for girls to see in themselves the divine image. Because God is imaged as female, Susan's daughters can experience innate goodness in themselves, which rarely happens for girls when God is equated with maleness. According to Susan, when a girl values herself, she is empowered to care about herself and, from that place of self-love, to care about others in ways that enhance and reinforce her core goodness."[22] Lana believes that if all children, like those at herchurch, "grew up with the idea that all of us embody the Divine," then "we wouldn't have so much degradation and violence against women and girls."

Lana feels blessed to be a member of Ebenezer/herchurch Lutheran because "it incorporates feminine images of the Divine into the worship and includes an appreciation of the earth." So she has not considered leaving church, although she recently had a troubling dream. "In my dream, Kathleen Hurty, coeditor of *Women, Spirituality and Transformative Leadership: Where Grace Meets Power*,[23] and I entered a church hall area because she was dropping off some glass serving bowls as donations. When we went up to the sanctuary, it was packed full for a service, but the people had been taken hostage by a gunman. That was when the dream turned to a nightmare, when my body felt sluggish and unresponsive. I struggled to get up from the pew as the other congregants began to flee. My body felt weighty and it was hard to get out of that pew and out the back door despite the urgency I felt and the repeated shots of the gunman. When I reached the church's side door and was heading down the exterior steps, following all the others who had fled, I woke up. Awake and conscious, I immediately equated the gunman with a church hierarchy that has held its congregants hostage to dictums that are unjust, a hierarchy that has shown itself to be complicit with corruption and perversion. In the dream, it made sense to break from its tyranny and violence."

Lana realizes that her call is in changing the church, not breaking from it. "I feel that I am part of the movement that is creating a ruckus and stirring things up in the church. I am part of a movement that is welcoming in freedom and fresh air. As St. Paul says, we must become a new creation. We are constantly being birthed anew by the Divine Mother/Father, the Creator who keeps on creating and who calls us, in like fashion, to renew and re-envision church."

As she stirs things up in the church with her prophetic ministry, Lana has taken some risks. She explains, "Writing and publishing *Birthing God* is an act of courage. Even though I am not a clergyperson and I do not depend on the church for an income or health insurance, I risk the threats of marginalization or trivialization." The term "Goddess," used by some of the women in the book, sparks the most resistance in people, Lana says. "I think that the witch hunts of past centuries have ingrained fears that are so deep most people are not even conscious of them. Many of us have a gut aversion to Goddess language or feel in our bones that it is heretical. All that repression worked to instill a deep fear that resides in most of us."

Meditation helps Lana transform fear into joy and to envision the fullness of the Divine. "The Divine that I encounter in meditation is a true joy, an upwelling of freedom, a sense of grace that carries me forward," she says. "I pray and work that we may experience the Divine in all its fullness. That we grasp the paradox that the Divine, which is ultimately beyond our full comprehension, can best be experienced through the particular, and the particular includes female and nonhuman metaphors such as Divine Mother, Compassionate Midwife, She-Bear, the Rock that bore us, High-Soaring Eagle, and Mother Hen who gathers us beneath Her wings." In the epilogue of *Birthing God*, Lana Dalberg further articulates her expansive vision:

> Most of us have been taught that God creates life, breathing our days into existence, our nights into being. We have been taught that Spirit, however we name it, births all that exists. And this is true. Yet we also birth the Divine, as the women in these pages have shown. All encounters and understandings of the Divine are essential to the whole. In bringing to light women's spiritual experiences, we increase our day-to-day awareness of the Divine and enhance our global consciousness of God. And when we see in ourselves and others the divine connection between us all, we increase the level of goodwill and equanimity in the world.[24]

Jeanette Blonigen Clancy

Writer; Educator; Lay Theologian

Cherishing Christianity Without Its Exclusive Claims

"To further causes we cherish, we must collaborate with other Christians and with other faiths. Religions today have lost moral standing for good reason—because some religious adherents model the very opposite of ethical principles. Bright spots amid such scandals and squabbling are examples of interfaith collaboration. They have the potential of restoring honor to religions, as well as advancing peace, justice, and spiritual harmony."

Jeanette Blonigen Clancy celebrates the power of interfaith collaboration to bring transformation. She believes that gender inclusive language and symbolism are also vital to change. "Words and symbols shape our minds and attitudes, which drive our actions," she says. "For this reason, change is impossible without language changes. If we talk about the highest value imaginable with exclusively male terms, we give males the right to act as lords over females—exactly what we experience around the world." Calling God "She" jolts us into realizing that this "exclusively male God-talk diminishes God," Jeanette writes on her blog.[25] To illustrate, she converts traditional male references to Deity to female references in this passage from the prophet Isaiah:

> On this mountain the Holy One will provide for all peoples
> ... She will destroy
> The veil that veils all peoples ...

She will wipe away
The tears from all faces;
The disgrace of Her people She will remove....
This is the Holy One for whom we looked;
Let us rejoice and be glad that She has saved us![26]

Jeanette was brought up "in a blanketing Catholic atmosphere" in the German-Catholic county of Stearns in Minnesota, where she still lives and teaches. One of her brothers became a priest. She recalls that ten people from her neighborhood entered religious orders, and that "the tiny parish of two hundred families" where she grew up in a farming community "produced over one hundred religious."

From elementary school through graduate school, Jeanette graduated from only Catholic institutions. She writes, "I grew up in a community so Catholic that a student of mine once expressed astonishment upon learning that most Americans are not Catholic."[27] Her community "has changed a lot, but in small towns of the county, the Catholic Church still dominates architecturally."

As she was growing up, Jeanette began to question exclusively masculine language for divinity. "Two tracks led me to my present stance against sexist God-talk—recognizing the error of worshiping a man-god and recognizing the injustice of elevating one gender over the other," she says. "The first realization began in my youth, when I tried to follow religious teaching by getting 'close to Jesus.' Even then, in high school and college, I resisted. Something in me said, 'God is not just a man' and 'a man is not God.' The realization of gender injustice happened later as a result of the feminist movement. I like to use the word 'feminist' to push back against the right's corruption of good words like 'liberal' and 'feminist.' To my shame, I first scoffed at 'the crazy bra-burners,' but soon I could see the justice of their statements. And then I read feminist theologians, for whom I have tremendous admiration. No one understands theology better than women theologians who explain that all God-talk is figurative."

While studying at St. John's School of Theology in Collegeville, Minnesota, for her master's degree in systematic theology, Jeanette had the idea for her book *God Is Not Three Guys in the Sky: Cherishing Christianity Without Its Exclusive Claims.* "I was annoyed by naïve questions and comments from seminarians," she recalls. "That's when the statement, 'God is not three guys in the sky' blurped up in me. I resolved to write a book 'someday.' It took more than twenty-five years. In the meantime, I educated myself past the traditional Christian mind-set by exploring feminist theology, comparative religion, Eastern spirituality, and pagan and atheist spirituality. Currently, I also try to keep up with mainstream Christian writing and bridge the disparate thought frames."

In addition to providing this interfaith bridge, Jeanette connects traditional Catholicism and the progressive Roman Catholic Womenpriests movement. She regularly attends Mass at St. Benedict's Monastery in St. Joseph, Minnesota, close to her home in Avon; she has relationships with Franciscan sisters, School Sisters of Notre Dame, and St. Joseph sisters; and she publishes letters in the *National Catholic Reporter*. As a member of Mary Magdalene, First Apostle, a women-priest community, she contributes to changing the language of monthly Mass readings from patriarchal to inclusive. "Participation in the liturgies of Mary Magdalene, First Apostle, now gives me another outlet for my feminist energy," she says.

Jeanette believes that rational arguments for justice are not enough. "We have to shake things up by actually changing things—thus the need for Roman Catholic Womenpriests and feminine names for the Holy," she explains. "Feminine names for the Holy force the realization of new possibilities. Women priests provide evidence that cannot easily be dismissed. Actually experiencing services with women priests builds the attitude that they are competent, normal, proper, and right."

In the conclusion of *God Is Not Three Guys in the Sky*, Jeanette gives further support for including women priests and female divine names in church in order to change the wider culture:

> I don't want to finish this book without mentioning the unique set of attitudes, skills, and perspectives that women contribute toward healing the world from the patriarchal bias of several millennia. To the independence-seeking male, let us add the connection-seeking female. To counter the adversarial inclination, let us apply relationship building. To counter warmaking, competition, and domination, let us apply peacemaking, cooperation, and partnership. To the image of a God or Gods up above, let us add that of living within the womb of Mother Earth, whose air, water, and soil we

strive to protect. Barred from power for many centuries, women are able to practice power *with* instead of power *over* and *against*, as demonstrated by their disproportionate presence in peace advocacy. This has implications for global politics and economics as well as religion.... Spirit/Source is infinitely greater than three male individuals.[28]

Jeanette feels strongly about the role of God-language in changing patriarchal culture. Commenting on the book *Half the Sky*[29] on her blog, she writes:

> The book's detailed evidence of sexual violence against women and girls—honor killings, bride beating, bride burning, genital cutting, forced prostitution, rape as a tactic of war, acid to disfigure, and selling of seven- and eight-year-old girls into sexual slavery—tells us that gender violence and discrimination is the paramount human rights problem of our time. Indeed, it tells us that nothing would do more to ameliorate the problems of the world than raising the status of women.... I invite readers to consider the pain of these women and also the hope of real transformation, only possible if we allow women to become confident and powerful. *Half the Sky* lists effective organizations and gives specific suggestions. I don't see how you could read these chapters without being changed in some way. In churches, we need to change the talk about a lord or lords in the sky. Women of the world have too many lords lording it over them—they don't need a god-lord besides.[30]

Through her writing and speaking, Jeanette challenges all language that perpetuates male dominance. "It's an uphill battle against rigidified structures of thought," she says. "I look for ways to disturb comfortable acceptance of the repetition of 'Father,' 'Son,' 'Lord,' 'He/Him/His.' This sexist God-talk promotes male domination and therefore gender abuse. God as exclusively 'He/Him/His' describes male power as natural, normal, proper, and right, and female power as unnatural, abnormal, improper, and wrong. The Christian 'Lord' promotes all types of inequality by establishing hierarchy and domination as the essential, even sacred, structure of the universe. Those of us still in the Christian tradition can help transform its immoral power structure by taking every opportunity to insert inclusive God-talk into liturgical and everyday language, to diminish the power of 'the Lord' by naming the Holy with feminine and nonhierarchical terms."

For Mary Magdalene, First Apostle, Jeanette and others in this womenpriest community change scripture readings to include female names for the Divine. She also writes prayers to empower women and girls, such as these:

> In the spirit of Lent and Women's History Month,
> may our religious leaders humbly grow to understand how religion contributes to sexual stereotypes that in turn contribute to sexual violence against women and girls, we pray ...

> In the spirit of Lent and Women's History Month,
> may secular leaders raise every country's prosperity by educating and empowering women, we pray ...

> In the spirit of Lent and Women's History Month,
> may the world grow in awareness of the many ways that confident and powerful women can bless all relationships to transform every aspect of society, we pray ...

In spite of Jeanette's deep roots in the Catholic Church, she left for a while. She returned through her relationship with the sisters at St. Benedict's Monastery. "What brought me back is a nearby monastery of Catholic religious women who formed my spiritual home in my youth and continue to model the best of Catholicism while feeding me spiritually," she says. "They even include me on the lector schedule for their liturgies, and some of them see things as I do. My association with the community of religious women tempers my speaking and writing. Without their friendship I might have become caustic in my critiques of the Catholic Church, reducing their effectiveness. Too bad the world doesn't know how cool nuns are!"

Jeanette draws strength from her relationships with Catholic sisters, from her womenpriest community, and from the many affirmations she receives from her writing. She takes every opportunity to challenge the patriarchal language, leadership, and dogma of the church because she believes in the power of religious and spiritual people working together to bring transformation. She writes, "Unthinking loyalty to exclusive

Christian claims damages spiritual harmony around the globe, contributing to the present climate of religious extremism."[31]

On her blog, Jeanette gives this invitation: "Interested in religions and spirituality? You've come to the right place. In Shakespeare's play, Hamlet says, 'There are more things in heaven and earth, Horatio, than are dreamt of in your philosophy.' This is a two-edged challenge. It invites believers to rethink their dogmas, and it challenges people without faith to rethink their certainty that everything religious is bunk."[32]

Although she acknowledges the slow process of changing church, she expresses optimism. "My writing is deliberately provocative because I am impatient with the glacial pace of change and want to shake things up. My letters to *National Catholic Reporter* are often published and articles in that paper show that change indeed is happening. Despite the rule of aging, ultra-conservative men in Rome, thoughtful theologians, religious leaders, and ordinary Christians continue to question and dissent, indicating an evolutionary shift in consciousness."

Jeanette's prophetic writing and speaking are contributing to this shift in consciousness. In addition to her active blog, her book, and her letters in the *National Catholic Reporter*, she frequently appears on the opinion pages of the *St. Cloud Times* and contributed an essay to the anthology *The Rule of Mars: Readings on the Origins, History and Impact of Patriarchy*.[33]

Through all, she strives to build global justice, spiritual understanding, and cooperation among nations and religions. She expresses this hopeful vision for the future: "The unmistakable trend is toward feminine equality and power. When ignorance, bigotry, and cruelty rear their ugly heads, I look at the wide sweep of history and take comfort in the clear direction shining over the long term and in the counsel of wise persons who know that."

Orion Pitts

*Director of Music, Office Administrator, First United
Lutheran Church, San Francisco, California*

All-Encompassing Love Uniting Us

"I was leading a children's group in some music, and I
wanted to make sure they understood the significance
of the Day of Pentecost. So I asked this group of kids
who've grown up in First United Lutheran: 'What's the
third most important day of celebration in our church
after Easter and Christmas?' One bright seven-year-old
piped up right away: 'Hanukkah!' I smiled, knowing that
our commitment to interfaith community was having an
impact."

Orion Pitts appreciates the openness of his congregation to diverse
religious traditions. "Our congregation has no problem with
singing a Buddhist chant during communion—it does not 'harm' God
or Jesus, or threaten our faith," he says. "It does have the potential to
broaden and enhance it, however, and celebrates the all-encompassing
Love that unites us; that is, God."

Moving from gender-exclusive to gender-inclusive worship language, Orion believes, is also vital to experiencing this expansive Love.
"Biblical writers reflected the dominantly patriarchal society in which
they lived, and too often that has been used as a force for exclusion
rather than reflecting the all-encompassing source of Love that is the
God whom Christ revealed," he notes. Including female images of the
Divine, such as Mother, will change some traditional Christian views

to open up new meaning. "The image of God as 'Mother' opens up a whole dimension of the nature of God for us to know and grasp," Orion says. "The all-pervasive historical Christian God as a judging, angry, powerful, destructive figure does a disservice to our concept of God—and has served to create for Christians a feeling that we are shameful beings who are lost and must grasp onto the Jesus of the cross for salvation. That is not at all what Jesus taught. Jesus taught that we are all beings suffused with Love, and that Love is God. The angry, vengeful God that condemns us to a need for salvation comes from what others said *about* Jesus, not from Jesus's own teachings."

As a music minister, Orion accepts the challenging responsibility of choosing hymns that reflect this theology of Love. "Over the years, I have become much more discerning about the music and the texts that we use," he says. "There are many—*many*—hymns that I have dearly loved since childhood, that I just will not use anymore, because the theology in them does not reflect an experience of the Divine that I wish to perpetuate. So I constantly ask myself whether my love for those hymns comes from the text and meaning, or whether it's a connection to the tune. We use many familiar tunes with many different texts. It can be challenging for congregations, but they adapt. Ever since I've been dedicated to inclusive language, I've become more and more discerning about texts. What a gift to be no longer blindly following along like sheep, but rather to be asking myself, 'What am I saying here? What am I teaching?'"

Orion's eclectic background, education, and career have helped shape his expansive theology. He earned degrees in music education and acting and a certificate in interspiritual wisdom, and has done graduate studies at Westminster Choir College and at the University of Hawaii. He has served as choir director and organist in Lutheran, Episcopal, and Presbyterian congregations around the country and as chair of the theater department at Newberry College.

When he was at Westminster Choir College, Orion first became aware of the power of language in hymns. "While in graduate school and rooming with some other church music majors, I was playing the hymn known as 'Once to Every Man and Nation,'" he recalls. "It goes on to say, 'Comes the moment to decide, in the strife of truth with falsehood, for the good or evil side.' A roommate, who was far more astute than I, stopped me and said, 'Do you really believe that?' Well, no I didn't believe that. I knew that many moments of decision come daily. I'd never really thought about these words; I just liked the tune. I hadn't paid attention to what hymn texts were actually saying until then."

Continuing to expand his thinking, Orion has been on what he calls a "ceaseless journey to the Spirit, with an intense interest in mysticism and Christian meditation." He believes inclusive sacred language and symbolism are signs of humanity's spiritual growth. "I think that the spiritual trajectory of human history is toward an ever-greater expansion of humanity realizing its all-encompassing spiritual nature," he says. "What does that mean? It means that the story of humanity is one of not limiting itself to the spiritual revelations of the past, but rather continued growth outward—with many, many bumps along the road—to full realization of all creation as a manifestation of God. Therefore, what we are doing, or experiencing now, in ever-widening uses of language and symbolism, is growing, maturing outward as the Spirit guides us toward full realization. In the never-ending attempt to experience our God-nature, the more that we get beyond the limiting view of God as a being—male, female, or otherwise—the closer we get to full realization. And that is the church's role."

To implement these beliefs in the worship services of his church, Orion tries to avoid exclusively male references, balances female and male divine names, and often gives precedence to the Female Divine. "We attempt to avoid exclusively male gender references to God as frequently as possible, and that is not easy," he says. "Beyond that, when we do make gender references, we include both female and male, God as 'Mother' as well as 'Father,' and we avoid the pronouns 'He' and 'Him' in reference to God. We frequently will stress the feminine to the exclusion of the masculine; and that's okay; with two thousand years of an exclusively masculine 'tradition,' it may take another two thousand to rectify that situation."

First United Lutheran Church, committed to inclusive and expansive language for many years, welcomes female references to Deity. Orion says that he only gets negative feedback, usually from some of the men, if he allows too many *male* references, such as "Lord" or "kingdom," to slip into the music in a worship service.

The church's commitment to inclusive language, however, has often proved challenging because members have varied interpretations of "inclusive," Orion says. "For the first four or so years in my position as music director here, I was happily plugging along using inclusive resources and textual changes that reflected my understanding of what that commitment meant," he explains. "Then at some point in some exploration of our identity, we engaged in a discussion of our inclusive language commitment. It became clear during that process that nearly everyone in our church community had different interpretations of just what 'commitment to inclusive language' meant. It involved details of such things as specific textual references, traditions, and comfort level. So, we've continued that dialogue regularly, and practice a balancing act that remains sensitive to many different concerns and understandings."

In this "balancing act" Orion consults numerous hymnals, other worship resources, and the Internet in selecting hymns. He also creates new texts and alters existing texts. Here are two examples of traditional texts in the public domain that Orion has altered to meet the varied interpretations of inclusive language in his church:

Sanctus[34]

Original Version

Holy, holy, holy Lord, God of power and might,
heaven and earth are full of your glory.
Hosanna in the highest.
Blessed is he who comes in the name of the Lord.
Hosanna in the highest.

Orion's Altered Version

Holy, holy, holy One, God of power and might,
heaven and earth reveal your glory,
blessed God of Love.
Sing hosanna in the highest, holy Adonai!
Sing hosanna, hosanna,
God of heavenly peace.

Irish Blessing
Original Version

May green be the grass you walk on;
may blue be the skies above you;
may pure be the joys that surround you;
may true be the hearts that love you.
May the road rise to meet you;
may the wind be always at your back;
may the sun shine warm upon your face;
may the rains fall soft upon your fields.
And, until we meet again,
may God hold you in the hollow of His hand.[35]

Orion's Altered Conclusion

And, until we meet again,
may God hold you in the palm of Her hand.

Another priority for Orion is worship music inclusive of many religious traditions and cultures. He has compiled what he calls the "Global Mass," with resources from numerous traditions such as Buddhist, Sufi, Jewish, and Native American. For example, he put the text of the traditional Christian chant *Agnus Dei* with the well-known Buddhist chant *Om Mani Padme Hum.*[36] Orion explains his use of this piece in worship services: "The congregation has the option of singing either text, and they may do that simultaneously, and sing it as a chant throughout the distribution of communion."

Orion says interfaith collaboration is a core value of his congregation, citing this example: "We engaged in a 'Summer Celebrating Pluralism.' In the context of our regular order of worship each Sunday, we had a guest speaker from a different faith tradition who told us about that tradition during the sermon time and provided one reading." Among the spiritual traditions featured were Judaism, Islam, Hinduism, Buddhism, Baha'i, Wicca, Religious Science, and Swedenborgian. In addition, one of the guest speakers was Maria Eitz, the first woman to be ordained as a Roman Catholic priest in the San Francisco Archdiocese. On the church's website under "Interfaith Awareness" is this statement: "We believe our wisdom will only be enhanced by continued conversation with all of our neighbors. Together we work for peace, justice, and the good of all people and all creation."[37]

Not all churches and areas of the country are as progressive as his, Orion recognizes. "It does make things difficult when we travel outside this area to encounter ideas and practices with which we are no longer familiar, and thought had gone away long ago," he says. "It teaches us that there is much work to be done." The main challenge Orion faces in his location is that many people have rejected any form of religion or spirituality because they are unaware that "old concepts and ideas" have changed.

Changes in the church, however, come slowly, Orion acknowledges. "The institution of 'the Church' is very slow to undergo change, but it is already happening. We see that in the desperation that many today feel as they see the old forms of belief that they have clung to for so long slipping away. But to give some very clear, and noncontemporary examples, most Christians today can fully understand how non-Christian the behavior and beliefs were that brought on the Crusades and the Spanish Inquisition. Far too many, however, do not see the very real reflection of those same beliefs in examples today, including exclusion of certain groups or persons as unworthy of God's love. 'Progressive' Christianity recognizes that the love of God is reflected only in peace, and in doing those actions that heal all humanity and bring us together under an all-loving force known as God."

Because of the slowness of the church to change to these progressive beliefs and actions, Orion has often considered leaving. But he believes that "the Spirit is working in and through" him to keep him engaged in the church. "It's so much a pattern in my life; I don't cling to it, but it's just inside me," he says.

In Orion's expansive vision for the future of the church, language and imagery will be inclusive of both female and male, varied religious traditions, and varied cultures. He envisions every Christian worship environment looking something like that of Ebenezer/herchurch Lutheran in San Francisco. His vision includes embracing "broad concepts of the Divine" and embracing what diverse spiritual traditions "have to teach us about our own." The creative ministry of Orion and First United Lutheran join Wisdom's work in fulfilling this vision.

Wisdom's Works of Changing Hierarchies into Circles

Divine Wisdom guides us to cocreate with Her new kinds of communities, to change hierarchies into circles. Hierarchies create the illusion that some people are more valuable or more spiritual than others. Circles symbolize the equal value of all. Wisdom works with us to change the top-down power that originates in hierarchical organizational structures to the organic power that flows from an egalitarian circle. In circles people share power and everyone's gifts have equal value. Wisdom increases as people join together in egalitarian, sacred circles.

Wisdom and other female personifications of the Divine contribute to the symbolic foundation for changing hierarchies into circles. The Divine Feminine comes in many circular forms, such as the Womb and Mother Earth or Gaia. The circular labyrinth, found in many religious traditions, is another ancient divine feminine symbol.

For many years I have experienced creative, healing, transforming power in sacred circles. One of these circles is New Wineskins Feminist Ritual Community.[1] The mission of this community is to explore new ways of seeing divinity so that the spiritual gifts of everyone are equally valued and nurtured and to offer rituals especially focused on the Female Divine in order to change culture from female devaluation to female empowerment. The rituals also symbolize the shared power and responsibility to change culture from one up/one down, win/lose relationships to mutual, win/win relationships. The New Wineskins circle and other circles around the world work with Wisdom to create healing, peace; and justice for all creation.

We Invite All to Join Our Circle Wide
(Sung to the tune of "Let Us Break Bread Together")

We invite all to join our circle wide;
we invite all to join our circle wide.
With our arms open wide,
we will join in a feast of love,
with Christ-Sophia beside.

Come and find healing in our circle wide;
come and find healing in our circle wide.
With our arms open wide,
we will join in a feast of love,
with Christ-Sophia beside.

May our circle keep growing deep and wide;
may our circle keep growing deep and wide.
With our arms open wide,
we will join in a feast of love,
with Christ-Sophia beside.[2]

Words © 2000 Jann Aldredge-Clanton   BREAK BREAD

Ann Landaas Smith

Writer; Cofounder and Director, Circle Connections

Cocreating a New Story

"Sacred circles are the Divine Feminine, the holy vessel,
the womb, the sacred container that births and nurtures
our growth, empowerment, collaborative work, worship,
celebrations, deep listening, wisdom, and spiritual
activism. I cofounded Circle Connections to promote and
help others start and connect circles with the dream that
circle structures will replace hierarchies in organizations
and the millionth circle will bring about a tipping point
of peace and justice for all creation. I call myself a circle
evangelist."

For many years Ann Landaas Smith has indeed been an evangelist for
circles, working with national and global organizations as an advocate of women and the egalitarian structure of circle. Her background
in personal growth, organization development, gender and racial justice activism, and group dynamics led her to dedicate her life to transform hierarchies into circles and to start, nurture, and connect circles
to bring about the millionth circle.

The Millionth Circle Initiative, which Ann cofounded with Jean
Shinoda Bolen and other women, hopes to shift world consciousness by
bringing "values of relationship, nurturing, and interdependency into a
global culture in which hierarchy, conflict and competition, power over
others and exploitation of the earth's resources are dominant values."[3]
The name "Millionth Circle," coming from Jean Shinoda Bolen's book
The Millionth Circle: How to Change Ourselves and The World, refers to the

circle whose formation tips the scales to this shift.[4] One of the stated goals of the Millionth Circle Initiative is "to seed and nurture circles, wherever possible, in order to cultivate equality, sustainable livelihoods, preservation of the earth and peace for all."[5]

Ann's work with the Millionth Circle, the "mother circle" organization, led to her cofounding of Circle Connections to teach circle principles and provide consultation on creating circle groups. Currently she is director of Circle Connections, whose stated mission is "to bring the gift of women's sacred circles and Circle Leadership worldwide; caring for ourselves, one another and Mother Earth."[6] As a mentor, an educator, a consultant, a professional speaker, a creator of circle leadership programs, and a trainer, Ann also hosts and facilitates circle events and gives presentations on such topics as "The Magnificence of Circle: Experiencing the Power of the Circle Model," "Circle Leadership: All Are Leaders," "Cocreating Sustainable Communities," and "Divine Feminine: The Greatest Power for Bringing Balance."

When working as the executive director of Global Education Associates think tank, Ann also brought circle-based resources to such initiatives as Earthchild Project that is now a United Nations nongovernmental organization (NGO), Native American women's leadership programs, and the AFRUS-AIDS coalition of global religious and secular women's organizations working together to stop the AIDS pandemic in Africa. She created the United Nations Women Circles Campaign; coproduced and cohosted *Circle Connections* radio show; cofacilitated the Indigenous Women's Pathways program in Alaska, where Native Alaskan women have gone from victims to leaders; served on the board of Interfaith Action, working on behalf of farmworkers; served as a board member of Happehatchee Center, an ecospirituality educational center in Florida; and coauthored *Stories from the Circle* and *Women Prints*.[7]

Ann grew up in the Episcopal Church, where she has stayed and worked for many years. Her vocational life has also included ecumenical and interfaith groups. As director of Global Education Associates, she worked with Catholic sisters and the Religious Orders Partnership with more than 150 orders of nuns.

For seventeen years Ann served as director of Women in Mission and Ministry in the Episcopal Church USA. During this time she formed her belief in the power of the Divine Feminine. "I was in a position to meet feminist Christians who followed Mary Daly's work on God as Mother and many others who were championing expansive theology," she recalls. "Before, I had worked in the secular world for several feminist organizations on behalf of women's empowerment and equality, but this position as director of women's ministries gave me a national and an international position to call together women leaders. It connected me to the worldwide ecumenical women's movement. Working in circle, we created and facilitated Episcopal women's experiential leadership programs that included feminist theology and inclusive language. The Women of Vision leadership program trained presenters around the world. The more She, the Divine Feminine, was evoked, the greater the feelings of believing in ourselves as women leaders. We saw ourselves as whole and powerful."

Thus, Ann led the Episcopal Women in Mission and Ministry to include female names and images of the Divine in all programs, publications, and activities. "We illuminated and celebrated the Divine Feminine in everything we presented: at leadership programs; at international, national, and local gatherings; in the *Journal of Women's Ministries* magazine; in the women's round calendar; in our national church and international Anglican Communion; and in the highly successful book *Women's Uncommon Prayers: Our Lives Revealed, Nurtured, Celebrated*," Ann says.[8] "We were the first UN NGO delegation of the Anglican Communion to attend a UN conference made up of U.S. and Kenyan women to the UN Third World Conference on Women. We illuminated the Divine Feminine in everything we did locally and globally through words, symbols, art, creative enactments, and spiritual activism. We partnered with our ecumenical sisters through the World Council of Churches and the United Nations."

These female divine symbols are vital to the survival of people and all creation, Ann believes. "They help us as a people, as a global society, learn equality between male and female and that all creation is sacred," she says. "When enough people worship the Divine Feminine—as sacred, as God—the rape of women, sex trafficking, and all forms of violence against women and girls and the land, all creation, will end. The majority of us on Mother Earth have grown up and lived with the 'old story' that defined God as male and women less than men in knowing the Divine. The 'old story' separated us, ranking white people over people of color, men over women, straight over gay, people over nature. People and the environment continue to be exploited with this perceived worldview of having less value, a commodity to be used by those with the power over others. Hierarchies maintain this means of power. This 'old story' is destroying our planet. We are cocreating a 'new story' that balances the Divine Masculine with the Divine Feminine. This is happening all over the world. This is the good news that seldom is heard in the media. Paul Hawken in his book *Blessed Unrest* documents how this 'new story' is being lived out and is the largest movement in the history of the world.[9] It is grassroots; it is small circles cocreating a better world."

Contributing to the emergence of the "new story," Ann writes worship resources that balance female and male images of the Divine, such as this prayer titled "God Is Not a Single Parent":

> Father God, Creator of us all.
> How long will we see you as a single parent?
> Send your loving wisdom to fill our hearts
> and minds with new words of inclusivity.
> Open our eyes to see images that nurture and heal our brokenness.
> Grant us courage and your freedom to try new words that
> restore balance in all our relationships.
> And like baby swans being guarded and cared for by both parents,
> let the wholeness of you be illuminated in us.
> Mother, Father, Creator of us all. Amen.[10]

In her position as director of Episcopal Women in Mission and Ministry, Ann promoted worship language that included the Divine Feminine and created egalitarian communities. "Fortunately, for seventeen years the conservative men—bishops and powerful laymen—paid little attention to what we, the women of the church, were doing," Ann recalls. "We were celebrating the Divine Feminine, creating sacred circles, circle leadership, and coming together in a sacred sisterhood as both liberal and conservative women. We were undermining the patriarchy as we cocreated new ways to be with one another. We became a powerful force, and when they realized it, I was fired."

During the devastating time after she was fired from her position with the Episcopal Church, Ann found strength in relationships and through taking part in the Millionth Circle Initiative. "When I was fired, I went into shock and felt as though I had lost my baby," she says. "It was a terrible time of despair similar in feeling to when my infant son died. It was my dear friend the Rev. Ginny Doctor, a Mohawk leader in the church, who helped me the most by including me in her life and work with Native American and Alaskan women's leadership programs. This was my salvation, as well as keeping my steadfast belief in circle, which led me to Jean Shinoda Bolen and the beginning of the Millionth Circle Initiative."

In spite of this painful loss of her job with Episcopal women's ministries, Ann stays in the church to bring change. She believes that bringing the Female Divine to the church will change the wider culture because of the profound influence of religion on the culture. "Religion dictates how we define and worship God, and because this belief has been engrained in all of us, it has the greatest influence on the wider culture," she says. "With the belief that God is only male, the old story that justifies the domination and exploitation of women and all of creation continues."

To illustrate her relationship with the church, Ann cites *Defecting in Place: Women Taking Responsibility for Their Own Spiritual Lives*, by Miriam Therese Winter, a Roman Catholic sister; Adair Lummis, an Episcopal laywoman; and Allison Stokes, a United Church of Christ pastor.[11] Ann identifies with the women in the book who stay in the church by forming spirituality circles to celebrate the Divine Feminine in themselves, one another, and all creation. "The women's spirituality movement is growing exponentially circle by circle," she says. "For women who have left the church and for others, such as myself, this is the place we find most welcoming. When in circle, the women, both conservative and liberal, feel free to express ourselves using 'God the Mother,' *Sophia*, and 'She' in worship and all interactions."

Within the Episcopal Church Ann says she also finds inspiration and strength through her involvement in the Society of the Companions of the Holy Cross (SCHC), a national Episcopal women's organization. "Our local chapter is a women's sacred circle made up of clergy and laywomen. We hosted a spring SCHC conference, a three-day retreat held in a sacred circle. It was inspiring and meaningful to all who attended."

Although Ann celebrates the many women now in leadership positions in the Episcopal Church, she laments the exclusively male language for God that persists in worship services. "In the Episcopal Church and the Anglican Communion we have women bishops, and we have a woman who is the presiding bishop of the Episcopal Church USA. However, most churches still use 'God the Father' in liturgical services, prayers, and hymns. There still is not a balance of the Divine Feminine and Masculine; so much work is still needed to make this happen."

Change will come and is coming to church and society, Ann believes. "By each one working within and outside the church we will bring about the new story: the Divine Feminine and Masculine worshiped and lived out in everything we do," she says. "This is happening, so all we need to do is keep on believing and acting that we are already bringing about real change, find a circle of like-minded people, and cocreate the new." Through all her prophetic ministries, Ann joins Wisdom's work of new creation.

Dr. Mary Ann Beavis

Professor of Religion and Culture, St. Thomas More
College, University of Saskatchewan

Charting New Spiritual Paths

"In my experience of progressive churches and small faith
communities that integrate the Divine Feminine into their
worship, the circle has replaced more hierarchical worship
structure. The circle is more conducive to participation,
equality, and relationship. God/dess isn't just 'out there'
or symbolized by the presider, but is there 'where two or
three are gathered,' in the participants."[12]

D r. Mary Ann Beavis makes clear the connection between including
the Female Divine in worship and egalitarian faith communities. In
her research and writing, Dr. Mary Ann Beavis uses the terms "Female
Divine," "Feminine Divine," and "Goddess" interchangeably, saying,
"'Goddess' is just the feminine form of the word 'God.'" She also uses
the word "Godde," which combines "God" and "Goddess," and the term
"thealogy," coined by Canadian scholar Naomi Goldenberg and further
defined by another Canadian scholar Charlotte Caron as "reflection on
the divine in feminine and feminist terms."[13]

For a focus group connected to her research project on the integration of the Female Divine into Christian faith, Dr. Beavis chooses a
circle arrangement. Seated around a table in a sunny room at a Catholic
college in western Canada, thirteen women reflect upon ways we combine female images of the Divine and Christianity in our spiritual lives.
The group includes ministers, theologians, a nun, a filmmaker, environmental activists, and facilitators of women's circles. We tell stories

of empowerment through the Female Divine and share our passion for cocreating with Her a more just and peaceful world. We address questions about our relationship with the Female Divine and about what we think Christianity and Goddess spirituality have in common. Mary Ann describes the origin and purpose of this project:

> The research project originated in my own experience and study. For decades, I have observed Christian women and men adopting Goddessian elements, such as croning rituals, Mother Earth, and artwork, as part of their personal spiritualities. Emerging at about the same time, feminist theology and feminist biblical scholarship have developed what I would call a distinctively Christian thealogy. I'm thinking of foundational works such as Virginia Ramey Mollenkott's *The Divine Feminine: The Biblical Imagery of God as Female* and Elizabeth A. Johnson's *She Who Is: The Mystery of God in Feminist Theological Discourse*.[14] To date, however, there have been no substantial academic studies of this phenomenon of what I call "Christian Goddess spirituality"—although there are loads of people practicing it in their own ways. Something I've found in my research is that there is often a disconnect between academic theology and practice. Many people in Christian-Goddess/Goddess-Christian circles aren't aware of the rich resources in the Christian tradition for the Divine Feminine, and feminist theologians aren't necessarily in touch with "popular" Christian thealogy.

Mary Ann grew up in what she calls "an evangelical-bordering-on-fundamentalist context." The churches she attended with her family were "literal" in biblical interpretation and "suspicious of theology, doctrine, other churches, other religions, and questioning." When she was an adolescent, Mary Ann withdrew from church, but then in graduate school she began attending more liberal Christian groups. In her early twenties, she became a Catholic. She describes this time as "pre–John Paul II, post–Vatican II," when "there was a lot of hope and impetus for change among Catholics."

After earning a master of arts in religion from the University of Manitoba, a master of arts in theology from the University of Notre Dame, and a PhD in biblical studies from Cambridge University, Dr. Beavis taught at the University of Winnipeg and several other universities before beginning to teach religion at St. Thomas More, a Catholic college.

She says that as a child she absorbed "that the Bible is powerful, and that it shapes the way Christians think about God, human beings, and the world," especially in Western culture. She was "initially attracted to biblical studies because it was a way to begin to question and critique all those things" she was taught were "biblical," and thus "sacred and unquestionable."

Some of the teachings Mary Ann questioned were that "God was an Almighty Father; Jesus was his Son; the world was sinful, as were human beings; religion was all about otherworldly salvation; women were subordinate to men, wives to husbands, and the earth to human beings; and Christians of a certain kind were better than everybody else because only they were going to be saved." She soon discovered "feminist theology, feminist biblical interpretation, and Goddess spirituality, all of which question the King-Almighty-God-Father-Protector theology that has shaped the doctrine, preaching, and worship" of Christianity. "As many Christian feminists have observed," she says, "challenging this dominant paradigm in any way, even after some forty years of feminist theology, is apt to provoke an explosive response from the 'malestream'—even though expressions of the Divine Feminine are well attested in the Bible and Christian tradition."

Ultimately, Mary Ann left the Roman Catholic Church. Although she has not experienced a call to ordination herself, one reason she left was the Catholic Church's opposition to women's ordination. "Due to the increasing conservatism of Catholicism under John Paul II and Benedict XVI, especially with reference to women's ordination, I became an Anglican," she says. "Another factor in my leaving the Roman Catholic Church is that I have been deeply disturbed by the inadequate and hypocritical response of the official church to clerical child sexual abuse, and its discrimination against LGBTQ persons."

In faith communities and academic institutions, Dr. Beavis has worked for justice and equality for all persons. For many years she participated in the advocacy work of the Catholic Network for Women's Equality. When she lived in Winnipeg, she started a group of women at her Catholic church to discuss issues relevant to the status of Catholic women, such as the inclusion of the Divine Feminine in worship. Since moving to Saskatoon, Saskatchewan, she has belonged to the Friends of Sophia, an ecumenical Christian organization that promotes feminist theology and social justice issues. At St. Thomas More College she teaches courses on women in the Bible, including lectures on the Divine Feminine in the Bible. She serves on the Feminist Biblical Hermeneutics Task Force of the Catholic Biblical Association, and has published numerous books, articles, book chapters, and book reviews.

Among the books Dr. Beavis has edited is *Feminist Theology with a Canadian Accent*. In the introduction she writes that one of the repeated themes in this anthology is "the need for ways to express the divine as female."[15] Among her published articles are three that examine the popular enthusiasm for Mary Magdalene as an embodiment of the Female Divine, sparked by Dan Brown's best-selling novel *The Da Vinci Code*.[16] While Dr. Beavis demonstrates that contemporary speculations about Mary Magdalene as bride of Christ or a Goddess figure are mistaken, she welcomes emerging interpretations of the Female Divine, "especially within a tradition as resolutely patriarchal as Christianity."[17] She calls for feminist theologians to "consider what it is about Mary Magdalene as the sacred feminine/Bride of Jesus/Sophia that captures the popular imagination."[18]

Churches are becoming more open to inclusion of female names and images of divinity, Dr. Beavis observes, although some "have become more conservative and resistant to anything that smacks of feminist theology." The United Church of Canada, she says, is a good example of movement to "gender-inclusive language and hymns that include women and the Divine Feminine." She says, "Christians who want more inclusive, social justice–oriented churches where the Divine Feminine is honored can find them if they look hard enough, at least if they live in urban areas, but people are also leaving the church to chart their own spiritual paths, or finding community in small Christian or non-Christian groups that are more congenial to these values."

These progressive churches and small groups understand the connection between female images of the Divine and equality, social justice, and peace, Mary Ann says. "Including the Divine Feminine in church—and outside the church—questions and corrects deeply held prejudices about God, humanity, and the world. If it's okay to image God as Goddess, this has implications for Christian leadership (women really *do* image the Divine) and Christian responsibility in church and society (contrary to the 'in the world but not of the world' theology). In my experience, churches that are involved in peace and social justice issues are also amenable to female leadership and the Divine Feminine."

The Bible and Christian tradition provide solid support for multicultural female divine images, Dr. Beavis points out. "Western churches especially have fixated on the notion that it's okay to portray God as an old white man on a heavenly throne—basically Zeus! However, if, as decades of feminist theology and biblical exegesis have abundantly demonstrated, the Divine Feminine is very much a part of the Bible and Christian tradition, then why is it wrong or threatening to portray God/dess as Mother, Daughter, Sophia, Great Spirit, verbally or in artistic form?" she asks. "I think that including multicultural images of God/dess is a recognition that *all* human beings are made in the divine image, and, as such, deserve respect."

Dr. Beavis also encourages including biblical images of divinity that support the sacredness of nonhuman beings. She explores biblical images, like the mother eagle and the mother hen, as vital resources for feminist and ecofeminist thealogy/theology. These are "fresh and powerful" metaphors of the Divine as female and as nonhuman. She writes:

> Like the image of the Holy Spirit as a dove (in Greek, *peristera*, a feminine noun), the metaphor of Godde as a mother bird not only avoids androcentrism, but it is non-anthropocentric. As a supplement and corrective to ecotheologies, particularly "stewardship theologies," which merely see the life-world as Godde's "handiwork" and humans as the "stewards" of creation, the ancient Christian, Jewish and "pagan" tradition of using birds and animals to symbolize the divine affirms that nonhuman as well as human beings reflect the "image and likeness" of the Holy One. Avian images of Godde belong to an ancient, cross-cultural tradition that sees the divine reflected in the animal world.[19]

Writing and teaching expansive theology have come with some risks, Dr. Beavis acknowledges. "I work for a Catholic college, so supporting women's ordination, teaching feminist theology and biblical studies, and being involved in Goddess studies have no doubt raised eyebrows. But I must say generally I've found my college to be a supportive academic environment for me personally, although it doesn't hurt to be a tenured full professor."

Working to change the church through progressive theology, Dr. Beavis has met resistance and ignorance. "I have had a few students who just didn't like feminist theology or feminist anything, or anything promoting progressiveness or reform in the church," she says. "Several years ago, I was almost 'uninvited' from writing a commentary when the editors realized that I was a feminist biblical scholar who had used the spelling 'Godde' in one of my books. More often, I find that many Christians—including 'Goddess-Christians'—simply don't know much about the accomplishments of feminist theology, which is discouraging."

Currently, Mary Ann's faith community is the ecumenical Friends of Sophia. She identifies with both Christianity and spiritual feminism. "Although I call myself a 'spiritual feminist,' the designation 'Christian' is still important to me," she says. "I've recently been troubled by a cultural hatred of Christianity, which is mostly fueled by stereotyping all Christians in terms dictated by radical right-wing churches in the United States. I've also found that the women I've interviewed who combine Goddess spirituality and Christianity are criticized and discriminated against not only by so-called mainstream Christians, but also by Pagans and Goddessians, who tend to interpret Christianity as the opposite of their spiritual paths. In my research and experience, I've found that the lines between Christianity, Paganism, and Goddess spirituality can be quite fluid and porous, and, personally, I find it offensive and simply wrong to be told that these spiritual paths can't be blended, or practiced together. They can be, and they are."

Dr. Beavis has, however, also experienced receptivity to her expansive spirituality and theology. "I made a presentation based on my Christian-Goddess research to the Canadian Theological Society, and got a very good response," she notes. Also rewarding to her are comments from colleagues and students about the positive impact of her published writing on their work and the positive feedback she gets from students on her teaching. She is especially excited about her recent completion, with coauthor HyeRan Kim-Cragg, of the first full-length feminist commentary on the Epistle to the Hebrews, where they maintain "that Hebrews is a submerged discourse of Sophia."[20]

Sophia and other female images of the Divine are inherent to Christianity, Dr. Beavis states. "The Divine Feminine is very much part of the Christian tradition. I would like to see more churches explicitly claim this aspect of Christianity, and become more welcoming places for women and men who relate to the Divine as female and in other 'nontraditional' ways." Through her prophetic writing and teaching, Mary Ann contributes to this transformation of churches.

Dr. Bridget Mary Meehan

Priest, Mary Mother of Jesus Inclusive Catholic Community, Sarasota, Florida; Bishop, Association of Roman Catholic Women Priests

Leading, Not Leaving, the Church

"Women priests call forth the gifts of the people in a circle of equals. The Eucharist belongs to the believing community. Therefore, when we celebrate Eucharist, we call people to join around the altar to pray the Eucharistic prayer, to say the words of consecration together because the Body of Christ is the whole people together. We have a dialogue homily that reflects that the Spirit is in the people. At the liturgy of the Word, we need to hear different voices of how the Spirit is calling people to live the Word today. It's not just one person's take on what it means to live the Word of God in the world, such as the preacher or presider or priest. We trust the Wisdom of the Spirit in the people gathered in the assembly."

Bishop Bridget Mary Meehan challenges the hierarchical church to move back to the early church model of a circle of equals. Women priests and female images of the Divine are vital to this egalitarian church, she says. Although Bridget Mary and other Catholic women priests envision an ideal church without distinctions between clergy and laity, they believe that women need to be ordained now to bring justice for women in the church. "Women priests remind us that women are equal symbols of the Holy," she says. "Women and men are created in God's image, and both may represent Christ as priests. Until we integrate the Divine Feminine in our religious systems, in our structures, and in our whole approach to life, we will be flying on one wing. We

243

will not be whole. We will have the patriarchal domination continuing, and that obviously is leading the world and religion to destruction. The patriarchal model is not working for people. It's not of the Spirit."

Born in Ireland, Bridget Mary was named for St. Brigit of Kildare, abbess and bishop, who was named for the Goddess Brigit. With her parents and two younger brothers she lived in "a lovely little gray cottage" in County Laois. She describes her close-knit family as "very loving and earth-centered." Her family prayed the rosary together every night. Her mom, whom Bridget Mary describes as having "mountain-moving faith," always led the rosary, and her dad filled the house with music of saxophone and trumpet. Bridget Mary flourished in this spiritual environment. "After the family rosary each evening, I'd have heart-to-heart talks with Mary," she recalls. "We grew up in the kind of household in Ireland where you always felt that the saints and angels and Jesus and Mary were like extended family. We had this prayerful atmosphere and this sense that all of life was encompassed by the Holy—the storytelling, the music."

At the age of seven, Bridget Mary made her first communion at Church of the Holy Trinity in Rathdowney, where there is a stained-glass window of St. Brigit. "Eucharist always drew me," she says. "I would go to Mass more times than we needed to. I didn't just go once a week with my family. Even as a child, I had that sense of connecting with the Holy in the Eucharist, that it was a source of power, a source of being loved."

When she was eight years old, Bridget Mary immigrated with her family to the United States and settled in Arlington, Virginia, where she attended Catholic schools. When she was eighteen, she entered a convent. "I loved my religious life," she says. "I always felt called to consecrate my life to God. I felt this amazing Love enveloping me and calling me to be that Love, to form relationships of love and kindness and service to other people." She has served with three religious orders: Sisters of the Immaculate Heart of Mary (IHM); Society of Sisters for the Church (SSC); and Sisters for Christian Community (SFCC), an order independent of the Catholic Church hierarchy. She describes SFCC as a community with "the vision of global interconnectedness of all life and of all people," working for "earth transformation" and "fostering relationships that support justice, harmony, peace, and equality for all people."

For many years Bridget Mary's ministry as a nun included teaching in Catholic schools. While teaching in Atlanta, Georgia, she became a member of an ecumenical, charismatic prayer group, a major influence on her spiritual journey and her pastoral ministry. "It broke my Catholic mentality and opened me up to see that the power and gifts of the Holy Spirit are present in all of us, that together we journey toward God and service to one another," she says.

After earning an MA in religious education at Catholic University of America, Bridget Mary served as pastoral associate at Fort Myer Chapel in Arlington, Virginia, for fifteen years. During that time she also worked toward the doctor of ministry degree at Virginia Theological Seminary, becoming the first woman and the first Roman Catholic at that seminary to graduate with this degree. There was only one other woman, an Episcopal priest, in the program at that time. "She celebrated the first Mass I attended at the seminary," Bridget Mary recalls. "It was the first time I'd ever experienced a woman priest. I thought the ground would swallow me up; it was absolutely awesome! At the seminary I had once again that great experience of stretching through ecumenical dialogue. Also, I was reading more and more feminist theology."

Then Dr. Meehan began writing about female divine imagery. "I felt that if we were to grow in partnership as men and women in equality in the church, we needed to restore the feminine dimension of the Divine," she says. Bridget Mary describes a mystical experience she had before writing her first book, *Exploring the Feminine Face of God*.[21] "I prayed about writing that book. In my prayer I felt Mary, Mother of Jesus, saying to me, 'Yes, you need to do this. Just do it, and it will be blessed.'" The book was so successful that as soon as it was published, it immediately sold out.

To teach biblical female divine images to children as well, Bridget Mary coauthored *Heart Talks with Mother God*. One of the meditations in this children's book is titled "God, a Nurturing Mother":

> Listen my child as your Mother God describes herself to you....
> "I am like a tender mother who cuddles, kisses, and holds you in
>   her arms.
> I am like a caring mother who provides for your needs.
> I am like a comforting mother who dries your tears when you are sad.
> I am like a kind mother who always tells you how special you are.
> I am like a wise mother who teaches and guides you.
> I am like a happy mother who smiles, sings, plays, and dances with you.
> I am like a loving mother who tells you lots of times: 'I love you....

> I believe in you.... Keep on trying.... I am proud of you....
> I will always love you
> no matter what happens.'"[22]

Bridget Mary was among the first eight women in the United States to be ordained Roman Catholic priests. "I was overjoyed that my dream of serving God as a priest was now being fulfilled," she says. "My image as we were ordained on the boat was of Jesus calling us to get out of the boat and walk on water to a new model of justice and equality for women as disciples and equals. The only way to keep from sinking in the waves and storms that life would bring was to keep our eyes on Christ-Sophia and trust in her wisdom and compassionate care."

The storms did come. Bridget Mary was excommunicated after being ordained, and a Catholic publisher discontinued five of her books. The bishop of the diocese where she began a church in her mobile home in Sarasota, Florida, told the local paper to pull an announcement about this weekly Mass. The paper refused, and printed an article about the bishop's opposition, drawing ABC news to do a story on the church. Then the church drew triple the number of people, and began renting space at St. Andrew United Church of Christ. "Opposition has always proved a blessing to us," Bridget Mary says.

Bridget Mary was among the first four American Roman Catholic women bishops to be ordained. One of the functions of women bishops is to ordain other qualified candidates as deacons, priests, and bishops without having to depend on male bishops, who must hide their identities from the Roman Catholic hierarchy. Bishop Bridget Mary participated in the ordination of the first women priests in Florida. The bishop of that diocese threatened to excommunicate not only her and others who officiated, but also everyone who attended. "I don't know how many excommunications I've had; I haven't counted them all," she says. "I think they're badges of honor actually, blessings. When the bishop threatened to excommunicate everyone, we held our breath, wondering who would come to the ordination. We had over two hundred people come! And the media were all there to chart the story. My experience is that opposition can really be the source of growth and blessing."

Although the Vatican has excommunicated women who have been ordained, the women priests reject the excommunication. "The Catholic Church teaches that a law must be received by the faithful," Bishop

Bridget Mary explains. "Seventy percent of Catholics in the United States support women's ordination. Therefore, the canon that states that only a baptized male may receive Holy Orders does not have the force of law because it has not been accepted by the community. In fact, we have a moral obligation to disobey this unjust law. We also reject the excommunication because we are validly ordained; the male bishop who ordained our first women bishops is in full apostolic succession. We are not leaving the church; we are leading the church."

She continues, "Roman Catholic women priests are prophetic because we are a movement that restores justice for women in the church, rooted in the example of Jesus who called women and men to be equal disciples and rooted in the early tradition of the church where women were deacons, priests, and bishops. Women priests in partnership with married priests and others are already positioned to reform the church, to move it from hierarchical and misogynist to egalitarian. There's a new partnership between women and men in grassroots communities, empowering and welcoming to all. People are now more open and ready. I think there's a tipping point coming in Catholicism. The largest religious group in the United States is Catholics, and the second largest group is Catholics who've left because they've been turned off or rejected."

With passion in her voice, Bishop Bridget Mary speaks about the great need for inclusive, egalitarian faith communities. "So many people are adrift and looking for community. Many have been alienated by the institutional church, including the divorced and separated, gays and lesbians, and women who feel like second-class citizens in their own church. We need to open our hearts, our homes, our churches to provide inclusive, welcoming, loving places of spiritual nurturance and spiritual challenge to live the vision of Jesus, the prophetic gospel of justice and love and peace in our world, which embraces equality at its heart because all are in the image of the Divine."

Bishop Bridget Mary's prophetic preaching, teaching, writing, and activism contribute to reforming and transforming the church. "I want to be an agent of change in solidarity with a vast group of sisters and brothers who are reformers and who love the church and want to restore it to its mystical, Christ-centered, justice-doing focus," she says. "We want to transform it from its hierarchical, male-dominated, insular view of the world to an open, democratic, participatory, people-empowered model of church. For now the institutional church has strayed. The Vatican is at the heart of global destructiveness. The institution has strayed because of the teaching on homosexuality as a disorder, the teaching on annulment, the ban on artificial birth control, the oppression of women—these are some ways the institutional church has alienated Catholics."

In her vision for the future, Bishop Bridget Mary sees women priests and the Female Divine as closely linked in creating egalitarian communities. "If the symbol system that patriarchy has given us of a male God is changed, our worldview could be radically altered. As we reimagine our divine beginning, we can incorporate a symbol system that reflects the Feminine Divine and the experience of women as images of the Divine Presence."[23]

Bridget Mary's book *Delighting in the Feminine Divine* includes a prayer for this transformation to become reality.

> Womb of Creation,
>> *Shekinah*, She-Who-Dwells Within
>>> God, the breasted One
>>>> Woman Mentor
>>>>> Sophia, Holy Wisdom,
> Help women to delight in their identity as *imago Dei* (images of God).
>> Angry Woman Preacher
>>> Liberator of the Oppressed
>>>> Welcoming Hostess
>>>>> Washerwoman God
>>>>>> Seamstress Elegant
> Transform patriarchal structures and sexist attitudes that prevent us from
> acknowledging women as *imago Dei*.
>> Jesus-Sophia, the Crucified One
>>> Mother Jesus, birthing the world
>>>> Merciful Mother Jesus,
>>>>> Jesus-Sophia, Healer of our Stress
>>>>>> Jesus, Mirror of Sophia
> Reveal your saving power through women, *imago Dei*.[24]

Christina Cavener

Founder and Leader of Feminine Divine Worship Services,
Minister of Formation, Grace United Methodist Church, Dallas, Texas

Seeing God in Her Fullness

Creating a Path Toward Liberation!

O Spirit-Sophia ...

We long to begin a spirituality of newfound wholeness.

Guide us toward liberation.

We thirst for fulfillment in new ways.

Guide us toward liberation.

We need to believe that we are made in the image of God.

Guide us toward liberation.

We hunger for more than masculine language during the holy hour.

Guide us toward liberation.

We demand that the voices of women be heard in the church and
everywhere.

Guide us toward liberation.

We want to break free from the chains of patriarchy.

Guide us toward liberation.

We yearn for a society free of us versus them, male versus female,
white versus black, straight versus gay.

Guide us toward liberation.

Seated in a circle in a lovely room with stained glass windows at Grace
United Methodist Church, Christina Cavener leads a liberating liturgy she created. Believing in the power of sacred circles, she found the perfect room at the church for a circular arrangement. She cleared out, cleaned, and transformed this room that was not being used. She also

transforms Christian liturgy with her creative Feminine Divine worship services.

Christina's personal experience contributed to her passion for including female divine imagery in worship. "Growing up in a Presbyterian church with exclusive male language for God caused me to internalize that I was less holy than men," she says. "I also felt that God could not quite identify with my experiences, and so I became increasingly distant from the God I knew. This inflicted so much pain on my spirituality that I began to doubt the mere existence of God."

Remaining active in church even in the midst of her spiritual struggles as an undergraduate at Texas Woman's University, Christina served as assistant youth director at First United Methodist Church in Rockwall, Texas, and as publicity director for the Denton Wesley Foundation. After completing her bachelor of arts degree in psychology and women's studies, she served as a missionary in the Congo for ten months. During this time, her spiritual struggles intensified. "In a desperate attempt to revive my spirituality and discover the God in whom I yearned to believe, I enrolled at Southern Methodist University Perkins School of Theology," she says. "It was during this academic journey that I was able to reconcile my theology with my experiences. God was no longer a distant, domineering Father who watched my every move, but a loving liberator of the oppressed in whom we live and move and have our being. God is Sophia, the Wisdom of the cosmos who seeks justice and indwells in all of creation."

To be true to biblical revelation, Christina believes it is vital to include female divine language and symbolism in the church. "There has not always been exclusive language for the Divine," she says. "The Bible is chock-full of various names and images—both feminine and masculine—for God that have been used in worship. Sexism has caused society to eradicate or simply ignore the biblical use of feminine images and names for God historically and into the present."

This exclusively male imagery limits and distorts the nature of the Divine, Christina says. "Referring to the Divine exclusively as male creates a confinement of God's identity. When we label the Divine exclusively as 'Father,' 'King,' or 'Lord,' we limit the ways we can express the multiplicity that God really is. The more names we can use to describe the Divine, the further we are from idolatry. I agree with

Mary Daly when she states, 'If God is male, then male is God.' If we only refer to God as male, then we are worshiping males. Instead, we should create as many names and images as we can conceive, including the Divine Feminine, to describe a multifaceted God beyond our linguistic comprehension."

In her current position as minister of formation at Grace United Methodist Church, Christina supervises religious education programs for children, youth, and adults. Working to expand understanding and experience of the Divine, Christina began with her youth ministry. "I believe it is imperative that teenagers see themselves in the image of God," she says. "Youth experience a lot of difficulties in being comfortable with their identities. They are often ostracized, judged for their appearances, or excluded. Therefore, it is important for them to know that they are beloved creations of the Divine. This is why I began to write my own curriculum and worship services that include the Feminine Divine among other names for God."

In addition to fulfilling this need for the youth, Christina began creating Feminine Divine worship services for adults at Grace United Methodist and for others in the community. Although Christina says that Grace United Methodist is her "favorite church" in Dallas, she saw a need that was not being fulfilled through the traditional services of the church. In order to include women and men who are active in churches on Sunday morning, she schedules the Feminine Divine worship services on Saturday morning.

Participants have affirmed the life-changing power of these services. "People do not always realize they need something different for their spirituality until they experience it," Christina says. "Even though we may have a logical understanding that God is not a giant male living in the distant heavens, we do not realize the effect ritual has on our spirituality. Worship forms us and we embody it in our daily lives. Exclusive male language in worship is the reason so many women feel less than holy or unable to identify with God. If God is male, then God cannot possibly understand me. If God is a domineering Father who punishes, then he is no different from my abusive dad. Worshiping the Feminine Divine opens the door for healing because it allows participants to experience what exclusive male language cannot offer: liberation from a male-dominated tradition and society."

The worship services that Christina creates with female divine names and images bring change to the whole church as well as to individual participants. She notes "small valuable improvements" in the Sunday worship services at Grace United Methodist Church. "The call to worship rarely refers to God as 'Father' or 'Lord.' The senior pastor now avoids male names for God. There are more conversations about why inclusive language is important. The people who do attend the Feminine Divine worship services see them as integral to the church's ministry."

Christina acknowledges the risk she takes by creating rituals that include female divine language and symbolism. "By simply using the Feminine Divine in ritual and conversation within the institution of the United Methodist Church, I am taking a risk. Institutions do not tolerate deviations from rules and doctrine without consequence." However, expansive liturgy is worth the risk to Christina because she believes it will bring liberating transformation not only to the church but also to the wider culture and contribute to "less sexualized and objectified images of women and girls" so that we all can claim our power in the image of the Divine.

Through a variety of ministries, Christina has been working to empower people. As a missionary, she lived in the Democratic Republic of Congo for ten months, and has traveled to Haiti, Zambia, Cameroon, South Africa, Ireland, and Mexico to empower communities all over the globe. As an activist, she serves as a trained Texas Woman's University and Southern Methodist University Ally to the LGBTIQ community and as an outreach advocate for survivors of sexual assault and relationship violence.

Including the Divine Feminine will bring healing power and will transform churches from hierarchical to egalitarian communities, Christina believes. "My vision is that there will no longer be any hesitancy to use the Divine Feminine during the 'holy hour.' When we can understand that in Christ there is no longer Jew or Greek, slave or free, male or female, then we will leave those hierarchies at the door as we enter the kindom of God.[25] Sexism will no longer hinder our communities from seeing God in Her fullest: as a multifaceted God who cannot be confined by our limited notions of God as exclusively male." Christina's creative, prophetic liturgies sound Sophia's call that justice must be done!

O Sophia, Justice Must Be Done!

O Sophia, Lover of all creation,

You have called us to a time of Jubilee.

By your power, may we hear your call.

'Cause justice must be done!

> *(Sound noisemakers)*

O Sophia, Relatedness of the cosmos,

You have created us as interdependent creatures.

By your power, may we awaken to our inherent connectedness.

'Cause justice must be done!

> *(Sound noisemakers)*

O Sophia, Source of all life,

You have given us the gift of creativity.

By your power, may we use our creativity for good.

'Cause justice must be done!

> *(Sound noisemakers)*

O Sophia, River of life,

You have quenched our thirst with abundant resources.

By your power, may we quench every creature's thirst.

'Cause justice must be done!

> *(Sound noisemakers)*

O Sophia, Cocreator of the universe,

You have blessed us with freedom.

By your power, may we free the oppressed in the land.

'Cause justice must be done!

> *(Sound noisemakers)*

O Sophia, Spirit of all that lives,

You have shown us the way of righteousness.

By your power, may we live righteously in every breath.

'Cause justice must be done!

> *(Sound noisemakers)*

'Cause justice must be done!

> *(Sound noisemakers)*

'Cause justice must be done!

Part 10

Wisdom's Works of Creative Worship

Divine Wisdom guides us to cocreate with Her new works for creative worship. Rituals that include female divine names and images form the foundation for Wisdom's works of social justice, peace, and equality. Because rituals engage our senses and emotions as well as our intellect, the words and images of rituals become imbedded in us at the conscious and subconscious levels. Our worship symbolism thus shapes our beliefs and values, which shape our actions. Actions change as the artistic and sensual dimensions of liberating rituals permeate our whole beings.

The stories in this book illustrate the power of including female names and images of the Divine in worship. Through personal experiences as well as biblical and theological explanation, the ministers in this book affirm the transformation that comes through this inclusive worship symbolism. Woven through their stories are prayers, hymns, litanies, and other liturgical resources that include Wisdom and other biblical female personifications of the Divine.

Here you will find additional inclusive, expansive, creative liturgical resources to use in faith communities and in personal meditation. It is my hope that you will also join the adventure of creating rituals that include the Female Divine, affirming the sacred value of all people and all creation. She lives! Holy Wisdom lives in all, giving each one creative gifts and calling us to join Her new creation.

She Lives and Moves Throughout the Earth

(Sung to the tune of "Hail, Holy Queen Enthroned Above")

She lives within us and above, Holy Wisdom;
Her many names bring life and love, Holy Wisdom.
Hokmah and Sophia wise,
Mary Queen of earth and skies,
Ruah Spirit, El Shaddai,
Mother Hen, Sister Friend,
join Her new creation.

She comes to sound her peaceful call, Holy Wisdom;
She is a Tree of Life for all, Holy Wisdom.
Blessing those who hold Her fast,
blending future, present, past,
helping all be free at last,
Wisdom-Word now is heard;
join Her new creation.[1]

Words © 2013 Jann Aldredge-Clanton   SALVE REGINA COELITUM

Christ-Sophia Loves Us, Restores Us, and Sets Us Free

Liturgy by Christina Cavener

Sophia, Our Love-Maker,

We are afraid of your love, your intimacy.

We are used to being judged,

but we are not used to being loved, totally.

Give us the courage to let go and embrace you;

may we learn how to want your loving touch,

that we in our turn may love generously those who cannot believe they are loved.

Let us now rise and greet one another, saying, "[Name], you are loved."

(Read Mark 14:3–9.)

Sophia, Our Pain-Bearer,

Give us the courage of this unknown woman,

to speak the gospel with authority;

to break open all our resources

from the place of no resources;

to break open and pour out

even the pain that we want to hold on to;

so that we can dare to name the truth about our world,

and truthfully stand with the Christ-Sophia who made herself nothing for our sake.

At this time, let us now name those women who have lived the gospel through their actions or spoken prophetic words. Let us name our sister pioneers. Let us claim our sister saints.

Miriam, poetess of the Exodus, our sister,

We remember you.

Sarah, our sister,

We remember you.

Ruth, our sister,

We remember you.

Mary of Magdala, our sister,

We remember you.

Phoebe, our sister,

We remember you.

St. Teresa of Avila, our sister,

We remember you.

St. Hildegard of Bingen, our sister,

We remember you.

Lift other names and we will respond with, "We remember you."

All women in the church, our sisters, how good it is to claim you,

for you are our tradition of prophets, disciples, ministers,

the cloud of witnesses to the work of Spirit-Sophia.

We thank you for your faithfulness. You are inspirations to us all.

Sophia, our Life-Giver,

Again and again we find ourselves stuck

in old patterns of domination and submission;

we stay resenting our powerlessness

or guilt-ridden by our power.

Give us courage to believe that change is possible:

Let us so wash one another's feet as sisters and brothers

that the fragrance of our ministry

may fill the whole church,

and free us from captivity

to a world where no one is held in bondage.

Let us now wash one another's feet with the love of Christ-Sophia. We will partner with one another and take turns washing each other's feet. After washing your partner's feet, say, "Christ-Sophia has set you free, my sister/brother."

Let us now come together as sisters and brothers, holding each other in solidarity. Let us together voice our unity in Christ-Sophia.

Christ-Sophia has restored our love.

Christ-Sophia has healed our pain.

Christ-Sophia has set us free.

Prayer for Christ-Sophia's Peace

Beverly Jane Phillips

Dear Sophia-God and Precious Mother, Christ-Sophia, Spirit-Sophia, You are so present with us! What a difference it would make in all the happenings of the world if all people knew that You are so close! I think we would not be shouting praise to Allah or Almighty God and then hurting and killing each other if we knew how You are the Spirit of Life within us.[2]

Litany for Peace

Deborah Hall

Leader: Sophia, we pray for each other, our sisters in this room. We pray for peace.

All: May peace prevail on earth.

Voice 1: Sophia, we pray for our families—for those struggling with careers, with health issues, with relationships. We pray for peace.

All: May peace prevail on earth.

Voice 2: Sophia, we pray for our community—for the mentally ill, for those who are grieving, for children who are bullied in our schools. We pray for peace.

All: May peace prevail on earth.

Voice 3: Sophia, we pray for healing—for the emotionally abused, for the physically abused, for the sexually abused, and for the spiritually abused. We pray for peace.

All: May peace prevail on earth.

Voice 4: Sophia, we pray for fairness—for those mistreated because of the color of their skin, sexual orientation, disability, size, or gender. We pray for peace.

All: May peace prevail on earth.

Voice 5: Sophia, we pray for knowledge—to assist the undervalued, the underrepresented, the underpaid, and the underdeveloped on this earth. We pray for peace.

All: May peace prevail on earth.

Voice 6: Sophia, we pray for action—for those who live in abject poverty and for those suffering the devastation of war. We pray for peace.

All: May peace prevail on earth.

Voice 7: Sophia, we pray for organizational assistance—for those suffering from earthquakes, famine, and other disasters. We pray for peace.

All: Sophia, Wisdom of God, in you resides our hope, in you resides our peace. Amen.

Seeking Sophia

Poem by Susan C. Hamilton

Again I mull through the mountains of paper arranged as books
        again I desperately seek for your face in
someone else's words,

someone else's images,
someone else's song
someone else with greater access to wisdom.

Again I am impressed by the sheer volumes written
again I am inspired with the beauty of your reflection in
another's experience,
another's dedication,
another's eloquence
another's ease in your presence.

But today you call me, stretch me, implore me to stop
today you urge me to set it all aside and be
be with you,   be open,   be real
be in the truth that you are closer than I dare believe.

The seeking is over, the journey ended and yet just begun
the seeking unnecessary. For you are the one
within,   among,   around
and through all that I creatively am and do.

I have found you, Holy Sophia, in time for the teaching
I have found the words to encourage the seeking
I have found you—not out there in someone else,
but in here,   in me,   no less.[3]

A Pentecost Prayer: Come, Sophia-Spirit

Diann L. Neu

Pentecost, fifty days after Easter, celebrates the coming of the Holy Spirit upon her people. It is the birthday of the Christian church. The Holy Spirit's Greek name is *Sophia*. "Wisdom" is her English name; *Hokmah* is her Hebrew name; *Sapientia* is her Latin name.

Divine Wisdom, Sophia-Spirit, calls for the liberation of all from patriarchy and kyriarchy. This is what we celebrate today as we bless bread,
wine, juice, and food.

Blessed are you, Womb of All Creation, Spirit-Sophia. With joy we give
you thanks and praise for creating a diverse world and for creating women
in your image.

Come, Sophia-Spirit, come.

Blessed are you, God of our Mothers, Spirit-Sophia. You call diverse
women to participate in salvation history: Eve, Lilith, Sarah, Hagar,
Miriam, Naomi and Ruth, Mary, Mary Magdalene, Tecla, Phoebe,
Hildegard of Bingen, Sor Juana, Sojourner Truth, Mother Theodore
Guerin, all WATER women, and countless others.

Come, Sophia-Spirit, come.

Blessed are you, Creator of all seasons and all peoples, Spirit-Sophia. You
call us to be prophets, teachers, house church leaders, ministers, saints,
and to image your loving and challenging presence.

Come, Sophia-Spirit, come.

Blessed are you, Companion on the Journey, Spirit-Sophia. In your abundant love you welcome all to come and dine. You proclaim from the roof-
tops, "Come and eat my bread, drink the wine which I have drawn."

Come, Sophia-Spirit, come.

Come, Holy Sister, Spirit-Sophia, upon this bread, wine, juice, and food.
Come as breath and breathe your life anew into our aching bones. Come as
wind and refresh our weary souls. Come as fire and purge us and our communities of sexism, racism, classism, heterosexism, ageism, and all evils.

Come, Sophia-Spirit, come.

As we eat, drink, and enjoy the Pentecost banquet, may Sophia-Spirit rise
within us like a rushing wind. May Sophia-Spirit spark the churches like
a revolutionary fire. May Sophia-Spirit flow through the world like a life-
giving breath.

Amen. Blessed be. May it be so.[4]

Blowing Where She Wills

Excerpts from a Pentecost Sermon by Shawna R. B. Atteberry

She has been here from the beginning, stirring, creating, bringing form to chaos, and life to dust. In the beginning she brooded over the watery chaos waiting for Godde to give the word. In the fire, thunder, and smoke of Sinai she guarded the holiness of Godde and showed that approaching this Godde should not be taken lightly. When Elijah looked for Godde in fire, earthquake, and storm, she came in sheer silence to show that she didn't always appear with the flash and panache that human beings expect.

She gave birth to the church and is the One who gives us our unity, giftings, and words. But we don't talk about her that much. In fact, the Church has never talked about the Holy Spirit much at all. She gets brushed to the side. She's the runt of the Trinity no one wants to claim. And there's a reason for this. The Holy Spirit scares us. We can't control her. We can't put restraints on her. We have our nice neat boxes for the other two members of the Trinity. Godde the Father and Mother is categorized with all of the attributes of Godde and put in the appropriate box. Godde the Son is neatly categorized by word and deed and placed in his box. For centuries theologians, scholars, teachers, and preachers have tried to do the same thing with the Spirit. But how do you put wind into a box?

I don't think it's an accident that in the Hebrew and Greek "spirit," "wind," and "breath" are the same word. All three are taken for granted and none is really under our control. My favorite metaphor for the Spirit is wind. I'm originally from Oklahoma and have lived in the Midwest for twenty-seven years, so I know something about wind. Wind is unpredictable. You don't know what it's going to do. It can give you a wonderful cool breeze on a hot summer day. It can also destroy acres of land and flatten towns and part of cities. As Jesus told Nicodemus, you can't see either the wind or the Spirit but you can feel them. You don't know where either comes from or where they are going. Wind is not something anyone can control. It decides when it blows and how. It can choose to be still and silent or roaring hundreds of miles per hour. No one tells the wind where to blow, but it will blow you a few blocks up the street on certain days. It's wonderful when it acts like we think it should, and it's disastrous when it decides to show its power in straight-line winds and tornadoes.

I think this is why we don't hear too much about the Holy Spirit. We just can't fit her into those nice, neat systematic theology boxes we put Godde the Father and Mother and Godde the Son in. We can't even pretend to control her. What do we do with this wonky member of the Trinity who doesn't fit into all of our nice, neat little boxes with the nice, neat little attributes fixed to her box? The Spirit does what she wants and blows where she wants. When she gives a nice breeze of inspiration during private prayer, we love her. When she blows us out of our comfort zones to be peacemakers and love those we'd rather not, we're not too sure about her and her methods.

In Acts the Spirit is blowing. A little group huddled in a room have been hiding out and praying for ten days. Their Messiah has been crucified, resurrected, and now has ascended into heaven. He's gone again, and left them the responsibility to build the Kingdom of Godde on earth. No pressure there. Jesus told them to wait until the Holy Spirit came. But what exactly did that mean?

It meant something they could not control. She came blowing through the room they were in and blew them out into the streets to proclaim what they had been hiding: the power of God in Jesus Christ, the Messiah. She inspired them with her fire and put her words in their mouths. They spoke in different languages with their Galilean accents to show that it was not the disciples alone who were doing this.

Godde's Spirit is poured out on all to proclaim what Godde has done. The young and old, male and female, free and slave are in-spirited to tell those around them about Godde's love and compassion shown in Jesus. No one is left out.

As the disciples proclaim and show the love of Christ, Godde comes back to earth for good, never to leave again. The Holy Spirit does not act without a human counterpart. The apostles and disciples are praying and waiting when the Spirit comes and impels them out into the street.

I'm still not sure whether it's to Godde's credit or discredit that she insists on working through us. But that's what she does. We might never know which way the Holy Spirit is going to blow, but we do know that she is going to blow around and through us. Blowing us out of our rooms and sanctuaries. Blowing us out of our regular haunts and the normal people we hang out with. She blows us onto new roads and into new places to continue to bring Godde's presence into our world. She continues to empower people to shout out the good news that judgment is not Godde's last word. That Godde's last word has always been and will always be forgiveness, love, and mercy. Godde's Spirit blows into our lives, so that we can live Christ-like lives in our world, and that is Godde's final word.[5]

Breathe on Me, Ruah, Fire

Hymn by Deborah Hall

(Sung to the tune of "Breathe on Me, Breath of God")

Breathe on me, Ruah, Fire
Awaken in my soul
Your presence and enduring love
Burn brightly and make me whole.

Breathe on me, Ruah, Fire
Fill me with your New Wine
To see and hear the vision wide
Uniting my will with thine.

Breathe on me, Ruah, Fire
Ignite within your power
To work for justice, healing, peace
And praying for strength this hour.

Breathe on me, Ruah, Fire
Reveal your love divine
Within your children, one and all
And this tender heart of mine.

TRENTHAM

In the Beginning

Poem by Shawna R. B. Atteberry

In the beginning there was

Silence
Chaos
Deep

In the beginning there was

Blackness
Void
Nothing

In the beginning

The Spirit brooded
Godde spoke
And Wisdom cheered

In the beginning was Godde
And Wisdom was with Godde
Before She was rationalized into

The Word

Before She was reduced to
A Housewife

In the beginning was Godde and Wisdom

Creating
Cheering
Saying, "It is good."[6]

Sophia Is the Breath of Life

Responsive Meditation by Christina Cavener

Listen to the wind whistle, the leaves rustle, and the waves crash against the shore.

These are the voices of Sophia: the whispers of the Holy One.

Touch the bark on the tree, the wildflower in the field, and the leaves of a bush.

These are the words of Sophia: the living literature of the Divine.

Hear the birds sing, the bees buzz, and the ducks quack.

This is the music of Sophia: the holy choir that sings under the sun.

Watch the fox run, the fish swim, and the eagle fly.

These are the creations of Sophia: the beloved friends of humanity.

Smell the buttercups, the honeysuckles, and the sunflowers.

These are the gifts of Sophia: the reminders of divine grace.

See the pink sunrise, the blue skies, and the purple sunset.

These are the paintings of Sophia: the masterpieces displayed for all.

Look at the moon, the stars, and the planets.

These are the revelations of Sophia: the heavens that shine in the night.

Feel your heart pump, surge, and beat.

This is the pulse of Sophia: the rhythm of life on earth.

Inhale the sea's breeze and the oxygen of the trees,

This is the breath of Sophia: the force that connects us all.

Sophia of Interconnectedness,

in each breath,

let us plunge into our connectedness with the universe.

For it is in praying that we are able to breathe the breath of the universe.

Sophia, connect us with all living beings.

In each breath,

we want to draw the world into ourselves.

For our existence is part of this immense web of relationships.

Sophia, connect us with all living beings.

In each breath,

plunge us into the deep heart of the universe.

For it is in our breath that we are tuning in to the vital core.

Sophia, connect us with all living beings.

In each breath,

we inhale and exhale with all living beings.

For we share this breath of life with every creature.

Sophia, connect us with all living beings.

O Sophia, as we deepen ourselves into prayer, into our breath, allow us to become further connected with you. Be fully present with us and within us as we strive to abide in your holy presence. Amen.

I now invite you to close your eyes and breathe deeply. Be aware of how you are sitting, and note where the tense areas of your body are. Breathe deeply and slowly into your lower midsection. Continue to breathe deeply, focusing on the parts of your body holding tension. Exhale into and through these areas, until you feel the tension begin to go. Experience the presence of Sophia within you as you take each breath. With each breath, allow your body to rest in Sophia.

As you continue breathing, feel your heart as it beats with the pulse of the universe. Experience the rhythm of creation. Connect yourself with every living being. As you breathe, a bird breathes. As you breathe, a plant grows. As you breathe, a turtle comes up for air. Feel your connection with every living thing. Allow the power of this connection to take hold. Clear your mind and just be. Listen to the sounds of Sophia …

When you feel ready, I invite you to go find a spot nearby where you can see my wave beckoning you to return. Be in meditative silence for ten minutes. Appreciate the beauty of Sophia's creation and listen to her whispers …

(after meditation)

At this time, we will voice words to describe our experiences of this morning thus far. After everyone has spoken, we will respond:

Sophia, we thank you for these experiences.

Let us go forth to recognize the Divine in all of creation, to plunge into our connection with every living being, and to thank Sophia for the gift of life.

In Her name we pray,

Amen.

Who Are You, God?

Poem by Bridget Mary Meehan

I am the womb of mystery
I am the birther of new life
I am the breast of unending delight
I am the passionate embrace of woman
I am the emanation of feminine beauty
I am the Mother of Creation
I am the cosmic dance of Sophia Wisdom
I am the sister of courage, justice, and peace
I am the feminine face of God
you have longed to kiss.[7]

Part 11

Wisdom's Works of Feminist Emancipatory Faith Communities

Divine Wisdom guides in creating feminist emancipatory faith communities to celebrate Her works of creative worship.[1] By including Wisdom and other female images of the Divine, these communities bring healing, justice, equality, freedom, and peace. For years many of these communities have been at the forefront of this transformation, and it is exciting to see others emerging in many locations. This section lists feminist emancipatory churches, communities, and groups I have discovered, along with information about them. I do not claim that this list is exhaustive, and I invite you to add to it. When I interviewed Monica A. Coleman, she expressed her desire for a website to help people find feminist churches. My hope is that this list may serve as a beginning.

If you do not find a community in this list near you and do not know of one, I invite you to begin one, perhaps using some of the inclusive worship resources in part 10 or elsewhere in this book. Divine Wisdom calls us to experience Her transforming power as we join together in communities for inclusive, liberating rituals.

Welcome New Wineskins

(Sung to the tune of "Blessed Assurance, Jesus Is Mine")

Welcome new wineskins filled with new wine;
welcome new visions and stories divine.
Old forms and symbols never will hold
all of our gifts that daily unfold.

Come and discover Wisdom ignored,
treasures and talents too long unexplored.
Come to a place where all can belong;
join in a new community song.

Sisters and brothers equally share,
working as partners to dream and to dare.
For a new peace and freedom we pray,
joining our hands to bring a new day.

Refrain:
Welcome new wineskins, filled with new wine,
giving the world new visions divine;
welcome new wineskins, filled with new wine,
giving the world new visions divine.[2]

ASSURANCE

Broadway Church

MEETING TIME AND LOCATION: 10:00 A.M., EACH SUNDAY

3931 Washington Street, Kansas City, Missouri 64111

MISSION

"Broadway is an inclusive, theologically progressive, healing community focused on the spiritual transformation that comes from following Jesus Christ. We experience God as love and reject all punishing, vengeful, and violent images of God. We see each person, as Jesus did, as a divine being on a human journey. We address God as 'Mother' and 'Father' while agreeing that God includes and transcends all human metaphors and is Ultimate Mystery. We practice justice, welcoming and affirming diversity."

CONTACT

http://broadwaychurchkc.org; 816-561-3274

Christ Sophia Inclusive Catholic Community

MEETING TIME AND LOCATION

5:00 p.m., 1st and 3rd Saturdays of each month

St. Andrew United Church of Christ

2608 Browns Lane, Louisville, Kentucky 40220

MISSION

"Christ Sophia Inclusive Catholic Community models radical hospitality and inclusion of all genders, races, and sexual orientations. We are part of the Roman Catholic Women Priests movement that is a Spirit-led movement working within the Church for Gospel equality, nonviolence, justice, and a people-empowered Church. We affirm that justice for the poor and marginalized in our world includes people living in poverty who are excluded from just wages, and women excluded from the ministry in the Roman Catholic Church. Our community promotes collaboration with other denominations and organizations who serve the poor and marginalized. Our liturgies model inclusion of feminine terminology for Godde, who is beyond all gender description."

CONTACT

Rosemarie Smead, shanti.rosemarie@gmail.com

Church in the Cliff

MEETING TIME AND LOCATION

11:00 a.m., each Sunday

Kidd Springs Recreation Center

711 W Canty, Dallas, Texas 75208

MISSION

"Church in the Cliff is an inclusive and affirming community where all are welcome. We are a theologically and socially progressive Christian church with questions, dialogue, and justice-making at the heart of our identity. We seek to follow the Way of Christ and the Wisdom of Sophia as we celebrate and create beauty in art, nature, the world, and each other."

CONTACT

http://churchinthecliff.org

Circle of Grace Community Church

MEETING TIME AND LOCATION

5:00 p.m., most Sundays
1240 Euclid Avenue NE, Atlanta, Georgia 30307

MISSION

"Circle of Grace Community Church is an inclusive feminist worshiping community. We are nondoctrinal and seek to reimagine understandings of language, stories, symbols, and metaphors. We welcome all persons regardless of race, gender, sexuality, ability, class, culture, age, and religious background. We use inclusive language in our reference to God and humanity. We use the term 'reimagine' to describe our process of opening understandings of language and stories, symbols and metaphors and how we creatively engage feminist theology and sacred text. We are impassioned to cocreate challenging, empowering, and inclusive church."

CONTACT

www.circleofgraceatlanta.org/index.html
For information on 5th Sundays of the month, contact Rev. Connie Tuttle, revgrace@bellsouth.net.

Compassion of Christ Catholic Community

MEETING TIME AND LOCATION

5:00 p.m., 1st, 3rd, and 5th Sundays of each month
Prospect Park United Methodist Church
22 Orlin Avenue SE, Minneapolis, Minnesota 55414

MISSION

"Compassion of Christ Catholic Community is an inclusive Catholic community in the Roman Catholic tradition that affirms the holiness of each individual's faith journey, spiritually nourishes with sacraments and ritual, and lives out its faith with works of social justice. Liturgies are officiated by Roman Catholic Womenpriests."

CONTACT

www.compassionofchristcatholics.org

Ebenezer/herchurch Lutheran

MEETING TIMES AND LOCATION

Worship Service, 10:30 a.m., each Sunday

Goddess Rosary, 7:00 p.m., each Wednesday

678 Portola Drive, San Francisco, California 94127

MISSION

"The mission of Ebenezer/herchurch Lutheran is to embody and voice the prophetic wisdom and word of the Divine Feminine, to uplift the values of compassion, creativity, and care for the earth and one another. Our purple church is home to a diversity of spiritual traditions and perspectives that are woven together to create a strong, stretchy fabric that provides everyone with ample room to grow. We are committed to acts of justice and peace as we help shift the worldview from domination systems to mending and caring for the web-of-life."

CONTACT

www.herchurch.org/index.html; 415-731-2953

First United Lutheran Church

MEETING TIME AND LOCATION

5:00 p.m., each Sunday

St. Cyprian's Episcopal Church

2097 Turk Street, San Francisco, California 94115

MISSION

"First United Lutheran is an inclusive, welcoming community seeking to reach out to those for whom organized religion has proved ineffectual, irrelevant, or repressive; to uphold evangelism as an agent of justice and peace; and to give a strong voice both in the churches and the public arena to the advocates of progressive Christianity. We are committed to creative worship, social justice, care for the environment, and service to the community."

CONTACT

http://fulc.com; 415-359-1025

Friends of Sophia

MEETING TIME AND LOCATION
Varied schedule, contact for information
University of Saskatchewan
105 Administration Place, Saskatoon, Saskatchewan S7N 5A2

MISSION
"The Friends of Sophia is an interdenominational group of women, based at the University of Saskatchewan, dedicated to nurturing Christian feminist spirituality through educational opportunities, shared experience, and liturgical celebration."

CONTACT
mbeavis@stmcollege.ca; grompre@stmcollege.ca
www.facebook.com/groups/615970608420027

Holy Cross Lutheran Church

MEETING TIME AND LOCATION
10:45 a.m., each Sunday
1045 Wayne Drive, Newmarket, Ontario L3Y 2W9

MISSION
"Our purpose is to encounter the Gospel in worship, play, study, music, work, prayer, and activism. We provide worship that includes female divine names and images, and that is diverse, flexible, thought-provoking, and relevant to our challenging times. We are a voice for compassion and actively seek justice and peace in the world. We welcome all those who have ever felt excluded by the Church because of their race, gender, sexual orientation, age, physical or mental challenges, financial resources, or family status."

CONTACT
www.holycrosslutheran.ca; contact@holycrosslutheran.ca; 905-898-1682

Mary Magdalene, First Apostle

MEETING TIME AND LOCATION
Mass, 1:00 p.m., 2nd Sunday of each month
Spiritual Reflection Service, 1:00 p.m., 4th Sunday of each month
St. John's Episcopal Church
1111 Cooper Avenue S, St. Cloud, Minnesota 56301

MISSION
"Mary Magdalene, First Apostle, is an inclusive Roman Catholic community where all are welcome. We support Roman Catholic Women Priests,

claiming our gifts and standing for justice and equality in the Catholic Church. We value the variety of gifts expressed in our community gathered for our liturgies. We believe humanity hungers for the Divine Feminine and women to image Her."

CONTACT

Jeanette Blonigen Clancy, www.godisnot3guys.com

Mary Mother of Jesus Inclusive Catholic Community

MEETING TIME AND LOCATION

4:00 p.m., each Saturday

St. Andrew United Church of Christ

6908 Beneva Road, Sarasota, Florida 34238

MISSION

"We are a Christ-centered community of equals, consisting of women and men, ordained and non-ordained, empowered by the Spirit whose mission is to worship, to serve, and to promote compassion, justice, and care for creation. Our liturgy reflects an adaptation of earliest centuries of Christianity where the community gathered in homes to celebrate the Eucharist. We use inclusive language and imagery."

CONTACT

www.marymotherofjesus.org; sofiabmm@aol.com; 941-955-2313

New Wineskins Community

MEETING TIME AND LOCATION

11:00 a.m., 1st Sunday of each month

Richland College, Yegua Building, Room 102

12800 Abrams Road, Dallas, Texas 75243

MISSION

"New Wineskins Community explores new ways of seeing divinity so that the spiritual gifts of everyone are equally valued and nurtured. Our rituals name and image the Divine as female and male and more to support the equality and value of all. We welcome people of all faiths, races, sexual orientations, ages, and abilities. The mission of New Wineskins is to expand experience of Divine Mystery and to contribute to healing, peace, and justice in our world."

CONTACT

www.jannaldredgeclanton.com/wineskins.php

Pullen Memorial Baptist Church

MEETING TIME AND LOCATION

11:00 a.m., each Sunday

1801 Hillsborough, Raleigh, North Carolina 27605

MISSION

"Pullen has a strong commitment to meaningful worship, active lay involvement in social justice ministries, and mutual care and respect for one another
and all of God's creation. With the understanding that all language for God is
metaphorical, and that language instills truths of equality and justice in human
relationships, we intentionally use a variety of feminine, masculine, and non-
gender images in referring to God and humanity."

CONTACT

www.pullen.org; 919-828-0897

Sisters Against Sexism (SAS) Women-Church Community

MEETING TIME AND LOCATION

5:30 p.m., 3rd Sunday of each month

Member homes, Greater Washington, D.C., area

MISSION

"We gather for a ritual and potluck dinner. The rituals are planned by different members on a theme of their choosing."

CONTACT

cherylnichols1@verizon.net; 301-559-0774

St. Hildegard's Community

MEETING TIME AND LOCATION

4:30 p.m., each Sunday

Kleberg Hall, St. George's Episcopal Church

4301 N Interstate 35, Austin, Texas 78722

MISSION

"St. Hildegard's Community combines inclusive, creative worship with the
beauty and drama of Anglican worship. We offer a supportive environment for
seekers, those open to the wisdom of other sacred traditions and to exploring
emerging Christian theology. We explore ways that inclusive and expansive language about God and humanity and newly emerging theological understandings
can be incorporated into liturgy that is faithful to the Book of Common Prayer."

CONTACT

http://hildegard-austin.org; viriditas@hildegard-austin.org; 512-524-5145

Sophia Sisters

MEETING TIME AND LOCATION
7:00 p.m., 3rd Tuesday of each month
Chandler, Arizona. Meetings held in members' homes; for addresses, see contact information below.

MISSION
"The mission of Sophia Sisters is to create a safe and nurturing environment for women as we awaken to the Divine Feminine, which is fostered by learning together, worship using inclusive language for the Divine, and by supporting one another as we do justice, love kindness, and walk humbly with the Holy One."

CONTACT
Deborah.hall@cox.net; 480-203-4189

WATER Women's Ritual Group

MEETING TIME AND LOCATION
7:30 p.m., monthly, date varies
Online and at WATER office
8121 Georgia Avenue, Suite 310, Silver Spring, Maryland 20910

MISSION
"We gather for justice-seeking rituals that use feminist religious values to make social change. The rituals focus on feminist, holiday, and seasonal themes."

CONTACT
www.waterwomensalliance.org; dneu@hers.com; 301-589-2509

Women-Church Communities

CONTACT
women-churchconvergence.org/memberorgs.htm

Women Priests Worship Communities

MEETING TIME AND LOCATION
Many locations

MISSION
All these communities include female divine imagery and language in liturgies, and all include women priests in worship leadership.

CONTACT
www.arcwp.org; www.romancatholicwomenpriests.org

Women's Covenant Group

TIME AND LOCATION

12:00 noon, 2nd Sunday of each month
Reformed Church of Highland Park
19–21 S 2nd Avenue, Highland Park, New Jersey 08904

MISSION

"The Women's Covenant Group gathers to explore and celebrate the Divine Feminine. Monthly gatherings include reflection, group contemplation, artistic expression, and joyful celebration."

CONTACT

rchpoffice@juno.com; www.rchighlandpark.org/groups/womens-group

Women's Sacred Circle

TIME AND LOCATION

7:00 p.m., 3rd Friday of each month
Happehatchee Center
8791 Corkscrew Road, Estero, Florida 33928

MISSION

"The mission of Women's Sacred Circle is to make deep love connections to self, Divine Feminine, and one another for personal growth and local/global transformation. We are a safe and loving community where all voices are heard and all dreams honored. The art of sacred listening without judgment is practiced and the magnificence of all women and girls celebrated through storytelling, music, dance, art, and lively interactive discussions."

CONTACT

www.happehatchee.org

Epilogue

As I am completing this book, I find myself resisting writing a conclusion. My resistance comes partly from not wanting the joy of writing this book to end. Throughout the process, I have felt the book to be a wonderful gift from Sophia Wisdom. She guided me in finding the people to interview, in discovering creative worship resources inclusive of female divine images, in finding feminist emancipatory worship communities. Sophia also gave me the book's title and led to the right publisher in record time.

Another reason I have resisted concluding this book is that I know it is unfinished. The stories of the people in this book continue, and there are numerous other stories to be told of people doing Wisdom's works in the world. Also, there are many more of Wisdom's expansive worship resources not included in this book and more continually being created. Feminist worship communities are springing up around the world, and the list in this book is only a beginning. Wisdom lives indeed and Her stories are ongoing. Her resources continually unfold, and Her communities continually emerge.

Recently I had a dream. People are gathering for a New Wineskins Community feminist worship service in a college classroom, converted for each meeting into a ritual space. Chairs circle a purple-draped altar adorned with gold and purple candles, a variety of female divine symbols, and a central statue of Sophia with multicultural facial features and flowing, star-bedecked purple robe. The chairs we have placed in the circle are filled, yet people keep coming, so we keep adding more chairs, creating a larger and larger circle. They continue coming, and there is standing room only. Soon there is no more room for people to stand, and they spill out into the hallway and throughout the building. Then in my dream I see thousands of worship communities springing up around the world, growing and flourishing—and then millions. And I hear Sophia's strong, gentle voice speaking to everyone in these communities: "I am here as always, and growing stronger every day with your help. I join with you as you join with me to continue cocreating works of justice, equality, peace, freedom, beauty, life, and love."

Wisdom, Sophia, Joins in Our Labor
(Sung to the tune of "Morning Has Broken")

Wisdom, Sophia, joins in our labor;
She with us freely cocreates life;
on this adventure, loving our neighbors,
kindness we nurture, ending the strife.

Wisdom, Sophia, gives us new power,
helping to free us, bringing us peace;
She with us healing that we may flower,
beauty revealing, talents released.

She is transforming, Wisdom, Sophia,
daily reforming, giving new birth;
changing and growing, She with us freeing,
touching and flowing, nourishing earth.[1]

Words © 2008 Jann Aldredge-Clanton   BUNESSAN

Notes

Introduction

1. That question would become the title of one of the chapters in my first book, *In Whose Image? God and Gender* (New York: Crossroad, 1990; revised and expanded edition, 2001).

2. In addition to *In Whose Image*, I wrote *In Search of the Christ-Sophia: An Inclusive Christology for Liberating Christians* (Mystic, CT: Twenty-Third Publications, 1995; Austin, TX: Eakin Press, 2004).

3. *Praying with Christ-Sophia: Services for Healing and Renewal* (Mystic, CT: Twenty-Third Publications, 1996; Eugene, OR: Wipf & Stock, 2007); *Inclusive Hymns for Liberating Christians* (Austin, TX: Eakin Press, 2006); *Inclusive Hymns for Liberation, Peace, and Justice* (Austin, TX: Eakin Press, 2011); *Seeking Wisdom: Inclusive Blessings and Prayers for Public Occasions* (Eugene, OR: Wipf & Stock, 2010).

4. Jann Aldredge-Clanton, *Changing Church: Stories of Liberating Ministers* (Eugene, OR: Cascade Books, 2011).

5. www.jannaldredgeclanton.com/blog.

6. Marjorie Procter-Smith uses the term "feminist emancipatory" in her book *The Church in Her House: A Feminist Emancipatory Prayer Book for Christian Communities* (Cleveland: Pilgrim Press, 2008), x. She explains her use of this term: "By 'feminist' I mean to place women at the center, to make women visible, audible, and active. By 'emancipatory' I mean being oriented toward the freedom of all people, recognizing the intersection and interrelationship of these multiple forms of oppression."

7. The Women's Alliance for Theology, Ethics and Ritual (WATER) is a feminist educational center and network of justice-seekers, responding to the need for theological, ethical, and liturgical development for and by women (waterwomensalliance.org/about-us).

8. Virginia Ramey Mollenkott, "Why Inclusive Language Is Still Important," *Christian Feminism Today* (www.eewc.com/inclusive-language-still-importan). Mollenkott's books *Omnigender: A Trans-Religious Approach* (Cleveland: Pilgrim Press, 2002, 2007) and *Transgender Journeys*, with Vanessa Sheridan (Cleveland: Pilgrim Press, 2003; Eugene, OR: Resource Publications, 2010) provide detailed explanations and moving stories on this topic.

9. Angela M. Yarber, *The Gendered Pulpit* (Cleveland, TN: Parson's Porch Books, 2013), 39.

10. "Every 9 Seconds in the US a Woman Is Assaulted or Beaten—Help End Domestic Violence," PRWEB (Austin, TX: October 8, 2012), www.prweb.com/releases/2012/10/prweb9986276.htm.

11. United Nations General Assembly, "In-Depth Study on All Forms of Violence against Women: Report of the Secretary General, 2006" (July 2006), www.un.org/en/women/endviolence/pdf/VAW.pdf.

12. The United Nations Population Fund, The State of World Population 2000 report, "Lives Together, Worlds Apart: Men and Women in a Time of Change" (2000), www.unfpa.org/swp/2000/english/ch03.html.

13. Nicholas D. Kristof and Sheryl WuDunn, *Half the Sky: Turning Oppression into Opportunity for Women Worldwide* (New York: Knopf, 2009), xvii.

14. Louise Arbour, United Nations high commissioner for human rights, "International Women's Day: Laws and 'Low Intensity' Discrimination against Women" (March 8, 2008).

15. Used with permission of Wipf and Stock Publishers. For fuller stories, see *Changing Church: Stories of Liberating Ministers* (Eugene, OR: Cascade Books, 2011).

16. www.eewc.com.

17. Caryn D. Riswold, *Feminism and Christianity: Questions and Answers, in the Third Wave* (Eugene, OR: Cascade Books, 2009), 20, 68.

18. Jann Aldredge-Clanton, "Celebrate the Works of Wisdom," *Inclusive Hymns for Liberation, Peace, and Justice* (Austin, TX: Eakin Press, 2011), #10.

Part 1: Wisdom's Works of Gender Equality

1. Mary Kathleen Speegle Schmitt, *Seasons of the Feminine Divine: Christian Feminist Prayers for the Liturgical Cycle*, Cycle C (New York: Crossroad, 1994), 18–19.

2. Jann Aldredge-Clanton, "Celebrate a New Day Dawning," stanzas 1 and 2, *Inclusive Hymns for Liberating Christians* (Austin, TX: Eakin Press, 2006), #52. This hymn is originally set to the tune HYMN TO JOY.

3. Lori Eickmann, "In Search of God: One Woman's Quest Leads Her to Change Her Life and Answer the Call to Become a Minister," *San Jose Mercury News*, May 2, 1998.

4. Virginia Ramey Mollenkott, *The Divine Feminine: The Biblical Imagery of God as Female* (New York: Crossroad, 1986; Eugene, OR: Wipf & Stock, 2014); Leonard Swidler, *Biblical Affirmations of Woman* (Philadelphia: Westminster Press, 1979).

5. Kendra Weddle Irons, "Fear, Fairness, and Feminism: Does It Have to Be So Lonely?" *Christian Feminism Today*, www.eewc.com/FemFaith/fear-fairness-feminism-lonely.

6. Ibid.

7. Kendra Weddle Irons, "Understanding Opposition to Feminism and What We Can Do about It, Kendra's Response: We Need to Do More," *Christian Feminism Today*, www.eewc.com/FemFaith/understanding-opposition-feminism.

8. Kendra Weddle Irons, *Preaching on the Plains: Methodist Women Preachers in Kansas, 1920–1956* (Lanham, MD: University Press of America, 2007).

9. Sue Monk Kidd, *Dance of the Dissident Daughter: A Woman's Journey from Christian Tradition to the Sacred Feminine* (San Francisco: HarperCollins, 1996).

10. Elizabeth A. Johnson, *She Who Is: The Mystery of God in Feminist Theological Discourse* (New York: Crossroad, 1992).

11. Kendra Weddle Irons, "Fearing the Feminine or Embracing Our Mother," *Christian Feminism Today*, www.eewc.com/FemFaith/fearing-the-feminine-or-embracing-our-mother.

12. Kendra Weddle Irons, "Creating Learned Helplessness, One Potluck at a Time, Response by Kendra: Language Must Be Part of the Change," *Christian Feminism Today*, www.eewc.com/FemFaith/creating-learned-helplessness. In this article Dr. Irons comments on her use of "Godde": "Godde is the spelling some Christian feminists, but not all, prefer to use in talking about the Deity because it suggests a combination of male and female in the very name."

13. Ibid.
14. Kendra Weddle Irons, "Worshipping Him: Ain't I a Woman: De/Constructing Christians Images" (October 8, 2012), http://aintiawomanblog.net/2012/10/worshipping-him.html.
15. Kendra Weddle Irons, "An Empty Pew," *Christian Feminism Today*, www.eewc.com/Articles/an-empty-pew.
16. Evangelical & Ecumenical Women's Caucus: Christian Feminism Today, www.eewc.com.
17. Kendra Weddle Irons, "An Empty Pew."
18. In addition to her work as a religion professor and her writing for *Christian Feminism Today* and other publications, Kendra Weddle Irons coauthors with Melanie Springer Mock the blog, "Ain't I a Woman: De/Constructing Christians Images," http://aintiawomanblog.net.
19. "The Good News According to the Tradition of Matthew," *The Christian Godde Project: Exploring the Divine Feminine within the Christian Godde*, http://godde.wordpress.com/the-divine-feminine-version-dfv-of-the-new-testament.
20. *The Christian Godde Project*, http://godde.wordpress.com/about/
21. Ibid.
22. Mark Mattison, "The Divine Feminine Trinity," *The Christian Godde Project*, http://godde.wordpress.com/godde-the-divine-feminine/the-divine-feminine-trinity.
23. http://godde.wordpress.com/the-divine-feminine-version-dfv-of-the-new-testament.
24. Mark Mattison, *"Because of the Angels": Head Coverings and Women in 1 Corinthians 11:2–16 and 14:34, 35* (Seattle, WA: CreateSpace, 2012); Mark M. Mattison, *The Gospel of Mary: A Fresh Translation and Holistic Approach* (Seattle, WA: CreateSpace, 2013).
25. Angela Yarber, *The Gendered Pulpit: Sex, Body, and Desire in Preaching and Worship* (Cleveland, TN: Parson's Porch Books, 2013), 41–42.
26. The acronym LGBTQ stands for Lesbian, Gay, Bisexual, Transgender, Questioning.
27. Yarber, *The Gendered Pulpit*, 12–13.
28. Angela Yarber, *Embodying the Feminine in the Dances of the World's Religions* (New York: Peter Lang Publishing, 2011).
29. Angela Yarber, *Dance in Scripture: How Biblical Dancers Can Revolutionize Worship Today* (Eugene, OR: Cascade Books, 2013).
30. Yarber, *The Gendered Pulpit*, 39.
31. Ibid., 25.
32. http://angelayarber.wordpress.com/artist.

Part 2: Wisdom's Works of Racial Equality

1. Caitlin Matthews, *Sophia, Goddess of Wisdom: The Divine Feminine from Black Goddess to World-Soul* (London: Mandala, 1991), 11–96.
2. Jann Aldredge-Clanton, "O Holy Darkness, Loving Womb," stanzas 1, 2, and 4, *Inclusive Hymns for Liberating Christians* (Austin, TX: Eakin Press, 2006), #99.
3. Grace Ji-Sun Kim, *The Grace of Sophia: A Korean North American Women's Christology* (Cleveland, OH: Pilgrim Press, 2002), 142–143.
4. Ibid., 131.
5. Ibid., viii.
6. Ibid., vii.

7. Grace Ji-Sun Kim, "Journey towards Reimagination: Society of Race, Ethnicity and Religion," *Feminist Studies in Religion* (May 29, 2013), www.fsrinc.org/blog/journey-towards-reimagination-society-race-ethnicity-and-religion.

8. Ibid.

9. Grace Ji-Sun Kim, *The Holy Spirit, Chi, and the Other: A Model of Global and Intercultural Pneumatology* (Basingstoke, Hampshire, England: Palgrave Macmillan, 2011).

10. Ibid., 5.

11. Grace Ji-Sun Kim, *Colonialism, Han, and the Transformative Spirit* (Basingstoke, Hampshire, England: Palgrave Pivot, 2013).

12. In addition to her work as a theology professor and her published books, articles, and book chapters, Grace Ji-Sun Kim writes a blog at http://gracejisunkim.wordpress.com.

13. Christine A. Smith, *Beyond the Stained Glass Ceiling: Equipping & Encouraging Female Pastors* (Valley Forge, PA: Judson Press, 2013), ix–x.

14. Ibid., x, xiii.

15. Ibid, 40.

16. bell hooks, *Ain't I a Woman: Black Women and Feminism* (Cambridge, MA: South End Press, 1981); Alice Walker, *In Search of Our Mothers' Gardens: Womanist Prose* (Boston: Houghton Mifflin, 1983); James Cone, *God of the Oppressed* (New York: Seabury Press, 1975); Paul Tillich, *The Courage to Be* (New Haven, CT: Yale University Press, 1952).

17. Smith, *Beyond the Stained Glass Ceiling*, 15–16.

18. Ibid., 36–37.

19. Ibid., 147.

20. In addition to her pastoral and denominational work and her published book, Christine A. Smith writes a blog at http://shepastor.blogspot.com.

21. TengoVoz, which Rev. Virginia Marie Rincon founded in 1999 in Portland, Maine, also presents lectures on the prevention of domestic violence; provides crisis intervention; organizes and collaborates in rallies and peace vigils related to immigrant rights, domestic violence issues, and racial profiling; translates and interprets documents; provides life skills coaching; and organizes cultural events.

22. A *mujerista* is a person who works for equal economic, social, political, and religious opportunities for Latina women. The work of Ada María Isasi-Díaz established the field of study, which she named "*mujerista* theology." See her book titled *Mujerista Theology: A Theology for the Twenty-First Century* (Maryknoll, NY: Orbis Books, 1996).

23. A *curandera*, literally translated "healer," is a traditional folk healer or shaman in Latino/a culture, who is dedicated to curing physical or spiritual illnesses. Many *curanderos/as* use Catholic elements, such as holy water and saints' pictures, along with other cultural religious elements.

24. Kristen Muszynski, "Rev. Virginia Marie Rincon Looks to Foster Latino Connection," *Biddeford Journal Tribune* (September 24, 2005), C4.

25. Melanie Springer Mock, "God's Gift of Motherhood Comes in Different Ways," *Christian Feminism Today*, www.eewc.com/Articles/god%E2%80%99s-gift-motherhood.

26. Ibid.

27. Melanie Springer Mock, *Writing Peace: The Unheard Voices of Great War Mennonite Objectors* (Telford, PA: Cascadia Publishing House, 2003); Melanie Springer Mock and Rebekah D. Schneiter, *Just Moms: Conveying Justice in an Unjust World* (Newberg, OR: Barclay Press, 2011); http://aintiawomanblog.net.

28. http://aintiawomanblog.net/2013/03/our-new-website-and-why-still-do-what-we-do.html.

29. "'Having It All' or 'Being It All?' When Leaning In Means Pushing Back: A Response by Melanie Springer Mock," *Christian Feminism Today*, www.eewc.com/FemFaith/having-it-all-or-being-it-all.

30. www.stjames-cambridge.org/music.

31. "Who Comes from God? (Sophia)," by Patrick Michaels, is published in *Chalice Hymnal* (St. Louis: Chalice Press, 1995), *Common Praise* (Toronto: Anglican Book Centre, 1998), and *Voices United: The Hymn and Worship Book of the United Church of Canada* (Etobicoke, Ontario: The United Church Publishing House, 1996).

Part 3: Wisdom's Works of Marriage Equality

1. The Religious Institute affirms inclusive worship language as foundational to LGBTQ inclusion, marriage equality, equality for all people, and celebration of sexual and gender diversity as sacred gifts. They sponsored a search for hymns that reflect these values. Eager to contribute to the Religious Institute's prophetic mission of celebrating the goodness of all creation and affirming a sexual ethic based on justice, equality, and full inclusion of all persons, I wrote "Praise the Source of All Creation." I was delighted that the Religious Institute selected this hymn as the winner of the contest.

2. Billy Hallowell, "Lesbian Pastor Refuses to Wed Straights Until Gays Allowed to Marry in NC," BeliefNet, www.beliefnet.com/columnists/watchwomanonthewall/2011/08/lesbian-minister-in-raleigh-n-c-wont-marry-hetrosexuals.html.

3. www.pullen.org/2011/11/20/marriage-equality-statement.

4. Nancy Petty, "Backsliding in the Wake County Schools," *News & Observer* (January 29, 2010).

5. See Introduction, p. xii.

6. Martin Luther King Jr., "Letter From Birmingham Jail" (April 16, 1963), in *Why We Can't Wait* (Boston: Beacon Press, 1963), 85.

7. Susan D. Newman, *Your Inner Eve: Discovering God's Woman Within* (New York: Random House Publishing Group, 2005), 84, 94.

8. Susan D. Newman, *Oh God! A Black Woman's Guide to Sex and Spirituality* (New York: Ballantine Publishing Group, 2002), 141.

9. Susan D. Newman, *With Heart and Hand: The Black Church Working to Save Black Children* (Valley Forge, PA: Judson Press, 1994).

10. Newman, *Oh God!*, 17–18.

11. Luke 15:8–10.

12. Paul R. Smith, *Is It Okay to Call God "Mother"? Considering the Feminine Face of God* (Peabody, MA: Hendrickson Publishers, 1993), 256, 261.

13. Ibid., 273.

14. Paul R. Smith, "The Cover-up of the Divine Feminine: Is It Okay to Call God 'Goddess'?" http://feniva.com/prs/teachings/DaVinciCode3.PDF ("Teachings," June 18, 2006).

15. Paul R. Smith, *Integral Christianity: The Spirit's Call to Evolve* (St. Paul, MN: Paragon House, 2011).

16. "Integral Life," http://integrallife.com/integral-post/transforming-power-integral-prayer.

17. John 10:34 records Jesus' answer to those who accused him of blasphemy for claiming to be God's son: "Is it not written in your law, 'I said, you are gods'?" Jesus here refers to Psalm 82:6: "I say, "You are gods, children of the Most High, all of you."

18. Caryn D. Riswold, "Yes, NALT, but SSA, and WAY?" "feminismxianity," *Patheos: Hosting the Conversation on Faith* (September 15, 2013), www.patheos.com/blogs/carynriswold/2013/09/yes-nalt-but-ssa-and-way.

19. Caryn D. Riswold, *Feminism and Christianity: Questions and Answers, in the Third Wave* (Eugene, OR: Cascade Books, 2009), 20, 68.

20. Ibid., 1.

21. Ibid.

22. Caryn D. Riswold, "feminismxianity," *Patheos:* Hosting the Conversation on Faith, www.patheos.com/blogs/carynriswold.

23. Riswold, *Feminism and Christianity*, 7, 125.

24. Ibid., 69.

25. Ibid., 70.

26. Ibid., 118.

27. Ibid., 109–10.

28. http://66.147.244.109/~herchurc/purple-church.

29. Rosemary Radford Ruether, *Sexism and God-Talk* (Boston: Beacon Press, 1983).

30. Luke 13:20.

31. Rev. Stacy Boorn has published two books of splendid photographs: *Natural Colors: "California"* and *Alaska: Wet and Wild* (www.blurb.com). Also, her works are on exhibit in "A Woman's Eye Gallery" (www.awegallery.com) and on her blog (stacy.awegallery.com).

Part 4: Wisdom's Works of Economic Justice

1. The word "kyriarchy," coined by feminist theologian Elisabeth Schüssler Fiorenza, is derived from the Greek words for "lord" or "master" (*kyrios*) and "to rule or dominate" (*archein*); Schüssler Fiorenza uses the word "kyriarchy" to redefine the category of patriarchy in terms of multiple "intersecting structures of domination and subordination, of ruling and oppression." See Elisabeth Schüssler Fiorenza, *Wisdom Ways: Introducing Feminist Biblical Interpretation* (Maryknoll, NY: Orbis Books, 2001), 211.

2. Jann Aldredge-Clanton, "Where Are Liberty and Justice?" This not-previously-published hymn was inspired by people with whom I serve on the Dallas Workers' Rights Board.

3. Dr. Docampo's recent publications include *Joshua, Judges, Ruth: Immersion Bible Studies* (Nashville, TN: Abingdon Press, 2012), in which she includes powerful commentary on social justice issues; and "Tracing Sister Connections: The Place of United States Latina Baptist Women in Ministry within the Overall Story of Baptist Women in Ministry," *Review & Expositor* 110, no. 1 (Winter 2013).

4. Mary E. Hunt, "New Feminist Catholics: Community and Ministry," in *New Feminist Christianity: Many Voices, Many Views*, ed. Mary E. Hunt and Diann L. Neu (Woodstock, VT: SkyLight Paths, 2010), 277–78.

5. Ibid., 276.

6. Ibid., 277.

7. www.waterwomensalliance.org/about-us.

8. Mary E. Hunt, ed., *A Guide for Women in Religion: Making Your Way from A to Z* (New York: Palgrave Macmillan, 2004); Mary E. Hunt, Patricia Beattie Jung, and Radhika Balakrishnan, eds., *Good Sex: Feminist Perspectives from the World's Religions* (New Brunswick, NJ: Rutgers University Press, 2001).

9. Mary E. Hunt, *Fierce Tenderness: A Feminist Theology of Friendship* (New York: Crossroad, 1991); Mary E. Hunt, ed., *From Woman-Pain to Woman-Vision: Writings in Feminist Theology* (Minneapolis, MN: Fortress Press, 1989).

10. Rosemary Radford Ruether, ed., *Feminist Theologies: Legacy and Prospect* (Minneapolis, MN: Fortress Press, 2007); Marvin M. Ellison and Judith Plaskow, eds., *Heterosexism in Contemporary World Religion: Problem and Prospect* (Cleveland, OH: Pilgrim Press, 2007); Lois K. Daly, ed., *Feminist Theological Ethics* (Louisville, KY: Westminster John Knox, 1994); Patricia Beattie Jung and Joseph Andrew Coray, eds., *Sexual Diversity and Catholicism: Toward the Development of Moral Theology* (Collegeville, MN: Liturgical Press, 2001).

11. Mary E. Hunt, "God Laughing Out Loud," *Concilium: International Journal for Theology* (2000/4), http://hosted.verticalresponse.com/695914/72c63dc1da/289509431/04f06e5487.

12. Mary E. Hunt, "Theology Has Consequences: What Policies Will Pope Francis Champion?" *Religion & Politics* (March 18, 2013), http://religionandpolitics.org/2013/03/18/theology-has-consequences-what-policies-will-pope-francis-champion.

13. The acronym LGBTIQ stands for Lesbian, Gay, Bisexual, Transgender, Intersex, Questioning.

14. Gail Anderson Ricciuti, "A Time of Confession" and "Assurance of Pardon," in *Birthings and Blessings: Liberating Worship Services for the Inclusive Church*, vol. 1, by Rosemary Catalano Mitchell and Gail Anderson Ricciuti (New York: Crossroad, 1991), 39–40.

15. In her presentation titled "The Transformational Stories of Jesus," Dr. Virginia Ramey Mollenkott illuminates Jesus's parables in Matthew 25:14–30, Luke 16:1–12, and Matthew 20:1–16; www.eewc.com/audio.

16. The parable of the widow's mite: Mark 12:41–44.

17. The parable of the lost coin: Luke 15:8–10; the parable of the woman baking bread: Luke 13:20–21.

18. Rev. Ricciuti, "A Quotidian Faith: Stories Sacred, Subversive, and Small"; www.eewc.com/audio.

19. Rosemary Catalano Mitchell and Gail Anderson Ricciuti, *Birthings and Blessings: Liberating Worship Services for the Inclusive Church*, vol. 1 (New York: Crossroad, 1991); Gail Anderson Ricciuti and Rosemary Catalano Mitchell, *Birthings and Blessings II: More Liberating Worship Services for the Inclusive Church* (New York: Crossroad, 1993).

20. David L. Bartlett and Barbara Brown Taylor, eds., *Feasting on the Word* (Louisville, KY: Westminster John Knox, 2011); Cynthia A. Jarvis and E. Elizabeth Johnson, eds., *Feasting on the Gospels* (Louisville, KY: Westminster John Knox, 2013).

21. Ricciuti and Mitchell, *Birthings and Blessings*, vol. 1, 30.

Part 5: Wisdom's Works of Caring for Creation

1. Jann Aldredge-Clanton, "Sophia Wisdom Shows the Way." I wrote this not-yet-published hymn originally for the 2012 Faith and Feminism, Womanist, Mujerista Conference on ecojustice, held November 2–4, 2012, at Ebenezer/herchurch in San Francisco.

2. Genny Rowley, "Food, Farms, and Faith: Priorities for Faith-Based Advocacy on the Farm Bill," *Huffington Post*, July 25, 2012, www.huffingtonpost.com/genny-rowley/ farm-bill-faith-based-advocacy_b_1684052.html.

3. www.gennyrowley.com.

4. Genny Rowley, "Congregational Environmental Communities: How They Happen and Why They Work," *Unbound: An Interactive Journal of Christian Social Justice* (December 20, 2012), http://justiceunbound.org/journal/current-issue/congregational-environmental-communities.

5. http://rkiser00.blogspot.com/p/sermon-posts.html.

6. Rebecca L. Kiser-Lowrance, "God of the Casserole," *Update: Newsletter of the Evangelical and Ecumenical Women's Caucus* 19, no. 2 (Summer 1995): 2–3.

7. Rebecca L. Kiser, "Interacting with Grace," *Update: Newsletter of the Evangelical and Ecumenical Women's Caucus* 26, no. 4 (Winter 2003): 4–5.

8. Daniel Charles Damon, "Pray for the Wilderness," *Faith Will Sing* (Carol Stream, IL: Hope Publishing Company, 1993), #18; *The New Century Hymnal* (Cleveland, OH: Pilgrim Press, 1995), #557. "Pray for the Wilderness" can be sung to the familiar hymn tune SLANE.

9. Dan Damon's numerous publications, recording, concerts, and more can be found on his website, www.damonstuneshop.com.

10. Dan C. Damon with Eileen M. Johnson, "A Cry for Justice in Hymnody," *The Hymn: A Journal of Congregational Song* 61, no. 4 (Autumn 2010), 11.

11. Daniel Charles Damon, "Goddess of Love," *Garden of Joy* (Carol Stream, IL: Hope Publishing Company, 2011), #9, also published in *The Hymn: A Journal of Congregational Song* 62, no. 3 (Autumn 2011), 37; Daniel Charles Damon, "Holy Mother of All Living" and "Wisdom Watches as We Pray," not-yet-published hymns.

12. www.pointrichmond.com/methodist.

13. Damon and Johnson, "A Cry for Justice in Hymnody," 8.

14. Connie L. Tuttle, "The Silence of Good People" (January 20, 2008), www.circleofgraceatlanta.org/012008.html.

15. www.circleofgraceatlanta.org.

Part 6: Wisdom's Works of Nonviolence

1. Proverbs 3:13, 17.

2. Nicholas D. Kristof and Sheryl WuDunn, *Half the Sky: Turning Oppression into Opportunity for Women Worldwide* (New York: Knopf, 2009), xiii.

3. See Introduction, n. 10.

4. "National Institute Partner and Sexual Violence Survey (NISVS): An Overview of 2010 Summary Report Findings," The Centers for Disease Control and Prevention, www.cdc.gov/violenceprevention/nisvs/index.html.

5. See Introduction, n. 11.

6. See Introduction, n. 12.

7. See Introduction, n. 13.

8. Harris Interactive poll, October 10, 2006, cited in "Why It Matters: Rethinking Victim Assistance for Lesbian, Gay, Bisexual, Transgender, and Queer Victims of Hate Violence & Intimate Partner Violence," a joint policy report by the National Center for Victims of Crime and the National Coalition of Anti-Violence Programs (March 2010), http://nicic.gov/library/026505. See also Stephen V. Sprinkle's

Unfinished Lives: Reviving the Memories of LGBTQ Hate Crimes Victims (Eugene, OR: Resource Publications, 2011), for compelling stories of LGBTQ people who suffered violence, and for a prophetic call to action to eradicate hate crimes.

9. "LGBT Hates Crimes on the Rise: An Interview with the Executive Director of the Matthew Shepard Foundation," *429 Magazine* (March 25, 2013), http://dot429.com/articles/1744-lgbt-hate-crimes-on-the-rise-an-interview-with-the-executive-director-of-the-matthew-shepard-foundation.

10. "Hate Crimes Against Gays, Transgender People Rise," *Los Angeles Times*, July 13, 2011, http://articles.latimes.com/2011/jul/13/nation/la-na-lgbt-hate-crimes-20110713.

11. Jann Aldredge-Clanton, "Awake to Work for Peace on Earth," *Inclusive Hymns for Liberation, Peace, and Justice* (Austin, TX: Eakin Press, 2011), #7.

12. Walter Wink, *Engaging the Powers: Discernment and Resistance in a World of Domination* (Minneapolis: Augsburg Fortress Press, 1992).

13. www.hildegard-austin.org.

14. Carolyn McDade, "This Ancient Love," *As We So Love* (Blue Jaye, 1996).

15. Carolyn McDade, "O Beautiful Gaia," *Love Songs to Earth* (Carolyn McDade, 2003).

16. J. Philip Newell, *Ground of All Being: The Prayer of Jesus in Color* (San Antonio: New Beginnings, 2008).

17. Kristof and WuDunn, *Half the Sky.*

18. Judith Liro, "Community, Creativity, Contemplation, and Call as a Feminist Spiritual Path," *EEWC Update* 29, no. 1 (Spring 2005): 13–14.

19. Ibid., 14.

20. Matthew 5:39, NIV.

21. Marg Herder, "Guns, Newtown, and Personal Responsibility," December 15, 2012, http://margherder.com/blog/guns-newland-responsibility.

22. Marg Herder, "Personal Tragedy Meets National Tragedy: The Boston Explosions," *Christian Feminism Today*, April 16, 2013, www.eewc.com/viewpoint/personal-tragedy-meets-national-tragedy-boston-explosions.

23. Marg Herder, "Two Anti-Gay Christian Groups at IndyPride—This Is Only a Test," May 28, 2013, http://margherder.com/blog/anti-gay-christian-groups-at-pride-this-is-only-a-test.

24. www.margherder.com; www.eewc.com/about-where-she-is.

25. From Alena Ruggerio, "Theapalooza: The Rhetorical Turn in the Third Wave of Biblical Feminism," presented at the 2008 EEWC-CFT Conference in Indianapolis, Indiana, www.eewc.com/audio.

26. Marg Herder, "A Name," www.margherder.com/musicLyricsAName.htm.

27. Ibid.

28. Ibid.

29. Herder, "We Can Know Her," www.margherder.com/musicLyricsWeCanKnowHer.htm.

30. Ibid.

31. Monica A. Coleman, *The Dinah Project: A Handbook for Congregational Response to Sexual Violence* (Eugene, OR: Wipf & Stock, 2010; originally Cleveland, OH: Pilgrim Press, 2004), xii.

32. Ibid., ix–x.

33. Ibid., xi.

34. Genesis 34.

35. Coleman, *The Dinah Project*.

36. Among Monica A. Coleman's publications are *Making a Way Out of No Way: A Womanist Theology* (Minneapolis: Fortress Press, 2008); *Creating Women's Theology: A Movement Engaging Process Thought* (Eugene, OR: Pickwick Publications, 2011); *Ain't I a Womanist, Too? Third Wave Womanist Religious Thought* (Minneapolis: Fortress Press, 2013); and numerous scholarly articles and book reviews. See http://monicaacoleman.com.

37. Coleman, *Making a Way Out of No Way*, 125, 170.

38. Octavia E. Butler, *Parable of the Sower* (New York: Four Walls Eight Windows, 1993).

39. Coleman, *Making a Way Out of No Way*, 142–143.

40. Ibid., 163, 170.

41. Virginia Ramey Mollenkott, *The Divine Feminine: The Biblical Imagery of God as Female* (New York: Crossroad, 1986; Eugene, OR: Wipf & Stock, 2014), 13–14.

42. Mollenkott, *The Divine Feminine*, 104.

43. Virginia Ramey Mollenkott, "Affirming Queer Spirituality in a Sometimes Hostile World," www.virginiamollenkott.com/queerspirituality.html.

44. Virginia Ramey Mollenkott, in *Transforming the Faiths of Our Fathers: Women Who Changed American Religion*, ed. Ann Braude (New York: Palgrave Macmillan, 2004), 55.

45. *Daughters of Sarah*, edited by Reta Halteman Finger, was a Christian feminist magazine published from 1974 to 1995.

46. Mollenkott, *The Divine Feminine*, 1–2.

47. Virginia Ramey Mollenkott, *Women, Men, and the Bible* (Nashville, TN: Abingdon Press, 1977); Virginia Ramey Mollenkott, *Godding: Human Responsibility and the Bible* (New York: Crossroad, 1990); Letha Dawson Scanzoni and Virginia Ramey Mollenkott, *Is the Homosexual My Neighbor? A Positive Christian Response* (New York: HarperCollins, 1978); Virginia Ramey Mollenkott, *Sensuous Spirituality: Out from Fundamentalism* (Cleveland: Pilgrim Press, 2008); Virginia Ramey Mollenkott, *Omnigender: A Trans-Religious Approach* (Cleveland: Pilgrim Press, 2007); Virginia Ramey Mollenkott and Vanessa Sheridan, *Transgender Journeys* (Cleveland: Pilgrim Press, 2003).

48. Virginia Ramey Mollenkott, "Trans-forming Feminist Christianity," in *New Feminist Christianity*, ed. Mary E. Hunt and Diann Neu (Woodstock, VT: SkyLight Paths, 2010), 133.

49. Mollenkott, "Affirming Queer Spirituality in a Sometimes Hostile World."

50. Mollenkott, *Transforming the Faiths of Our Fathers*, 71.

51. Mollenkott, *Transgender Journeys*, 38–39.

52. Mollenkott, *Transforming the Faiths of Our Fathers*, 69.

53. Marcia C. Fleischman, *Wild Woman Theology: In the Arms of Loving Mother God* (Bloomington, IN: AuthorHouse, 2009), 125.

54. Ibid., iv.

55. Sue Monk Kidd, *The Secret Life of Bees* (New York: Penguin Books, 2002).

56. Marcia Fleischman also created angel pictures for her children's storybook, *Angels Everywhere* (Bloomington, IN: AuthorHouse, 2008).

57. "The Girl Effect" is a movement leveraging the unique potential of adolescent girls in developing countries to bring social and economic change to their families, their communities, their countries, and the world; see www.girleffect.org/about.

58. Fleischman, *Wild Woman Theology*, 1–2.

Part 7: Wisdom's Works of Expanding Spiritual Experience

1. Jann Aldredge-Clanton, *Inclusive Hymns for Liberation, Peace, and Justice* (Austin, TX: Eakin Press, 2011), #50.
2. Beverly Jane Phillips, *Learning a New Language: Speech about Women and God* (NewYork: iUniverse, Inc., 2005).
3. Larry E. Schultz, "Wisdom Graciously Gives to All," *Inclusive Hymns for Liberation, Peace, and Justice* (Austin, TX: Eakin Press, 2011), #27.
4. Albert Schweitzer, *The Quest of the Historical Jesus* (London: A. & C. Black, 1926).
5. The musical setting is by Joseph M. Martin, *Song of Wisdom from "Old Turtle"* (Nashville, TN: Shawnee Press, 2000). The book is by Douglas Wood, with illustrations by Cheng-Khee Chee, *Old Turtle* (NewYork: Scholastic Press, 2007).
6. Larry E. Schultz and Jann Aldredge-Clanton, *Imagine God! A Children's Musical Exploring and Expressing Images of God* (Dallas, TX: Choristers Guild, 2004).
7. Larry E. Schultz and Jann Aldredge-Clanton, *Sing and Dance and Play with Joy! Inclusive Songs for Young Children* (Raleigh, NC: Lulu, 2009).
8. Phillips, *Learning a New Language*, 132–133.
9. Ibid., 21.
10. Beverly Jane Phillips, *From Heaven to My Heart: God's Journey with Me* (Bloomington, IN: iUniverse, Inc., 2011).
11. Elizabeth A. Johnson, *She Who Is: The Mystery of God in Feminist Theological Discourse* (NewYork: Crossroad, 1992).
12. Phillips, *From Heaven to My Heart*, 289–90.
13. Ibid., 297.
14. Phillips, *Learning a New Language*, 2.

Part 8: Wisdom's Works of Interfaith Collaboration

1. Proverbs 8:23.
2. Jann Aldredge-Clanton, *Inclusive Hymns for Liberation, Peace, and Justice* (Austin, TX: Eakin Press, 2011), #17.
3. In Korean, the last name is spoken first. "Chung" is Hyun Kyung's last name.
4. Chung Hyun Kyung, "Welcome the Spirit; Hear Her Cries," address given at World Council of Churches Assembly in Canberra, Australia, February 1991, http://archive.is/sptYB.
5. Chung Hyun Kyung, interview, "(Chung) Hyun Kyung," *Zion's Herald* 177, no. 5 (Sept/Oct 2003):14, complete interview pp. 14–16.
6. Chung Hyun Kyung, *Struggle to Be the Sun Again: Introducing Asian Women's Theology* (Maryknoll, NY: Orbis Books, 1990), 1.
7. Ibid., 2.
8. Anne Hilty, "Feminist Leaders Visit Jeju: Conversations with Chung Hyun Kyung, Lee Hyae-kyung, and Amy Richards," *The Jeju Weekly* (June 2, 2011), www.jejuweekly.com/news/articleView.html?idxno=1630.
9. Chung, *Struggle to Be the Sun Again*, v.
10. Ibid., 1.
11. Ibid., 47.
12. Ibid., 48.
13. Ibid., 49, 50, 51, 64, 66.

14. Chung Hyun Kyung, "Image of God," *inspirationandspirit*, interview, August 24, 2011, www.youtube.com/watch?v=iwFBK1kPbLE&feature=relmfu.

15. Chung Hyun Kyung, *In the End, Beauty Will Save Us All: A Feminist Spiritual Pilgrimage*, vols. 1 and 2, published in Korean (2002); *Letter from The Future: The Goddess-Spell According to Hyun Kyung*, published in Korean (2003); and *Hyun Kyung and Alice's Fabulous Love Affair with God* (2004), coauthored with renowned American novelist Alice Walker.

16. Chung, "Welcome the Spirit; Hear Her Cries."

17. Lana Dalberg, *Birthing God: Women's Experiences of the Divine* (Woodstock, VT: SkyLight Paths Publishing, 2013).

18. Ibid., 4–5.

19. Ibid., 5–6.

20. Lana Dalberg, poem dedicated to her mother, Anabelle Dalberg, on Mother's Day, 2004; published in Lana's book *Birthing God*, 110–11, and in Jann Aldredge-Clanton, *Changing Church: Stories of Liberating Ministers* (Eugene, OR: Cascade Books, 2011), 26–27.

21. Dalberg, *Birthing God*, 6.

22. Ibid., 160.

23. Kathe Schaaf, Kay Lindahl, Kathleen S. Hurty, and Guo Cheen, eds., *Women, Spirituality and Transformative Leadership: Where Grace Meets Power* (Woodstock, VT: SkyLight Paths Publishing, 2012).

24. Dalberg, *Birthing God*, 266.

25. Jeanette Blonigen Clancy, "Sexist God-Talk," blog, *God Is Not Three Guys in the Sky: Cherishing Christianity Without Its Exclusive Claims*, November 18, 2011, http://godisnot3guyscom-jeanette.blogspot.com/2010/06/thinkers-dissent.html.

26. Adapted from Isaiah 25:6–9.

27. Clancy, *God Is Not Three Guys In The Sky: Cherishing Christianity Without Its Exclusive Claims* (Edina, MN: Beaver's Pond Press, 2007), 9.

28. Clancy, *God Is Not Three Guys in the Sky*, 193.

29. Nicholas D. Kristof and Sheryl WuDunn, *Half the Sky: Turning Oppression into Opportunity for Women Worldwide* (New York: Knopf, 2009).

30. Clancy, "Rule by Rape," blog, *God Is Not Three Guys in the Sky*, March 18, 2012, http://godisnot3guyscom-jeanette.blogspot.com/2012/03/rule-by-rape.html.

31. Clancy, *God Is Not Three Guys in the Sky*, 14.

32. http://godisnot3guyscom-jeanette.blogspot.com.

33. Cristina Biaggi, ed., *The Rule of Mars: Readings on the Origins, History and Impact of Patriarchy* (Manchester, CT: Knowledge, Ideas & Trends, 2006).

34. "Sanctus" has been a part of the Christian Mass from the first century CE. The chant is based on Isaiah 6:3 and Matthew 21:9.

35. Orion combined two traditional Irish blessings using www.arizonacap.com/mgame/irishblessings.htm as source material.

36. *Agnus Dei* is a Latin term meaning "lamb of God"; *Om Mani Padme Hum* is a Sanskrit mantra meaning "Hail, the jewel in the lotus."

37. http://fulc.com/our-values/social-justice-and-incusivity/interfaith-awareness.

Part 9: Wisdom's Works of Changing Hierarchies into Circles

1. The name "New Wineskins," coming from the metaphor in Matthew 9:17, describes our search for new language and symbols to proclaim the good news of liberation and shalom; see www.jannaldredgeclanton.com/wineskins.php.

2. Jann Aldredge-Clanton, "We Invite All to Join Our Circle Wide," *Inclusive Hymns for Liberating Christians* (Austin, TX: Eakin Press, 2006), #111.

3. www.millionthcircle.org/About/vision.html.

4. Jean Shinoda Bolen, *The Millionth Circle: How to Change Ourselves and the World—The Essential Guide to Women's Circles* (York Beach, ME: Conari Press, 1999).

5. www.millionthcircle.org/About/intentions.html.

6. http://circleconnections.com.

7. Fredrica Harris Thompsett, Ann Smith, Katerine Tyler Scott, Sally Bucklee, Edna M. Brown, Claire Woodley, Alexsandra K. Stewart, Linda L. Grenz, Dorothy J. Brittain, and Claire Woodley, *Stories from the Circle: Women's Leadership in Community* (Harrisburg, PA: Morehouse Publishing, 1991); Ann Smith, Lucy Germany, Sr. Helena Marie, and Nancy Grandfield, *Women Prints: A Detailed Plan of Action for the New Millennium* (Harrisburg, PA: Morehouse Publishing, 1997).

8. Elizabeth Rankin Geitz, Marjorie A. Burke, Ann Smith, Debra Q. Bennett, Kathryn McCormick, and Tracy J. Sukraw, *Women's Uncommon Prayers: Our Lives Revealed, Nurtured, Celebrated* (Harrisburg, PA: Morehouse Publishing, 2000).

9. Paul Hawken, *Blessed Unrest: How the Largest Social Movement in History Is Restoring Grace, Justice, and Beauty to the World* (New York: Penguin Books, 2007).

10. Ann Smith, "God Is Not a Single Parent," in *Women's Uncommon Prayers*, 215–16.

11. Miriam Therese Winter, Adair Lummis, and Allison Stokes, *Defecting in Place: Women Taking Responsibility for Their Own Spiritual Lives* (New York: Crossroad, 1995).

12. Matthew 18:20.

13. Naomi Goldenberg, *The Changing of the Gods* (Boston: Beacon, 1979), cited in Mary Ann Beavis, *Feminist Theology with a Canadian Accent: Canadian Perspectives on Contextual Feminist Theology* (Montreal, Quebec: Novalis Publishing, 2008), 20; Charlotte Caron, *To Make and Make Again: Feminist Ritual Thealogy* (New York: Crossroad, 1993), cited in Mary Ann Beavis, *Feminist Theology with a Canadian Accent*, 20.

14. Virginia Ramey Mollenkott, *The Divine Feminine: The Biblical Imagery of God as Female* (New York: Crossroad, 1986; Eugene, OR: Wipf & Stock, 2014); Elizabeth A. Johnson, *She Who Is: The Mystery of God in Feminist Theological Discourse* (New York: Crossroad, 1992).

15. Beavis, *Feminist Theology with a Canadian Accent*, 19.

16. Dan Brown, *The Da Vinci Code* (New York: Anchor Books, 2003).

17. Mary Ann Beavis, "The Cathar Mary Magdalene and the Sacred Feminine: Pop Culture Legend vs. Medieval Doctrine," *Journal of Religion and Popular Culture* 24:3 (Fall 2012): 428–29.

18. Mary Ann Beavis, "The Deification of Mary Magdalene," *Feminist Theology* 21:2 (2012): 151.

19. Mary Ann Beavis, "'I Like the Bird': Luke 13:34, Avian Metaphors and Feminist Theology," *Feminist Theology* 12 (2003): 127, 128.

20. Mary Ann Beavis and HyeRan Kim-Cragg, *Feminist Commentary on the Epistle to the Hebrews: Wisdom Series* (Collegeville, MN: Liturgical Press, 2014).

21. Bridget Mary Meehan, *Exploring the Feminine Face of God* (Kansas City, MO: Sheed & Ward, 1991).

22. Bridget Mary Meehan and Regina Madonna Oliver, *Heart Talks with Mother God* (Collegeville, MN: The Liturgical Press, 1995), 18.

23. Meehan, *Exploring the Feminine Face of God*, xi.

24. Bridget Mary Meehan, *Delighting in the Feminine Divine* (Kansas City, MO: Sheed & Ward, 1994), 136.

25. "Kindom" is a well-known feminist respelling of "kingdom" to highlight the mutual relationships in egalitarian communities rather than the hierarchical relationships of the patriarchal system.

Part 10: Wisdom's Works of Creative Worship

1. Jann Aldredge-Clanton, "She Lives and Moves Throughout the Earth," stanzas 1 and 3, not previously published.

2. Phillips, *From Heaven to My Heart*, 252.

3. Susan C. Hamilton, *Seeking Sophia: 33 Lessons for Discovering the Divine Feminine* (Seattle, WA: CreateSpace, 2012), 111.

4. Diann L. Neu, codirector of WATER (Women's Alliance for Theology, Ethics and Ritual), 8121 Georgia Avenue, Suite 310, Silver Spring, MD 20910 USA; phone 301.589.2509; fax 301.589.3150; www.waterwomensalliance.org; dneu@hers.com.

5. Shawna R. B. Atteberry, "Pentecost: Blowing Where She Wills," June 1, 2009, http://shawnaatteberry.com/2014/06/08/pentecost-blowing-where-she-wills.

6. Shawna R. B. Atteberry, "In the Beginning," 2009, http://shawnaatteberry.com/2009/09/19/poem-in-the-beginning-was.

7. Bridget Mary Meehan, *Exploring the Feminine Face of God* (Kansas City, MO: Sheed & Ward, 1991), 79.

Part 11: Wisdom's Works of Feminist Emancipatory Faith Communities

1. See introduction, n. 6.

2. Jann Aldredge-Clanton, "Welcome New Wineskins," *Inclusive Hymns for Liberating Christians* (Austin, TX: Eakin Press, 2006), #57.

Epilogue

1. Jann Aldredge-Clanton, "Wisdom, Sophia, Joins in Our Labor," stanzas 1, 3, & 4, *Inclusive Hymns for Liberation, Peace, and Justice* (Austin, TX: Eakin Press, 2011), #11.

Additional Inclusive Worship Resources

Book Collections

Aldredge-Clanton, Jann. *Praying with Christ-Sophia: Services for Healing and Renewal*. Eugene, OR: Wipf & Stock, 2007.

————. *Seeking Wisdom: Inclusive Blessings and Prayers for Public Occasions*. Eugene, OR: Wipf & Stock, 2010.

Aldredge-Clanton, Jann, with composer Larry E. Schultz. *Inclusive Hymns for Liberating Christians*. Austin, TX: Eakin Press, 2006.

————. *Inclusive Hymns for Liberation, Peace, and Justice*. Austin, TX: Eakin Press, 2011.

Duck, Ruth. *Dancing in the Universe*. Chicago: CIA Publications, 1992.

Fleischman, Marcia C. *Wild Woman Theology: In the Arms of Loving Mother God*. Bloomington, IN: AuthorHouse, 2009.

Ford-Grabowsky, Mary. *WomanPrayers: Prayers by Women from Throughout History and Around the World*. New York: HarperOne, 2003.

Meehan, Bridget Mary. *Delighting in the Feminine Divine*. Kansas City, MO: Sheed & Ward, 1994.

————. *Exploring the Feminine Face of God*. Kansas City, MO: Sheed & Ward, 1991.

Meehan, Bridget Mary, and Regina Madonna Oliver. *Heart Talks with Mother God*. Collegeville, MN: Liturgical Press, 1995.

Mitchell, Rosemary Catalano, and Gail Anderson Ricciuti. *Birthings and Blessings: Liberating Worship Services for the Inclusive Church*. New York: Crossroad, 1991.

Neu, Diann. *Return Blessings: Ecofeminist Liturgies Renewing the Earth*. Cleveland, OH: Pilgrim Press, 2002.

————. *Women's Rites: Feminist Liturgies for Life's Journey*. Cleveland, OH: Pilgrim Press, 2003.

Newell, J. Philip. *Ground of All Being: The Prayer of Jesus in Color*. San Antonio, TX: New Beginnings, 2008.

Procter-Smith, Marjorie. *The Church in Her House: A Feminist Emancipatory Prayer Book for Christian Communities*. Cleveland, OH: Pilgrim Press, 2008.

Ricciuti, Gail Anderson, and Rosemary Catalano Mitchell. *Birthings and Blessings II: More Liberating Worship Services for the Inclusive Church*. New York: Crossroad, 1993.

Richardson, Jan L. *Sacred Journeys: A Woman's Book of Daily Prayer*. Nashville, TN: Upper Room Books, 1996.

———. *In Wisdom's Path: Discovering the Sacred in Every Season*. Orlando, FL: Wanton Gospeller Press, 2012.

Ruether, Rosemary Radford. *Women-Church: Theology & Practice*. New York: Harper & Row, 1986.

Rupp, Joyce. *The Star in My Heart: Experiencing Sophia, Inner Wisdom*. San Diego, CA: LuraMedia, 1990.

Schaaf, Kathe, Kay Lindahl, Kathleen S. Hurty, PhD, and Reverend Guo Cheen, eds. *Women, Spirituality and Transformative Leadership: Where Grace Meets Power*. Woodstock, VT: SkyLight Paths Publishing, 2012.

Schmitt, Mary Kathleen Speegle. *Seasons of the Feminine Divine: Christian Feminist Prayers for the Liturgical Cycle*. 3 Vols. New York: Crossroad, 1993, 1994, 1995.

Shapiro, Rami. *The Divine Feminine in Biblical Wisdom Literature: Selections Annotated & Explained*. Woodstock, VT: SkyLight Paths Publishing, 2012.

Winter, Miriam Therese. *Woman Prayer, Woman Song: Resources for Ritual*. Eugene, OR: Wipf & Stock, 2008.

———. *WomanWisdom* and *WomanWitness: A Feminist Lectionary and Psalter, Women of the Hebrew Scriptures*. 2 Vols. New York: Crossroad, 1991, 1992.

———. *WomanWord: A Feminist Lectionary and Psalter, Women of the New Testament*. New York: Crossroad, 1991.

Online Resources

Jann Aldredge-Clanton: www.jannaldredgeclanton.com.

Stacy Boorn (feminist pastor, artist): http://stacy.awegallery.com.

Christian Godde Project, The Divine Feminine Version (DFV) of the New Testament: http://godde.wordpress.com/the-divine-feminine-version-dfv-of-the-new-testament.

Jeanette Clancy, "God Is Not Three Guys in the Sky": www.godisnot3guys.com.

Monica A. Coleman (womanist theologian): http://monicaacoleman.com.

"Communion of Creative Fire": http://kreativefire.com/about-us.html.

Lana Dalberg (writer, activist, lay feminist theologian):
http://womenspiritandfaith.com.

Dan Damon (composer): www.damonstuneshop.com/record.htm.

Evangelical & Ecumenical Women's Caucus-Christian Feminism Today
(EEWC-CFT): www.eewc.com.

Marg Herder (writer, musician, artist): www.margherder.com.

Kendra Weddle Irons and Melanie Springer Mock, "Ain't I a Woman? De/
Constructing Christian Images": http://aintiawomanblog.net.

Grace Ji-Sun Kim (feminist theologian): http://gracejisunkim.wordpress.com.

Carolyn McDade (songwriter, spiritual feminist, social activist): www.
carolynmcdademusic.com.

Bridget Mary Meehan, "Bridget Mary's Blog: Living Gospel Equality Now:
Association of Roman Catholic Women Priests": http://bridgetmarys.
blogspot.com.

Progressive Christianity: http://progressivechristianity.org.

Caryn D. Riswold "Feminismxianity": www.patheos.com/blogs/carynriswold.

Genny Rowley (liturgist, ecofeminist theologian): www.gennyrowley.com.

Ann Smith, "Circle Connections": http://circleconnections.com.

Women's Alliance for Theology, Ethics and Ritual (WATER):
http://waterwomensalliance.org.

Angela Yarber (feminist theologian, artist, dancer): http://angelayarber.
wordpress.com.

Credits

Inspiration

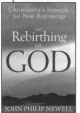

The Rebirthing of God
Christianity's Struggle for New Beginnings
By John Philip Newell
Drawing on modern prophets from East and West, and using the holy island of Iona as an icon of new beginnings, Celtic poet, peacemaker and scholar John Philip Newell dares us to imagine a new birth from deep within Christianity, a fresh stirring of the Spirit.
6 x 9, 160 pp, HC, 978-1-59473-542-4 **$19.99**

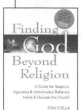

Finding God Beyond Religion: A Guide for Skeptics, Agnostics & Unorthodox Believers Inside & Outside the Church
By Tom Stella; Foreword by The Rev. Canon Marianne Wells Borg
Reinterprets traditional religious teachings central to the Christian faith for people who have outgrown the beliefs and devotional practices that once made sense to them.
6 x 9, 160 pp, Quality PB, 978-1-59473-485-4 **$16.99**

Fully Awake and Truly Alive: Spiritual Practices to Nurture Your Soul
By Rev. Jane E. Vennard; Foreword by Rami Shapiro
Illustrates the joys and frustrations of spiritual practice, offers insights from various religious traditions and provides exercises and meditations to help us become more fully alive.
6 x 9, 208 pp, Quality PB, 978-1-59473-473-1 **$16.99**

Journeys of Simplicity: Traveling Light with Thomas Merton, Bashō, Edward Abbey, Annie Dillard & Others *By Philip Harnden*
Invites you to consider a more graceful way of traveling through life. PB includes journal pages to help you get started on your own spiritual journey.
5½ x 7¼, 144 pp, Quality PB, 978-1-59473-181-5 **$12.99**
5½ x 7¼, 128 pp, HC, 978-1-893361-76-8 **$16.95**

Perennial Wisdom for the Spiritually Independent
Sacred Teachings—Annotated & Explained
Annotation by Rami Shapiro; Foreword by Richard Rohr
Weaves sacred texts and teachings from the world's major religions into a coherent exploration of the five core questions at the heart of every religion's search.
5½ x 8½, 336 pp, Quality PB Original, 978-1-59473-515-8 **$16.99**

Openings, 2nd Edition: A Daybook of Saints, Sages, Psalms and Prayer Practices *By Rev. Larry J. Peacock*
Draws on a wide variety of resources—lives of saints and sages from every age, psalms, and suggestions for personal reflection and practice.
6 x 9, 448 pp, Quality PB, 978-1-59473-545-5 **$18.99**

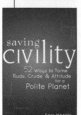

Saving Civility: 52 Ways to Tame Rude, Crude & Attitude for a Polite Planet
By Sara Hacala
Provides fifty-two practical ways you can reverse the course of incivility and make the world a more enriching, pleasant place to live.
6 x 9, 240 pp, Quality PB, 978-1-59473-314-7 **$16.99**

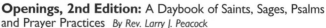

Or phone, fax, mail or email to: SKYLIGHT PATHS Publishing
Sunset Farm Offices, Route 4 • P.O. Box 237 • Woodstock, Vermont 05091
Tel: (802) 457-4000 • Fax: (802) 457-4004 • www.skylightpaths.com
Credit card orders: (800) 962-4544 (8:30AM–5:30PM EST Monday–Friday)
Generous discounts on quantity orders. SATISFACTION GUARANTEED. Prices subject to change.

Women's Interest

She Lives! Sophia Wisdom Works in the World
By Rev. Jann Aldredge-Clanton, PhD
Fascinating narratives of clergy and laypeople who are changing the institutional church and society by restoring biblical female divine names and images to Christian theology, worship symbolism and liturgical language.
6 x 9, 320 pp, Quality PB, 978-1-59473-573-8 **$18.99**

Birthing God: Women's Experiences of the Divine
By Lana Dalberg; Foreword by Kathe Schaaf
Powerful narratives of suffering, love and hope that inspire both personal and collective transformation. 6 x 9, 304 pp, Quality PB, 978-1-59473-480-9 **$18.99**

Women, Spirituality and Transformative Leadership
Where Grace Meets Power
Edited by Kathe Schaaf, Kay Lindahl, Kathleen S. Hurty, PhD, and Reverend Guo Cheen
A dynamic conversation on the power of women's spiritual leadership and its emerging patterns of transformation.
6 x 9, 288 pp, Quality PB, 978-1-59473-548-6 **$18.99**; HC, 978-1-59473-313-0 **$24.99**

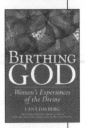

Spiritually Healthy Divorce: Navigating Disruption with Insight & Hope
By Carolyne Call A spiritual map to help you move through the twists and turns of divorce. 6 x 9, 224 pp, Quality PB, 978-1-59473-288-1 **$16.99**

New Feminist Christianity: Many Voices, Many Views
Edited by Mary E. Hunt and Diann L. Neu
Insights from ministers and theologians, activists and leaders, artists and liturgists offer a starting point for building new models of religious life and worship.
6 x 9, 384 pp, Quality PB, 978-1-59473-435-9 **$19.99**; HC, 978-1-59473-285-0 **$24.99**

Bread, Body, Spirit: Finding the Sacred in Food
Edited and with Introductions by Alice Peck 6 x 9, 224 pp, Quality PB, 978-1-59473-242-3 **$19.99**

Dance—The Sacred Art: The Joy of Movement as a Spiritual Practice
By Cynthia Winton-Henry 5½ x 8½, 224 pp, Quality PB, 978-1-59473-268-3 **$16.99**

Daughters of the Desert: Stories of Remarkable Women from Christian, Jewish and Muslim Traditions
By Claire Rudolf Murphy, Meghan Nuttall Sayres, Mary Cronk Farrell, Sarah Conover and Betsy Wharton
5½ x 8½, 192 pp, Illus., Quality PB, 978-1-59473-106-1 **$14.99** Inc. reader's discussion guide

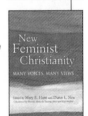

The Divine Feminine in Biblical Wisdom Literature
Selections Annotated & Explained
Translation & Annotation by Rabbi Rami Shapiro; Foreword by Rev. Cynthia Bourgeault, PhD
5½ x 8½, 240 pp, Quality PB, 978-1-59473-109-9 **$16.99**

Divining the Body: Reclaim the Holiness of Your Physical Self
By Jan Phillips 8 x 8, 256 pp, Quality PB, 978-1-59473-080-1 **$18.99**

Honoring Motherhood: Prayers, Ceremonies & Blessings
Edited and with Introductions by Lynn L. Caruso
5 x 7¼, 272 pp, Quality PB, 978-1-58473-384-0 **$9.99**; HC, 978-1-59473-239-3 **$19.99**

Next to Godliness: Finding the Sacred in Housekeeping
Edited by Alice Peck 6 x 9, 224 pp, Quality PB, 978-1-59473-214-0 **$19.99**

The Triumph of Eve & Other Subversive Bible Tales
By Matt Biers-Ariel 5½ x 8½, 192 pp, Quality PB, 978-1-59473-176-1 **$14.99**

Woman Spirit Awakening in Nature: Growing Into the Fullness of Who You Are
By Nancy Barrett Chickerneo, PhD; Foreword by Eileen Fisher
8 x 8, 224 pp, b/w illus., Quality PB, 978-1-59473-250-8 **$16.99**

Women of Color Pray: Voices of Strength, Faith, Healing, Hope and Courage
Edited and with Introductions by Christal M. Jackson
5 x 7¼, 208 pp, Quality PB, 978-1-59473-077-1 **$15.99**

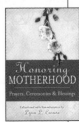

*A book from Jewish Lights, SkyLight Paths' sister imprint

About SKYLIGHT PATHS Publishing

SkyLight Paths Publishing is creating a place where people of different spiritual traditions come together for challenge and inspiration, a place where we can help each other understand the mystery that lies at the heart of our existence.

Through spirituality, our religious beliefs are increasingly becoming a part of our lives—rather than *apart* from our lives. While many of us may be more interested than ever in spiritual growth, we may be less firmly planted in traditional religion. Yet, we do want to deepen our relationship to the sacred, to learn from our own as well as from other faith traditions, and to practice in new ways.

SkyLight Paths sees both believers and seekers as a community that increasingly transcends traditional boundaries of religion and denomination—people wanting to learn from each other, *walking together, finding the way.*

For your information and convenience, at the back of this book we have provided a list of other SkyLight Paths books you might find interesting and useful. They cover the following subjects:

Buddhism / Zen	Gnosticism	Poetry
Catholicism	Hinduism / Vedanta	Prayer
Chaplaincy		Religious Etiquette
Children's Books	Inspiration	Retirement & Later-Life Spirituality
Christianity	Islam / Sufism	
Comparative Religion	Judaism	Spiritual Biography
	Meditation	Spiritual Direction
Earth-Based Spirituality	Mindfulness	Spirituality
	Monasticism	Women's Interest
Enneagram	Mysticism	Worship
Global Spiritual Perspectives	Personal Growth	

Or phone, fax, mail or email to: SKYLIGHT PATHS Publishing
Sunset Farm Offices, Route 4 • P.O. Box 237 • Woodstock, Vermont 05091
Tel: (802) 457-4000 • Fax: (802) 457-4004 • www.skylightpaths.com
Credit card orders: (800) 962-4544 (8:30AM–5:30PM EST Monday–Friday)
Generous discounts on quantity orders. SATISFACTION GUARANTEED. Prices subject to change.